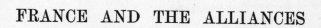

FRANCE AND THE ALLIANCES

FRANCE AND THE ALLIANCES

THE STRUGGLE FOR THE BALANCE OF POWER

BY

ANDRÉ TARDIEU

**HONORARY FIRST SECRETARY IN THE FRENCH
DIPLOMATIC SERVICE**

New York
THE MACMILLAN COMPANY
1908

All rights reserved

Norwood Press
J. S. Cushing Co. — Berwick & Smith Co.
Norwood, Mass., U.S.A.

PREFACE

HAVING been requested, in 1908, to deliver, under the auspices of the French Circle of Harvard University, the annual course of lectures there, founded by Mr. James H. Hyde a dozen years ago, I explained in my eight lessons the subject treated of in this book. Although to-day, in its published form, my subject contains developments which would not have been possible in a three weeks' series of lectures, I have modified neither its spirit, nor its plan, nor its conclusions.

Its spirit first. Cultivated Americans, who have in their universities such an admirable instrument of work, are all acquainted with France of the past; her history, her literature, and her art. To show them France of to-day, in presence of Europe and the world, such as she has been shaped, after painful experiences, by thirty-eight years of sustained effort and diplomatic action, is the aim that I have proposed to myself.

The plan resulted from the subject itself. It was through the Russian Alliance that France issued from the isolation in which she had been placed by defeat. It was by her understandings with Great Britain, Italy, and Spain that she subsequently pursued the satisfaction of her interests. It is in presence of the Triple Alliance, dominated by Germany, that she has raised the edifice of her agreements. It is against Germany that she has been compelled to defend and complete it. Such is the woof of this book of contemporary history, which is supplemented by a necessary study of Franco-American relations.

My conclusions come out on each page from the narration of events. In this diplomatic drama, the unity of which is equal to that of the antique tragedies, France has fought for the balance of power. Both militarily and politically destroyed in 1871 by Germany's triumph, this equilibrium has been gradually reconstituted. It exists to-day. But it is unstable. The heirs of Bismarck have not yet resigned themselves to the loss of the hegemony which — though it could be only temporary — he had secured for his country. Will they accept the new order of things which, through symmetric groupings of Powers, expresses the necessity for stability in the various international elements? This is a question that, in the near future, will be settled either by peace or war.

A Frenchman could not treat such a subject otherwise than from a French point of view. But to try to understand one's adversaries is already to do them justice. With this spirit of justice I have endeavoured to inspire myself, yet not seeking to hide errors, which indeed do not fundamentally affect the whole of the French achievement.

If Americans should see in this book, which has been written in good faith, fresh reasons for loving and esteeming France, then I shall have attained my object. The historic souvenirs which unite the two Republics have created imperishable ties between them. Being convinced that they may find in the study of the present time a positive justification for their old sympathies, I have striven to the best of my ability to make this justification clear, by telling, in the field of diplomatic action, the struggles of France for peace through the balance of power.

PARIS, September 1, 1908.

CONTENTS

vii

CHAPTER IV

CHAPTER VI

CHAPTER VII

CHAPTER VIII

FRANCE AND THE ALLIANCES

CHAPTER I

FRANCE AND THE RUSSIAN ALLIANCE

I

THE Franco-Russian Alliance may be considered as a perfect type of the "*mariage de raison*"; not that by this should be understood a bond imposed

upon the contracting parties through a will foreign
to their own, but one which, suggested first by a
correct appreciation of interests, corresponded, when
once formed, to the sentiments of each.

To be convinced of this, one needs only to examine a map. From time immemorial, France, as
a continental power, badly protected on her north-
eastern frontier, had found herself on land in rivalry,
if not in open struggle, with her eastern neighbour,
formerly Austria, to-day Germany. And always
also, in order to keep this rival or adversary at
arm's length, she was obliged to seek allies in the
east of Europe, — Turks, Swedes, Poles, these last
more recently replaced by Russians. In 1717, Peter
the Great, during his travels in France, said to the
Regent Philippe d'Orléans, when offering him his
alliance, "I will stand to you in the stead of
Poland, Turkey, and Sweden." [1] A century and a
half later, at the close of the Crimean war, Bismarck expressed the opinion that a "Franco-Russian Alliance was in the nature of things." As a
matter of fact, the Russian Empire and the French
Republic worked for the increase of their own
security by fortifying the equilibrium of Europe, on
the day that they recorded in a treaty of alliance
the lasting community of their essential interests.

In order to succeed in concluding this Alliance,
both French and Russians had a good deal to undo.
Of the various *régimes* in power since 1815, the
Government of the Restoration alone, and notably

[1] See Albert Vandal in his *Louis XV and Elizabeth of Russia*.

that of Charles X, had clearly understood the profit France would derive from a *rapprochement* with Russia. The Duc de Richelieu, Chateaubriand, and Polignac were the first partisans of the Russian Alliance. And it was largely because he was assured of Russia's support that, in spite of England's threats, the last mentioned statesman undertook the Algerian expedition. On the other hand, the reign of Napoleon III had a deplorable influence on French relations with Russia. The Crimean campaign was a mistake; and the policy followed in the affairs of Poland was another. When the war of 1870 broke out, Russia did nothing to defend us. During his stay in Saint Petersburg, Thiers obtained neither "understanding nor engagement." The Czar saw in our disasters nothing more than an opportunity to bring about the revision of the Treaty of Paris. Gortchakoff had full confidence in Prussia; and this confidence was destined to last until the Congress of Berlin. The diplomatic combination known under the name of the Alliance of the Three Emperors left France isolated. Vanquished and alone, she had only herself to rely on.

Many circumstances, indeed, then prevented the hope of her being able to escape from this isolation by an alliance with Russia. An initial obstacle existed in the wide difference between the two countries' domestic *régimes*. For the Republican form of government the Russian Court felt very little sympathy. And if communications were set up between Paris and Saint Petersburg, it was usually between the respective oppositions, Russians blaming the Radical trend of French politics, Frenchmen praying for the success of Russian Liberals. Already, before the end of the Franco-Prussian war, one of the members of the Government of the National Defence, put forward the absurd proposal of a pardon for Berezowski.[1] Ten years later, the refusal to extradite the nihilist Hartmann, who had taken refuge in Paris, grievously offended the Czar's Government.[2] A no less unfavourable impression was produced by the pardon granted to Prince Kropotkine. These incidents turned to the advantage of Bismarck, who openly declared himself opposed to a Franco-Russian *rapprochement*. "I won't live," he said, "between two enemies."

Personal reasons were added to those arising from circumstances. In choosing diplomatists to represent France in Russia, the French Government was not always well-inspired. At Saint Petersburg the souvenir still remains of blunders in language committed by Admiral Jaurès. He it was who, seeing in the Palace the portraits of the ancient Czars of Moscow, asked a Master of the Ceremonies:—

"Who are those ugly creatures?"

He it was also, who, when dining with the Minister of the Interior and speaking of certain Nihilist outrages, finished up by sententiously remarking:—

---

[1] Berezowski had fired a pistol at the Czar during his stay in Paris in 1867.

[2] Hartmann had blown up a train which he supposed to be the Czar's.

"You will only get out of the mess by establishing a Republic."

On the contrary, his successor, General Appert, was quite in the Czar's good graces. But the bruskness of his recall irritated Alexander III, who, by way of protest, ordered his Ambassador in France to take a long leave of absence from the country. Then, there was the Floquet question. Under the Empire, Mr. Charles Floquet, a young barrister at that time, had greeted the Czar, during his Imperial visit to the Palais de Justice, with, "*Vive la Pologne, Monsieur!*" [1] When the fiery law-student of 1867, became Chairman of the Lower Chamber and subsequently Prime Minister, a regular negotiation had to be carried through for relations to be established between him and the Russian Ambassador. Mr. Grévy, who remained at the Elysée until 1887, was, moreover, hostile to any diplomatic action — and especially to the Russian Alliance. To him the policy of absolute reserve and of isolation alone seemed reasonable. He was of the opinion that we had nothing to expect from negotiations with autocratic Russia, and that, in entering upon them, we should only alarm Germany without any positive benefit accruing.

Interest, however, which was pushing France and Russia nearer each other, was ultimately fated to carry the day. As early as 1873, the Duc de Broglie, uneasy at Germany's attitude, had solicited through Comte de Chaudordy an intervention of Prince

[1] "Hurrah ! for Poland, Sir."

Gortchakoff; and the Russian Chancellor, receiving the French envoy, had said to him: —

"We want France as strong as she was in the past."

Two years later, in 1875, German threats were more openly expressed.[1] It was the time when Bismarck thought of exhausting us by a fresh bleeding, and the Berlin papers spoke without disguise of another war. The only thing left to conjecture was, whether the war would break out in the spring or the autumn. Russia could not overlook the fact that, the issue of this unequal struggle would bring with it a definite rupture of the European balance of power to the benefit of the German Empire, and would mean, as the Duc Decazes said, "the enslaving of the Old World." Prince Orloff, who was then Ambassador at Paris, encouraged our Minister for Foreign Affairs not to yield an inch.

"Be firm," he repeated, "be very firm."

The French Ambassador at Saint Petersburg was General Le Flô, who, being in possession of the Czar's entire confidence, pressed him to intervene. And, Alexander II inclined more every day to the idea of intervention.

"If you are really menaced," he said, "you shall know it by me."

And, in fact, he refused to meet the overtures that Mr. von Radowitz, a German diplomatist, was at this moment commissioned to make him; and conveyed to General le Flô, through Gortchakoff, that

[1] See Hanotaux' *History of Contemporary France*.

France had nothing to fear. On the 10th of May, he arrived in Berlin, and, in an interview with Bismarck, spoke out so plainly that, a few days later, the cloud passed away.[1]

The Eastern question and the Congress of Berlin — which Gortchakoff called the darkest page of his history — completely loosened the ties of Russo-German intimacy. Even in the Conference of Constantinople, that is to say, before the commencement of the Russo-Turkish war, Bismarck had played a double game. He continued doing so during the Congress. On the morrow of this European assize, Russia was as isolated in the East as France was in the West. The Russian newspapers, the *Moscow Gazette*, for instance, preached the French Alliance. On the 7th of October, 1879, the conclusion of the Austro-German Alliance, two years subsequently, transformed into a Triple Alliance by Italy's adhesion, and directed even more against Russia than against France; brought an extra argument to the Francophile campaign. The Russian Czar and the German Emperor continued their reciprocal assurances of "cordial affection"; but the old confidence was lacking. During his ephemeral premiership of 1881, Gambetta felt that the moment had arrived to profit by this change. And, in appointing Comte de Chaudordy Ambassador at Saint Petersburg, he said to him: —

[1] See Hanotaux' *History*, already cited. The Czar said to Mr. de Gontaut-Biron, the French Ambassador at Berlin: "I hope our relations will become increasingly cordial. We have common interests. We must remain friends."

"Leaning on Russia and on England, we shall be unattackable."

Another five years, however, elapsed without any advantage being taken of such favourable conditions. By another diplomatic masterpiece, Bismarck had, indeed, contrived, in 1887 first, and, subsequently in 1888, to form with Russia a counter-assurance which warded off all danger of a Franco-Russian alliance. To Mr. Flourens, who was appointed Minister of Foreign Affairs in the Goblet Cabinet on the 13th of December, 1886, the honour belongs of having for the first time turned the suggestions of interest into acts. The Eastern crisis supplied him with an occasion. Bulgarian delegates had come in January, 1887, soliciting the support of the great Powers against Russia. Mr. Flourens declared to them that their first duty was to reach an understanding with the Saint Petersburg Cabinet. The German campaign on behalf of the military *Septennat*, and the warlike ardour it aroused in Berlin, enabled the French Government to ascertain that their attitude with regard to Bulgaria had been appreciated in Russia. Important movements of troops on the Polish frontier, showed that the Czar's Government, while not yet making alliance with us, yet intended to be in a position to have a word to say in the matter, if France were attacked. A week after, the Czar, in annotating a confidential report of Mr. de Giers, his Minister of Foreign Affairs, wrote on the margin, "We must not let France be diminished."

At this date, owing to the clear-sighted initiative of her financiers, France was able to gain a fresh hold on Russia's gratitude.[1] With a trend more and more directed towards an intensive policy of economic development, the Russian Empire needed capital. In order to procure it, she had, up to then, applied to bankers who, after subscribing the loans, sometimes found, sometimes did not find, people to invest in these values, of whose Exchange rates they thus remained masters. In reality, it was especially on the Berlin market that such operations were effected. A group of French financiers, at the head of whom was Mr. Hoskier, a banker of Danish origin, thought it would be to the interest both of France and of Russia to substitute for this system, precarious in its principle and limited in its extension, that of floating the Russian loans on the French market and among the French public. In the month of June, 1888, Mr. Hoskier opened negotiations for this purpose with Mr. Wichnegradski, the Russian Minister of Finance. In the following December, after the scheme had been thoroughly dealt with, a first loan of 500,000,000 francs was issued in Paris, of the 4 per cent type, at 86 fr. 45 c., which was subscribed by more than a hundred thousand persons. Other loans followed: in 1889 (700,000,000 and 1,200,000,000 francs), in 1890 (300 millions and 41 millions), in 1891 (320 millions and 500 millions), in 1893 (178 millions), in 1894 (454 millions, 166

[1] See Ernest Daudet's *Diplomatic History of the Franco-Russian Alliance.*

millions, 400 millions), in 1896 (400 millions), in 1901 (424 millions), in 1904 (800 millions), in 1906 (1,200 millions). And France thus became Russia's creditor for a sum which may be estimated, with municipal loans and industrial enterprises, at twelve billions of francs.[1] It was a new principle of solidarity between the two countries, and, from 1889, offered to political combinations the broad, solid basis of financial interests.

The French Government resolved to take advantage of it. On his nomination to the Ministry of Foreign Affairs, which he held till the 11th of January, 1893, Mr. Ribot resolutely lent his efforts to the forming of an alliance with Russia. His chief agent was our Ambassador at Saint Petersburg, Mr. de Laboulaye, one of the most remarkable of our diplomatists of the Third Republic, for qualities of shrewdness, firmness, and tact. Moreover, the whole Cabinet were in agreement on the subject. In 1890, Mr. Constans, the Minister of the Interior, placed a trump card in the Ambassador's hand, by effecting the arrest of a band of Nihilists that were manufacturing in Paris bombs intended to serve against the Czar and his family. At the same date, Mr. de Freycinet, the Minister of War, rendered Russia a service of another kind, no less appreciated, by putting our Châtellerault Arms Factories at her

[1] To the loans above mentioned must be added the 5 per cent loan of 1822, quoted on the Exchange, on and after February 22, 1890; the Interior loan, admitted on 'Change June 2, 1894; and, last of all, the Austrian portion of the 1900 loan, which has remained on the Paris market.

disposal. Every day the atmosphere grew more favourable.[1] With statesmanlike perspicacity, Mr. de Laboulaye saw that the time had come for action, and that only the approval of the people was required to bring to a successful issue these combinations, previously conceived in the secret councils of the two Chancelleries. In the summer of 1890, he organized the visit of the French fleet to Russia; but, for reasons of opportuneness, the project was not realized until the next year. On the 25th of July, 1891, Admiral Gervais' squadron arrived off Cronstadt.

The memory of this triumphal visit is so recent that I need not dwell upon it. All Europe was astounded at the Russian nation's enthusiasm. All at once, in spite of distance; in spite of a past of mistrust, in spite of differences of every sort, political, intellectual, and moral, Russian opinion and French opinion, breaking a long silence, united in applauding the act which manifested the *rapprochement*. Although the Alliance was not yet made, it was already looked upon as certain. A few weeks later, in the Reichstag, the Count von Caprivi, Chancellor of the German Empire, said in the course of an Army speech: "There can be no doubt that a close *rapprochement* has come about between France and Russia. It has been in preparation for a long while. But to-day, everything, Cronstadt included, seems to indicate that an alliance is intended." This Alliance was signed on the 22d of August, 1891, by

[1] See Ernest Daudet's book already cited.

Mr. Ribot, Minister of Foreign Affairs, and the Baron
de Mohrenheim, who was the Russian Ambassador
at Paris. At the end of June, 1892, General de
Boisdeffre, being at the head of the Army Staff,
went to Saint Petersburg, for the purpose of negotiating a military arrangement completing the initial
protocol, and gave the Cabinet's seal to a defensive
pact between France and Russia.[1] The two countries thus abandoned their isolation, and thereby
reëstablished the balance of power in Europe.

II

During four years longer, the signatory Governments forbore to render their Alliance public; but,
in the meantime, they determined its character
more precisely. On the 31st of August, 1891, at a
fête given in his honour at Cauterets, the Russian
Ambassador, Mr. de Mohrenheim, said: —

Mr. Prefect, you have just alluded to the mutual current of
sympathy set up throughout Russia and France. . . . There
are many reasons why this should be so.

A few days later at Vandeuvre, Mr. de Freycinet,
who combined with his Premiership the Ministry
of War, held in his turn the following discourse: —

Don't let us tire of improving and strengthening our Army.
It is one of the elements, and not the least, of our influence in the
world. It has its share in the events that are a joy to our patriotism. Its progress, which Europe sees and France applauds,
inspires some with confidence, others with respect. Such prog-

[1] See Jules Hansen's book, *The Baron de Mohrenheim's Ambas-
sadorship at Paris.*

ress, moreover, proves that the Government of the Republic, in spite of superficial changes, are capable of long designs, and that in the accomplishment of national tasks, they manifest a consistency that is not inferior to a Monarchy's. No one to-day doubts our strength. Let us show that we are prudent. We shall know how to maintain, *in a new situation*, the coolness, dignity and moderation which, during days of misfortune, prepared our recovery.

Finally, on the 29th of September at Bapaume, Mr. Ribot, Minister of Foreign Affairs, said: —

After hesitating for some time, Europe has, at last, done us justice. A Sovereign, who is far-seeing and firm in his designs, and pacific like ourselves, has publicly demonstrated the deep sympathies uniting his country and our own. (Enthusiastic applause. Cries of: 'Long live the Czar! Hurrah for France! Hurrah for Russia!')

The Russian nation have joined their Emperor in giving us proofs of cordial friendship. (Fresh applause.)

You know how well we reciprocate these sentiments. (Yes! Yes!)

The events of Cronstadt have had an echo even in our smallest hamlets, our tiniest villages. . . .

From them has resulted, as justly remarked, a new situation, which does not mean that a new policy needs to be adapted to it. . . .

. . . Just at the moment when we are able to practice peace with more dignity, we are not likely to expose ourselves to its being compromised. Conscious of her strength and confident in her future, France will continue to exhibit the qualities of prudence and coolness which have gained her other peoples' esteem and have helped to restore her to the rank due to her in the world.

In other words, to a state of forced peace succeeded one that was voluntary. Doubtless, the Franco-Russian Alliance was not an alliance formed for revenge. Its object was not to give us back Alsace-

Lorraine. But it insured us in Europe a moral
authority which, since our defeats, had been wanting to us. It augmented our diplomatic value.
It opened to us the field of political combinations,
from which our isolation had excluded us. From
mere observation, we could pass to action, thanks
to the recovered balance of power.

To prove that such was the character of the
Franco-Russian Alliance, I cannot do better than
quote the Chancellor of the German Empire. Returning from Saint Petersburg to Paris early in
June, 1902, I had the honour of a long interview
with Count von Buelow at Berlin. After speaking
to me of the journey Mr. Loubet had just made, as
President of the Republic, to Russia, he added : —

"The Triple Alliance and the Dual Alliance are the
chief supports of the European balance of power."

This was implicitly admitting that, until the latter
was an accomplished fact, the equilibrium did not
exist. Mr. Jaurès, in his sacrilegious letter on the
Triplice, as being a necessary counterweight to
Franco-Russian jingoism, stands alone in ignoring,
despite history and geography, this plain truth.
By uniting their previously isolated forces, France
and Russia had made Europe stable again.

For some years, the two Allies would seem to
have been too exclusively absorbed in contemplat-
ing the fact of their union, and multiplied outward
manifestations that might convince the world at
large of its reality. In June, 1892, the Grand Duke
Constantine came in the Czar's name to Nancy, to

pay his respects to President Carnot. In the ensuing September, Messrs. Ribot and de Freycinet had a meeting, at Aix-les-Bains, with Messrs. de Giers and de Mohrenheim. In November, the Grand Duke Vladimir was Mr. Carnot's guest. In October, 1893, Admiral Avellan's sailors were boisterously fêted at Toulon, and afterwards in Paris. In September, 1895, Prince Lobanoff, Minister of Foreign Affairs, and General Dragomiroff paid us a visit in their turn. In October, 1896, the Czar and Czarina, amidst extraordinary ovations, made a stay in France, which was terminated by the admirable Châlons review. Then came, in 1897, Count Mouravieff's journey to Paris as Prince Lobanoff's successor, and Mr. Félix Faure's visit to Russia; in 1899, Mr. Delcassé's journey to Russia, and that of Count Mouravieff to Paris; in 1901, Admiral Birilev's call at Villefranche with his squadron, Mr. Delcassé's second visit to Saint Petersburg, and the Czar and Czarina's stay at Compiègne; lastly, in 1902, Mr. Loubet's journey to Russia, that of Count Lamsdorf to Paris; and, more recently (in 1906 and 1907), the two stays in our Capital of Mr. Isvolski, appointed, on Count Lamsdorf's retirement, Minister of Foreign Affairs.

That all these official comings and goings, accompanied by an abundant exchange of telegrams, increased the practical value of the Alliance, is not so certain as some have maintained. At most, may it be said, that Mr. Félix Faure's journey to Russia, fur-

nished the Czar and himself with an auspicious occasion to define publicly the ties subsisting between
their two "friendly and allied" countries. With
that exception, these frequent meetings, amid much
ado, produced no result of immediate utility. A
policy of parade may satisfy vanities; it can also
offend them; rarely does it serve interests. And
I am inclined to share the opinion expressed to me
by Count Witte, when he said to me one day: —

"For ten years you have been making Franco-
Russian manifestations, in season and out of season."

I have seen the principal of these manifestations
close to. I was at Compiègne in 1901, at Tsarskoie-
Selo in 1902. And the impression they have left
upon me is, that it is neither necessary nor profitable
to celebrate alliances with the help of protocol and
ceremonial. One is exposed in so doing to incidents
comical or painful. Was it indispensable to Franco-
Russian politics for the Czarina Alexandra to hear
at Compiègne, — without any pleasure, — the repeated, *"Oh! oh! c'est une impératrice"* with which
Mr. Edmond Rostand had thought fit to greet her?
Was it opportune to offer a certain Russian diplomatist, at the time belonging to the Russian
Embassy at Paris, the occasion to behave discour-
teously towards the Republican Government, and
then to put ourselves forward in order to secure him
a pardon that was not justified? Ought we to have
given our guests the spectacle of ridiculous quarrels
between the wives of our Ministers and those of our
Ambassadors? And later, could it be thought an

edifying sight, when a Secretary of the French Embassy at Saint Petersburg, — who claimed to possess President Loubet's entire confidence and that of Mr. Delcassé, — entered into open conflict with his hierarchic superior, the Marquis de Montebello? A Republic never finds it advantageous to measure itself with a Monarchy on the ground of protocol observance. The lack of habit therein leads to errors, on this or that side of the mean, to omissions or excess-commissions of zeal. Thence results for the Democratic *régime*, thus induced to lavish complaisances of somewhat servile character, an embarrassed and, as it were, subaltern situation, which creates a factitious inequality between two governments called upon to treat political questions on the same footing. Too many fêtes — too many flowers, might one say — have been loaded upon the Franco-Russian Alliance. Neither on the one hand nor on the other have they yielded matter for congratulation.[1]

Between 1893 and 1902, the combined action of the two allied countries was wanting in intensity and consistency. Each of them looked after their own affairs, while profiting by the moral credit which the Alliance brought, yet without developing the credit by a methodical coöperation. Thanks to the assistance afforded by French capital, Russia was able to carry out her Railway programme and her conversions, to construct the Trans-Siberian, and to devote herself more and more exclusively to ques-

[1] The same thing may be said of Franco-English relations.

c

tions interesting her in the Far East. France, after giving herself up for three years to the Dreyfus Affair, managed to paralyze her activity through religious struggles. A few years later, Russia found herself engaged with the armies of Japan; France with the diplomacy of Germany. Manchuria in the one case, Morocco in the other; such were the assets of the Alliance. How had it been possible for such consequences to issue from a right principle? How was it that the pact of 1891, instead of protecting its signataries from reverses and humiliations, had left the way open to this double and astonishing set-back?

III

The reply to this question is easy. If the Alliance had become sterile, the reason was, that Russia's wilful blindness and France's weakness, had allowed it to deviate from its aim. Instead of keeping Europe for its sphere of action, it had gradually drifted towards Asia. So that, finally, instead of reminding our Allies, for their good and our own, of the respect they owed to the fundamental pact — respect of the letter and respect of the spirit — we had, with sheeplike docility, made ourselves the accomplices of their imprudence.

On the day when Mr. Witte, by modifying the track of the Trans-Siberian, directed Russia's money, Army and Navy, towards the seas of China, France ought to have protested. And this she did not do. In 1895, she joined Russia and Germany, in order to stop Japan on the threshold of victory, in the name of the Chinese Empire's integrity. Two years later, with singular incoherence, she violated this integrity — again imitating these two powers — by seizing Kouang-Tcheou-Ouan, as Germany had taken the Chantung, and Russia, Port Arthur.[1] In 1900, during the negotiations that followed the Pekin expedition, she passively accepted Russia's lead. In 1901, she made no attempt to show the Russians the mistake they were committing in neglecting the Japanese Alliance which the Marquis Ito had come to offer them. Last of all, in 1902, when Japan had turned to England and had signed the Treaty of the 30th of January, 1902, she was rash enough to reply to this treaty by the declaration of the 19th of March, which, if it had any meaning, extended to the Far East the action of the Dual Alliance.

This declaration was thus conceived : —

The allied Governments of France and Russia, having received communication of the Anglo-Japanese Convention of the 30th of January, 1902, concluded with a view to assuring the *status quo* and general peace in the Far East, and to maintain the independence of China and Corea, which should remain open to the commerce and industry of all nations, were fully satisfied to find therein affirmed the essential principles which they themselves have on several occasions declared to constitute and to remain the basis of their policy.

The two Governments deem that the respecting of these principles is at the same time a guarantee for their special interests in the Far East. However, being themselves obliged to provide for the case in which either the aggressive action of

[1] See René Pinon's book, *The Struggle for the Pacific.*

third Powers, or new troubles in China, raising the question of the integrity and free development of this Power, should become a menace for their own interests, the two allied Governments reserve to themselves the right eventually to provide means for their preservation.

A few days afterwards, Mr. Delcassé, Minister of Foreign Affairs, denied in the Chamber that, in signing the above text, he had intended or accepted an extension of the Alliance to Eastern Asia. But then, what was the meaning of the declaration? Was it a mere surface manifestation for the purpose of make-believe? Such kinds of "bluff" are redoubtable snares, in which those who have recourse to them are usually caught. The joint note of the 19th of March misled Russian opinion by allowing it to count on France's eventual aid. It irritated Japanese opinion by leading it to dread a double European hostility. It accustomed everybody to the idea of a war by opposing to one another the two groups, Japan and England, Russia and France. At the very least, it was an encouragement to the Russian colonial party, who, through greedy speculation or ignorance of the facts, refused to perceive the inevitable issue of the movement towards Corea. It favoured the plans of men like Bezobrazoff [1] and other risk-alls, who precipitated Russia into the war of 1904.

France, who, in 1902, had not foreseen the danger,

[1] Mr. Bezobrazoff had succeeded in interesting a number of big manufacturers in the Yalu Company. His intrigues were one of the causes of the war. See Kouropatkin's revelations (*McClure's Magazine*, September, 1908).

continued her scepticism until the day when it
burst. Three months before the war, while all our
agents in the Far East were declaring it to be unavoidable, Mr. Delcassé asserted that it was impossible. Instead of listening to our ministers and
consuls, who said, "Japan means war," he paid
attention only to the Czar, whose language was, "I
desire peace." When it was still time to restrain
our Allies on the eve of a rupture, and to say to
them, "You are not ready," he allowed himself to
be the dupe of certain civil or military personages,
who, having staked their whole career on the Alliance, were to him the Leboeufs of this second Sedan,
and guaranteed that everything would be ready,
even to the last gaiter-button. Instead of reminding
Russia, that her contribution to the Alliance was her
strength in Europe, we let her sacrifice at once her
pledges and her interests.

Both morally and materially, the Alliance risked
wreck in this storm. The French public, who for
twelve years had been accustomed to count on Russia,
were deeply disappointed by her repulses and were
not able to hide their sentiments. That the war would
necessarily be long and difficult at such a distance;
that there would be huge obstacles in the way of
provisioning the army, which had been transported
to the front at a great expense; that the Staff in
command had not been suitably prepared for their
task, — all this was known and expected. What
was not foreseen, was the continued series of reverses, the implacable development of an irre-

mediable inferiority, the demonstration of strategic incapacity, surpassed only by administrative carelessness — a misreckoning cruel for the Russians, and almost as cruel for the French, who had put their faith and sense of security in the Alliance.

Then those who, from the outset, had been opposed to our pledging ourselves to Russia, began to cast up accounts and strike the balance, with the most unfavourable interpretation possible. The three loans of 1890 were passed in review, the two loans of 1891, those of 1893, 1894, 1896, 1901, 1904. To these were added the municipal loans and Finlandese loans, the sums invested in metallurgic mining, manufacturing or transport undertakings, the whole totalling nearly twelve billions, that is to say, nearly a fourth of the French capital invested abroad; and, while doing justice to the Czar's Government for its exact punctuality in paying dividends and coupons, the doubt was expressed, as to whether the services rendered by Russia were worth the price paid for them, as to whether the Alliance, so useful to Russia for her conversions, the redemption of her railways, the equilibrium of her budget, and the construction of the Trans-Siberian, had given France an equivalent in return, especially after the Asiatic adventure, which, on the Manchurian soil or in the Chinese seas, engulfed the men, ironclads, and millions intended, as we hoped, for the safeguarding of European peace.

This impression was put into words with somewhat bad taste. Mr. Combes, the Prime Minister,

made blunt statements to journalists, which a
Russian diplomatist characterized in an interview
with me: —

"It is disagreeable," he said, "when we ask you
for nothing, to hear your Premier proclaim from the
housetops that you don't intend to give us anything."

I remember being one evening, after a Russian
defeat, at the Russian Embassy, where I met the
German Ambassador, who, prompter or shrewder
than the French Government, had come to convey
to his colleague the expression of his sympathy.
Such things as these were only failures in tact;
but, under the circumstances, they were deeply
felt by Russia. They were all the more regrettable,
as they caused us to lose the benefit of our altogether correct attitude in the question of neutrality.
Not only were we assuring to our allies our financial
help, as in the past; but, immediately after the North
Sea or Dogger Bank incident, Mr. Delcassé successfully intervened to prevent the conflict that threatened to embroil them with England. A few weeks
later, through the facilities — legitimate indeed in
French Law — which we afforded Admiral Rodjestvensky's squadron at Madagascar and in Indo-
China, we exposed ourselves to the gravest difficulties with Japan. None the less, there was a
general impression — and against impressions discussion is useless — that the Alliance was growing
cooler, that its bonds were loosening and coming
undone. The moral impetus which had animated

its first years of existence, seemed to be checked for long to come.

Materially, the detriment was still more severely felt. For Russia, there was not only the disastrous end to her dream in Asia; there was her military disorganization besides, coinciding with domestic troubles. For France, there was the annihilation of the guarantee that had been gained in 1891. In September, 1904, the Russian forces succumbed at Liao-Yang. In March, 1905, they were crushed at Mukden. It was in the same month of March that the Emperor William, disembarking at Tangier, played check to the mission of Mr. Saint-René Taillandier at Fez; check also to Mr. Delcassé's policy. If, to make use of the Chancellor's expression, German diplomacy had been a deductive one, it was in 1904 that the objections raised in 1905 to our treaty with England and our Moroccan projects would have been put forward. But being, and flattering itself on being, an opportunist one, it had waited until the war in Manchuria and the paralysis of the Alliance, should place France within reach of its attack.[1]

For having allowed their Alliance to be turned aside from its proper object, both Russians and French suffered jointly for their joint mistake. Military defeats on the one side, diplomatic defeats on the other, demonstrated *a contrario* the necessity of a pact which had become useless only by reason of its having been tampered with. Would the

[1] See André Tardieu's *Conference of Algeciras.*

lesson be profitable to those who had just felt its weight so severely?

IV

On the French side first, wise reflections took the place of earlier disappointment. Among the Radicals, Radical-Socialists, and Socialists even, who, only a little while before, were criticizing the barrenness of the Russian Alliance, hesitation was visible. From the comparison of dates, the truth was perceived. And when it was realized how closely Germany's rough manifestation had followed the weakening of Russia's strength, it was better understood what force and security France had derived for thirteen years from the many-times depreciated Alliance.

It was thought that, if Russia had remained pacific and preserved her position of advantage in Europe, William II, other things being equal, would have put less vehemence and brutality into his action at Tangier; that, even if uneasy, as he pretended to be, at Mr. Delcassé's tendencies, he would have found a discreeter way of expressing his uneasiness, either to the head of the State or to the head of the Ministry. Lulled with pacific songs, the Parliament had given itself up to the illusion that the war in Manchuria was none of its concern. Being sharply awakened, it saw that, from Mukden to Fez, the way was not so long as it had believed, and that the road between the two places passed through Paris.

Undoubtedly, the domestic history of Russia

during the last few years has added a fresh difficulty to those already existing. French opinion in the majority has, more often than not, disapproved the somewhat arbitrary police operations of the Czar's Government. Without always taking sufficiently into account the circumstances surrounding each case, people have found that the Autocracy, in its halting evolution towards liberty, was forgetting the juridical maxim that *"Donner et retenir ne vaut."* [1] The seriousness of this incongruity, however, ought not to be exaggerated. The treaties binding nations, in view of their foreign relations and action, by their very essence make abstraction of domestic policy. The similarity of *régimes* and institutions has but little importance, if international interests do not agree. On the contrary, the concordance of these interests suffices to justify a contract of alliance. Francis I had no objection to ally himself with the Grand Turk. Richelieu treated with the Protestants, and Mazarin with Cromwell. Even Mr. Jaurès, who, it is true, has since changed his mind, declared on the 23d of January, 1903, that he had no fundamental objection to the Russian Alliance, and added: "There was a time when the Republican party wondered whether it would be possible to establish solidarity of foreign policy between two countries so dissimilar in their political and social conditions. This is a preoccupation that we have no right to entertain. . . . It is the duty

[1] Compare the English proverb, *Give a thing, take a thing, Naughty man's plaything.*

of all Frenchmen to do nothing which can shake
and destroy the Franco-Russian understanding."

On the Russian side, fidelity to the French Alliance was evinced in the most energetic way during
the Conference at Algeciras. And the appointment
of Mr. Isvolski to the Russian Foreign Office, was
followed by his country's becoming once more a
factor in Europe, which return to the normal state
of things is a matter for congratulation to France.
The agreements with Japan in 1907, consolidating
the Treaty of Peace in 1905, have checked the
reappearance of the Asiatic mirage.[1] The signing
of an agreement with Great Britain in the same year,
has accentuated the evolution and freed French
policy from the awkwardness of having to keep up
at once, between a divided Russia and England,
the Russian Alliance and English friendship.[2] At
the time of his first journey to Paris in 1906, Mr.
Isvolski, indeed, had an opportunity of testifying
to the sincerity of his sentiments towards France.
He had been in the Capital for a few days when he
received the unexpected visit of Prince Ouroussov,
the Russian Ambassador at Vienna. The Prince
came to inform him that it would be appreciated in
Austria and Germany if, after his call at Paris and
Berlin, he were to return to Saint Petersburg through
Vienna. Mr. Isvolski replied: —

"I shall not do what you propose. I have come
to Paris, because France is Russia's ally. I shall
call at Berlin, because, having to pass through this

[1] See below, Chapter VII.   [2] See below, Chapter VII.

city, I owe it to our friendly relations with Germany
to stop there. But I shall not go to Vienna, because
I have no reasons for going there, and because, by
going, I should alter the significance of my journey,
especially as I have not been to London."

The Russian Minister thus affirmed his resolution
not to modify the character of the Franco-Russian
Alliance, by superimposing on it more or less de-
terminately a kind of resuscitation of the "Alliance
of the Three Emperors." Since then, his policy,
made increasingly precise by the *rapprochement*
with England, has preserved the same character.
The replacement, long desired by him, of the French
Ambassador at Saint Petersburg, Mr. Bompard,
by Admiral Touchard, has tended to confirm him
in these intentions.

Brought back to its original scope, the Alliance
seems, therefore, destined to regain its full value in
Europe. The mistakes committed have been taken
to heart on both sides; and, on both sides also, their
logical conclusion has been drawn. In spite of
press polemics which break out from time to time,
a close understanding remains the norm of the relations of the two countries with each other. Whether
the newspapers discuss military questions or deal
with financial questions, their arguments are usually
frivolous. When the *Novoie Vremia* attacks the
French Army, it wilfully exaggerates defects that
are easy to correct, and deliberately leaves out of
count merits of the highest order. When French
newspapers criticise the Russian army and claim

that the war in Manchuria, carried on for two years by this army at thousands of kilometres from its base, has pronounced against it a verdict from which there is no appeal, they are no less completely deceived. As for the financial question, and the puerile bickering that makes the Russians say, "You were only too happy to lend us your money," while the French retort, "And you were only too glad to keep it," there is no need to dwell on it. The essential quality of financial operations is to serve the interests of both borrowers and lenders. If Russia has borrowed our money, she required it, and, therefore, has nothing to reproach us with on this score. If we have lent it to her, we did so because it suited us, and we have no reproaches to make either.

Economic relations between the countries, moreover, are susceptible of being developed. It has been seen above what a formidable sum of money France has invested in Russia. The amount of our loans, quite as much as the interests of the Alliance, would have justified on her part a less subaltern utilization of the pledges of 1891. But, financially, French lenders have nothing to regret. The financial situation of Russia is not bad. The ordinary budgets — deduction made of the expenses incurred during the war and by the construction of railways — are in a condition of equilibrium. The difficulties of the last few years are to be explained rather by Exchequer reasons than budgetary. They have their origin, as a matter of fact, either

in expenses that are directly productive, or in
reimbursements of debts, or else in exceptional
circumstances. The capital of the Russian debt,
which on the 1st of January amounted to 327,000,000
francs, represents less than 200 francs per inhabitant,
— a high figure, it is true, but not excessive. The
gross expenses of the debt — comprising the amor-
tizements, that is to say, the counterpart of the
loan resources — absorb $17\frac{1}{4}$ per cent of the ordinary
budgetary receipts, which is a less proportion than
in many other States. Without doubt, France has
the duty and the right to desire that a thorough
reform of the Russian bureaucracy, both in financial
matters and in other administrations, shall insure
the regularity, honesty, and competence which
have so often been wanting. No less legitimate is
the desire to develop by commercial agreements
economic relations, which, in spite of a somewhat
unfavourable Customs legislation, have made appreciable progress during the last twenty-five years.
But, without underestimating the importance of
the services rendered by France to Russia, it is
altogether unjust to pretend, as some do, that the
Alliance is liable to have bankruptcy as its counterpart.

In military matters, it is natural that the Russians
should wish to see the French Army equal to its
task. The development of our strength, and the
compensation of the weakness resulting from our
two years' service by a better utilization of our
resources, are duties imposed upon us in our own

interest, still more than in that of our Allies. On her side, Russia must make herself capable of successfully playing the rôle incumbent on her, in the event of a European war. For that, she has still much to do. The Russo-Japanese war has certainly diminished her power of attack for some time to come. It drew successively on the military formations belonging to the Far East, the Reserve divisions stationed in the various central provinces, and, ultimately, on the several Army corps destined to the defence of the Western frontier and, more peculiarly, prepared for an intervention beyond this same frontier, on those which, consequently, have an especial interest for the Franco-Russian Alliance. Transported in detachments to the front, these Western Army Corps were obliged to borrow men, officers, artillery, and material from those that were not being mobilized. And the latter thus became incapable of immediately passing from a peace to a war footing. Moreover, domestic disturbances required their employment against the Revolutionaries, under conditions which had nothing in common with the plan of mobilization. In a word, that which was left to Russia in the way of military strength at the end of the war no longer weighed in the European balance of power, and no longer counted in the estimates of international policy.

In order for this state of things to end, the drafts made by the Far East on European Russia had to be restored. The demobilization commenced directly after the signing of the Treaty of Ports-

mouth. A general strike on the railways retarded
it, and caused the returning convoys to be almost
as long on the journey as the outgoing ones had
been. Not until within the closing months of 1906,
were the European Army Corps completely rein-
stalled along the Western frontier. They had lost
in Manchuria a considerable portion of their units
and the whole of their belongings, spent their war
provisions, experienced the fatigues of a hard campaign, and suffered the demoralization of defeat.
Their military capacity could only be regained
through a twofold persevering effort — of reconstitution and reorganization. The reconstitution
requires considerable expense, and is, therefore,
subordinated to the state of the finances. It implies
changes in weapon equipment and military accesso-
ries. Count Witte recently estimated the cost of
this necessary undertaking at a billion roubles, or
nearly three billions of francs. Although these
figures are enormous, the Government and the Duma
owe it imperatively, both to Russia and to France,
to set to work without delay.

As regards the reorganization, various measures
have been taken since the conclusion of peace.
The fundamental military law of March, 1906, has
reduced the duration of the service to three years,
instead of the five fixed by the old law, which in
practice became four. The long time passed by
soldiers of the active Army under the flag, resulted
in the Reserves being composed of men compara-
tively old and numerically weak. These two in-

conveniences had been keenly felt in Manchuria,
where the bad component elements of the Reserve
divisions first transported to the front, were partly
the cause of the defeat of Liao-Yang. With a
shorter service, it has been found necessary to
increase numerically the annual contingents, since
the active Army will have henceforward to be filled
up by means of, no longer four, but three contingents.
The last three levies have been fixed at about four
hundred and seventy thousand men. This change
will extend to the Reserve classes, which will become
younger, more numerous, and more capable of
homogeneity. Its tendency will be also to bring
about a modification in the recruiting regulations,
which date back to 1874, and to diminish the exemp-
tions. In fine, three years being just sufficient to
form a non-commissioned officer in Russia, service
reënlistments will have to be made use of. Although
certain measures have already been taken, the lack
of a well-coördinated plan is keenly felt. It is
indispensable for Russia's security, for her pledges
exchanged with France, and for the balance of power
in Europe, that this plan should be clearly defined
and energetically carried out through a cordial
understanding between the ancient bureaucracy and
the young Duma.

On these conditions, the Franco-Russian Alliance
will have its full practical effect. To-day, as yester-
day, and to-morrow, as to-day, this Alliance, if
sincerely executed, both is and will be equally
necessary to the two contracting parties. Let us

D

once again repeat that one has only to look at a map
to be convinced that, in a Continental war, Russia
alone would be able to immobilize part of our
adversaries' forces — and reciprocally. It is by
coming back to this principle that, the whole bearing
of the 1891 pact is understood. As Count Witte
said to me in 1905: "The essence of our Franco-
Russian relations is not modified. The Alliance
remains in conformity to the interests of the two
nations. In this Alliance, there is nothing to change,
and nothing must be changed." For such a change
to be justified, Europe would have to cease to be
Europe.

CHAPTER II

FRANCE AND THE ENGLISH "ENTENTE"

I

NEVER has a reconciliation been more unexpected than the one which, on the 8th of April, 1904, put an end to the ancient quarrel between England and France; and still more unexpected was the permanent character it has since assumed. Now and again, during the last hundred years, there were hints of an *Entente Cordiale*, but these incipient understandings were of short duration. In 1801, the inhabitants of London unharnessed the horses of the First Consul's Aide-de-Camp, Colonel de Lauriston, who had come to ratify the terms of peace; and yet, a few months later, the war began which was to finish only at Waterloo. Again, in 1838, when Marshal Soult went as Louis-Philippe's representative to the coronation of Queen Victoria, he was most enthusiastically received; but, within a couple of years after, there was very nearly an open rupture between the two countries. Similarly, under Napoleon III, both understanding and subsequent alliance were ephemeral; and, with the advent of 1860, Queen Victoria counselled a "regular crusade" against France. The opinion of Albert Sorel, as expressed in his writings, was that "between France and England understandings may exist, as they have existed in the past, for the purpose of preserving the *statu quo*, but that England has never been, and can never be, an ally for France, except on condition of the latter's abandoning her foreign expansion." [1] The same thing had been said by Lord Chatham a century earlier in somewhat different words, "England's only fear here below is that France should become a naval, commercial, and colonial power."

After the fall of the Stuarts, the habitual relations

[1] See the *Temps* of December 24, 1903.

of France and England were those of war;[1] following each other, came the war of the League of
Augsbourg (1688–1697), the war of the Spanish suc-
cession (1701–1711), the war of the Austrian suc-
cession (1742–1748), the Seven Years' War (1756–
1763), the American war (1778–1783), the wars
of the Revolution and Empire (1793–1815); and,
in between these periods of fighting, there were
intervals of precarious peace overshadowed by deep
reciprocal mistrust. Such is the record of the past,
explained by the fact that England regarded France
as her most dreaded adversary in Europe, and more
especially outside of Europe, and that she was
defending, against contingent successes of our own
country, the naval supremacy which is the *sine qua
non* of her existence. "Beware," said Mr. Urquhart,
a Member of Parliament, in 1862, "the sea threatens
while it serves you; it bears you, but it environs
you. The position of this island is such that, there
is no *via media* for her between being all-powerful
and being nothing at all. This is why she was
always conquered until, having subjugated the sea,
she in turn became mistress of the world. England
will be the sea's victim on the day she ceases to
be its queen." From the conviction of such necessity arose the adoption of the *two-powers standard,*
"England's fleets must be superior to those of the
two strongest naval Powers in Europe combined."
And from it also was born the Anti-French policy.

[1] See Mr. Jean Darcy's excellent volume, *A Hundred Years of
Colonial Rivalry.*

Throughout the nineteenth century, without interruption and without hesitancy, England opposed the expansion of France. She began with disputing, step by step, the execution of the treaties of 1815, which restored to us Saint-Pierre and Miquelon, Guadeloupe, Martinique, Guyana, our factories in Senegal and Guinea, the isle of Bourbon and the five towns in India. In 1830, for months, she threatened us with war, at the time when we were installing ourselves in Algeria. In the preceding years, she had boldly supported the Barbary pirates against France; and, when Prince de Polignac decided on a military expedition, she brought to bear on him a pressure which can only be compared to that exercised by Germany in 1905 with regard to Morocco. At Algiers, Tunis, Tripoli, her consuls set the Mussulmans against us: "The French are mad," cried Wellington, "a terrible reverse awaits them on the coast of Algeria." A few days later Algiers was in our hands. Then all through Europe and in Africa, English diplomacy turned against France. At Gibraltar, the forces were mobilized.

To the Duc de Laval, French Ambassador at London, Lord Aberdeen, the Prime Minister, said: —

"I wish you good-bye, Monsieur le Duc, with more than ordinary regret, since I fear we shall not see each other again. Never, even in the days of the Republic and Empire, did France give us such reason to complain."

To which the Ambassador replied: —

"My Lord, I am unable either to tell or to foresee

what you may be hoping from the moderation of France; but what I do know is that you will obtain nothing from her by threats."

The conquest continued; and, as long as it lasted, England's attitude was violently hostile. Mr. St. John, the English consul at Algiers, made a number of defamatory accusations against our troops; nor was it until 1851, when applying for the *exequatur* of this official's successor, that the English Cabinet reluctantly acknowledged the *fait accompli*. For no direct cause of local enmity, through simple hatred of French expansion, "without any fixed plan other than that of acting everywhere and, on all occasions, in an interest opposed to that of France," England had thwarted our policy and weakened our influence.

In the Tunis affair, she it was, on the contrary, who at the Berlin Congress made us the first advances, for reasons of general policy, and in order to render her occupation of Cyprus more palatable. However, some years later, when Jules Ferry tried to realize the profit which Lord Salisbury had, of his own accord, held out as an inducement to Mr. Waddington, objections of various kinds were raised by the British Foreign Office; and the Sultan, in particular, was advised that *carte blanche* had not been given to France. True, the English Government turned a deaf ear to the Bey when he begged aid. But regret was publicly expressed "that France should have thought fit to open a fresh Eastern question to her profit"; and the English press assumed a denun-

ciatory tone when the success of the French arms
was decisive. On the 14th of May, 1881, Lord
Lyons, the British Ambassador at Paris, handed a
note to Mr. Barthélemy Saint-Hilaire, Minister of
Foreign Affairs, protesting in advance against Bizerta
being made into a fortified town; and, a few weeks
later, Lord Granville said to our Ambassador, Mr.
Challemel-Lacour, "I should lack frankness if I
were to leave you under the impression that the
action of France in Tunis has produced a favourable
impression here." Indeed, England emphasized
her opinion by abstaining for sixteen years from any
revision of the treaties of commerce, which secured
her exorbitant privileges in the Regency.

In West Africa, the question of the Niger also
brought British interests and our own into conflict.
Our situation in the basin of the Niger was, in 1882,
if anything, superior to theirs, and at any rate not
inferior. Yet, in a few months, our fellow-countrymen were ousted by the National African Company,
soon transformed into the Royal Niger Company,
with its charter and sovereign powers, thoroughly
supported by the British Government. In spite
of the successes of our explorers, and notwithstanding the protectorate treaties they signed with native
chiefs, our diplomacy, through its shortsightedness
and lack of energy, lost ground and was held in
check under a campaign of systematic intimidation.
The treaty of the 5th of August, 1890, set the seal
to this policy; and, through its defective drawing
up, became the cause of subsequent difficulties.

Between 1890 and 1894, we made no effort to react against the aggressive behaviour of the Royal Niger Company towards our fellow-countrymen, and, in particular, against Lieutenant Mizon. Our victories over Rabah, Samory, and Behanzin even did not suffice to give us a due consciousness of our strength. When these successes were followed by a more active pacific penetration, Sir Edward Grey replied in a tone of serious menace, which was more loudly echoed in the English press; and we decided to evacuate one of our most important posts, the Royal Niger Company's troops at once occupying it. Thereupon negotiations were entered into, which enabled us to gauge Great Britain's intransigence. The *Pall Mall Gazette* accused our officers of conducting themselves like "vulgar brigands"; and, in his speeches, Mr. Chamberlain announced that he was asking for military preparations to be made. On the 14th of June, 1898, a treaty was signed which, in reality, favoured England by shutting us out from the Lower Niger. Through a continuous forward policy, helped by the supineness of our statesmen, our implacable rival seized, in the most brutal way, on the great way of penetration into West Africa.

In the Congo, Savorgnan de Brazza's successes had provoked in London both surprise and irritation. As early as 1884, England signed a treaty with Portugal, intended to cut off both the French and Belgian Congo from their outlet on the Atlantic. In presence of protests from Belgium, France, and Germany, the Cabinet of Saint James yielded, and forbore to carry the treaty to its conclusion. On the other hand, no recognition was forthcoming of the right of preëmption conceded to France over the Belgian Congo. At the same date, as our explorers were displaying their activity on the Obanghi, Great Britain determined to shut us out from the Nile route. She proceeded to negotiate an agreement with the Free State, which "made, as it was said, the Congo the mandatary of British policy, and introduced this State as England's tenant into the Nile Valley." Such a treaty was manifestly directed against France; and Mr. Hanotaux, the Minister of Foreign Affairs, said so in Parliament, adding: "This agreement places the Independent State in a condition of rupture — pacific, I am willing to allow, but rupture none the less — with the signatory powers that gave their consent to its formation; it is in formal contradiction with African international law." King Leopold gave way; and, some weeks later, signed another treaty with France which practically cancelled the previous one. Here again, Great Britain had concentrated her efforts against us, and, in her policy, set our enfeeblement as a goal to be attained.

The acute stage of the conflict between the two countries was reached with the affair of Egypt. Since the cutting of the Suez Canal, the importance of the route to India had doubled for England. On the 9th of February, 1877, Lord Beaconsfield, acting on his own authority, bought for a hundred million francs the hundred and seventy-seven thousand shares held by the Khedive in the canal property. Four years later, through an inconceivable error, the French Government allowed the English to install themselves alone in the Nile Valley, where, from 1882 to 1885, they carried on a sanguinary struggle against the Dervishes, and lost the Soudan, but strengthened their position on the Lower Nile. On the 14th of January, 1883, profiting by the weakness of Mr. Duclerc, Minister of Foreign Affairs, they induced the French Government to abandon the condominium, which, indeed, then had a merely theoretic value. In 1884, they announced their intention of evacuating Egypt, the date mentioned being 1888; but this promise, as all the others of the same reference, made diplomatically or in Parliament, remained unfulfilled. Between 1891 and 1894, they established themselves strongly on the Upper Nile and over all the plateau extending between Lake Albert Nyanza and Lake Victoria. At the end of 1895, Lord Salisbury informed the French Government confidentially that he had decided to crush the Mahdi and reconquer the Soudan. England's hold over Egypt grew tighter every day.

Now, at the same time, though with insufficient means of execution, the lack of which could not be supplied by the heroism of their agents, and, moreover, with deplorable vacillation in their manner of giving instructions, the French Government sent out expeditions with a view to reopening the Egyptian problem for European consideration. Cap-

tain Marchand's force started from the Ubanghi,
and that of Mr. de Bonchamps from Djibouti.
Unfortunately, a French Deputy, speaking in the
Chamber on the 28th of February, 1895, had the
imprudence to say: "To-day the English dream of
possessing the whole of the Nile is, I believe, once
for all spoiled." Certain members of the Government thought that, by anticipating Great Britain,
we should be in a position to enter into negotiations
with her on the whole question under favourable
conditions. . . . Three years after, Captain Marchand arrived at Fashoda; but, instead of finding
himself able to communicate from there with Abys-
sinia, and backed up by previous diplomatic action,
he encountered Sirdar Kitchener's Anglo-Egyptian
army victoriously camped on the battle-field of
Omdurman.

What the morrow was is in the memory of all:
a painful, breathless, humiliating discussion between
Mr. Delcassé, Minister of Foreign Affairs, and Sir
Edmund Monson, the English Ambassador, blunt
demands from the British Government, Lord Salisbury, Sir Michael Hicks-Beach, and Mr. Ritchie;
finally, on the 4th of November, 1898, the evacuation of Fashoda under the direct threat of a war
for which our Navy was unhappily far from being
prepared. Between 1894 and 1896, we had lost
two years. In 1896, we had made up our minds
to act, but had left to a single officer and two hundred men the task of reopening the Egyptian question. We suffered the just penalty of so much lack

of foresight. Strengthened by our mistakes, England had pursued us without mercy. Thenceforward, she was preponderant in Eastern Africa. On the 21st of March, 1899, we signed a treaty recognizing her hold over the Bahr-el-Gazal and Darfour regions. No special mention was made of the Nile; but what was true of the Darfour region was *à fortiori* true of Egypt. In reality, Great Britain required us, by abandoning Bahr-el-Gazal, to yield to her a country into which she had never penetrated, and where we had concluded treaties with the natives and created some thirty posts. Once again, the English had treated us as enemies; and the 1899 convention was a suitable culmination to centuries of hatred.

If, to these grave motives of conflict, be added secondary questions of dispute in Newfoundland, Zanzibar, Madagascar, Siam, and Morocco, a fair idea may be gained of what Franco-English relations were up to the day when the *Entente Cordiale* was concluded. Now victorious over English opposition in Algeria, Tunis, the Congo, now vanquished, on the Niger, in Egypt, and the Soudan, we might say with Lord Salisbury: "Not every cause for controversy has been removed; and certainly, in the future, we shall have many things to discuss." Peace had been maintained, but an armed peace, characterized by alarms, distrust, rancour, and irritation. How came it that within five years a sincere understanding was established. between the two hereditary enemies?

II

Neither in England nor in France is the principle of the understanding to be sought. Rather was it the fear of Germany which determined England — not only her King and Government, but the whole of her people — to draw nearer to France.

During the twenty years that followed the foundation of the German Empire, Anglo-German relations remained correct. And German diplomacy also, under Prince Bismarck's direction, made a special point of being on good terms with London, and of pursuing outside Europe no design calculated to arouse anxiety at the British Foreign Office: "I am an Englishman in Egypt," the Chancellor once said; adding on another occasion: "England is of more importance to us than Zanzibar and the whole eastern coast of Africa." In spite of polemics caused by the Germans' installing themselves on various parts of the African coast, in spite even of the diplomatic intervention which prevented Great Britain from ratifying her Congolese treaty with Portugal, there was a systematic effort of Wilhelmstrasse to preserve cordial relations with Downing Street. On the 14th of June, 1890, an Anglo-German treaty was signed, acknowledging Great Britain's supremacy over all the basin of the Nile. A second treaty, on the 15th of November, 1893, marked a fresh English success by stipulating that the German Cameroons should not extend eastward beyond the basin of the Chari, and that the Darfour, Kordofan, and Bahr-el-Gazal regions should be excluded from the German sphere of influence. Even the Emperor William's telegram to Mr. Kruger provoked only a temporary storm, and did not hinder the conclusion of a secret treaty which, in 1898, in conditions but little known, disposed of the future of the Portuguese colonies. Whilst the German press made violent attacks on England throughout the Transvaal war, the Emperor paid a visit to his grandmother and negotiated an Anglo-German agreement relative to Samoa. A few months later, there was a further treaty between the two countries relative to China; and, at the end of 1901, a triple naval demonstration associated together the English, German, and Italian fleets against Venezuela.

From this time, however, the *Entente* policy was definitely abandoned, the cause being, as Bismarck said, "cousin land-rat's taking it into his head to turn water-rat," and obtaining, within a few years, such prodigious success that England was both confounded and exasperated. On the morrow of the Treaty of Frankfort, no Englishman foresaw this lightning transformation.

A soil with badly worked riches; ways of communication still incomplete ; irregular shallow rivers with silted-up harbours at their estuaries, and flowing into a sea shut up between continents, where, for eight months out of the twelve, both climate and fog interfered with navigation ; a defective economic organization ; anarchy in production ; insufficiency in capital ; in fine and above all, a population of soldiers, *savants* and peasants ;

everything seemed to forbid Germany's aspiring to the brilliant destiny of the United Kingdom.[1]

Freed from French competition, the latter power was incontestably the carrier of the seas, the necessary intermediary between the two worlds. Her security was absolute.

And yet the security was deceitful. Never was economic progress more prompt, steady, and lucky than that of the German Empire. Never was there a better exemplification of the proverb that "Iron calls forth gold." In 1870, the population of Germany was 41,000,000 inhabitants. Between this date and 1907, it advanced to 63,000,000. During the same period, the railways increased their length from 20,000 kilometres to 58,000 kilometres. Thanks to the carrying out of a magnificent river improvement scheme, the country's interior navigation has gone beyond the watersheds, and drained the products of Central Europe towards her ports. These latter, to which Belgian Antwerp and Dutch Rotterdam serve as auxiliaries, are the best fitted up in the world. German ship-building yards have a universal reputation. German docks monopolize the major portion of Europe's exportation. The trading fleet of Hamburg alone surpasses in tonnage the whole of that of France. German commerce (importation and exportation) amounted to six billion marks in 1878, seven billions in 1892, ten and a half billions in 1900, and fifteen billions in 1906.

[1] See Maurice Lair's *German Imperialism.*

Parallel in its progress, Germany's Navy has developed in formidable proportions. In 1898, it comprised only nine small iron-clads. Under the programmes of 1898, 1900, and 1906, as finally amended, and with the further increase anticipated for 1912, the Empire will possess in 1918, according to the well-known military writer, Colonel Gaedke's computation, eighty iron-clads or iron-clad cruisers of 20,000 tons, these without counting a reserve fleet of twenty-five ships either of less strength or of less recent construction. She will therefore be capable of coping on sea with any enemy whatsoever. That this adversary must be England, no one takes any trouble to hide, whether it be the sailors, or the Navy League with its nine hundred thousand members and its annual budget of 1,000,000 marks. And a moral transformation has accompanied the material one. To the Emperor's appeal, saying: "Our future is on the sea," the German people have replied with their usual discipline. "As my grandfather worked for the reconstitution of this Army," added the Kaiser, "so I will work, without letting myself be checked, to reconstitute this Navy, so that it may be made comparable to our land army and permit the Empire to rise to a greater degree of power." While her merchants were sailing forth to conquer fresh markets, Germany began to prepare herself for this new rôle. Read the statutes of the Naval League:—

The Naval League considers that Germany cannot do without a redoubtable fleet, both for defending her coasts and for

E

maintaining her rank among the great World Powers, both for protecting her general interests and commercial relations, and for defending her citizens abroad. Consequently, it proposes to arouse and strengthen throughout the country an opinion favourable to the increase of the fleet; and it assumes the duty of coming to the help of sailors belonging to the fleet and colonial army in case the Administration should be unable to grant them sufficient assistance.

Next, listen to Chancellor von Buelow. You will see that both Government and nation are in perfect accord. On his speaking for the first time in the Reichstag, he claims for Germany her share of room. Two months later, he sets forth what is required by the economic, maritime, and moral progress of Germany "as she passes through the world with her sword in one hand and her spade and trowel in the other." And his ensuing speeches, whether treating of Samoa, East Africa, Kiao-Tcheou, or the Carolines, all assert the necessity of the Empire's exercising an action outside of Europe. Each time, he brings out the close connection between the successive steps of this forward movement. Each time, he shows his fidelity and zeal towards the colonial policy so often railed at fifteen years previously. Soon, indeed, he pronounces the decisive words, "Like the English, French, and Russians, we claim the right to a greater Germany."

Then by the despatch of numerous circulars, the Imperial Chancellery is seen taking a preponderant part in the negotiations with China, and assuming, during the repression of the Pekin disturbances, a still more important rôle through the appointment of Count Waldersee to the head command of the international troops.

We shall not let ourselves be thrust out from an equality with other Powers. We shall not suffer ourselves to be denied the right to speak as they do in the world. There was a time when Germany was only a geographical expression, when she was denied the name of a great Power. Since then, we have become a great Power; and, with the help of God, we hope to remain so. We shall not permit the abolition or limitation of our claim to a world policy based on reflection and reason.

The expression was out at last. Henceforward, we shall meet with it continually, and, on each fresh occasion, backed up with greater precision. As a matter of fact, the expansion phenomenon is one that is general, so that Germany, as a great Power present and future, participates in it, perforce. Read over the speech of the 3d of March, 1902, the Budget discussions of 1903, and 1904; everywhere you will find the same affirmation; everywhere, the German adaptation of this thought of President Roosevelt that a nation cannot remain huddled up like a petty tradesman in a narrow shop.

So, imperialist Germany aspires to fulfil Treitschke's prophecy: "When Germany's flag covers and protects this huge empire, to whom will the sceptre of the universe belong? Who will impose her will on other nations enfeebled or decadent? Is it not Germany who will have the mission of assuring peace to the world? Russia, a huge giant in process of formation, and with feet of clay, will be absorbed by her internal and economic difficulties.

England, stronger in appearance than in reality, will doubtless see her colonies separate from her, and will wear herself out in barren struggles. France, a prey to her domestic strife and quarrels, will sink more and more into final ruin. As for Italy, she will have enough to do, if she wishes to bestow tranquillity enough on her children. The future, therefore, belongs to Germany, with whom Austria will unite, if she has a desire to live."

The appearance of so formidable a competitor could not fail to disturb England. Chatham's saying, "Our first duty is to see that France does not become a naval, commercial, and colonial Power," applied now much more accurately to Germany than to France. Thenceforward, therefore, Great Britain's efforts had to turn themselves against Germany. Long since, indeed, her merchants, consuls, and politicians had uttered a cry of alarm.[1] In 1886, at the Commission of Inquiry into the decline of British Commerce, the Birmingham delegates said: —

Germany has found the way to our markets, the addresses of our customers, and, seeing our profits, has fabricated our trademarks. She has sent her cutlery everywhere; has even pirated the names of our manufacturers. . . . Sometimes, she has employed simple imitation: the Malta cross and the star, with the name Rodgers, is one of the favourite marks with our customers: here are German knives with two Malta crosses and the name Rötgens. . . . The Germans of Westphalia have the advantage over us of water-transport on the Rhine right down to the sea. . . . The Germans also have the enormous advantage over us of technical education; and are discreet into the

[1] See Victor Berard's *English Imperialism.*

bargain. They have spread over the world and have swarmed into our country, flooding it with their imitations. In the City of London I know firms which, ten years ago, used to supply the colonies and foreign countries with English products, and which, to-day, ship nothing but German inferior articles. These articles arrive with the Sheffield mark; and, when the consumer finds that he has been taken in, he accuses us. After two or three of such experiences, he refuses to deal further with us, and applies direct to the Germans, . . . who then offer him good stuff.

Ten years later, all the official reports made similar statements in more precise language.

Our market, wrote the English Consul at Cherbourg, in 1897, is overrun with German hardware and toys. The region lives mainly by its trade with England ; and yet the shopkeepers buy nothing in England. At the big bazaar, where I asked the reason of this, the manager handed me articles in wood and fayence made in Germany from models he had given, and in sizes suited to the taste of our population, with views of Cherbourg and scenes from Norman history.

The same note is struck in reports from the British consuls in Italy, Sweden, Norway, Greece, Roumania, Portugal, and Spain. In 1898, the English consuls in Germany summed up their impressions thus : —

The year of 1897 has been an admirable success for Germany. In every industry, progress has continued, and the net result can be expressed in three words, " All fires alight," and not only those of the manufactory and well-to-do citizen, but those, too, of the peasant and workman. . . . Everything evinces this country's gigantic effort to take the lead of the world's industrial development and surpass all its rivals.

If the English ports were declining in importance, this also was Germany's fault : —

In the last twenty-six years Germany has made enormous strides in every direction. The establishment of productive industries has given work to an ever increasing population, which between 1872 and 1897 has gained thirty per cent. The creation of a flourishing commerce has bestowed on the population a growing proportion of the comforts of life ; and, during the last twenty years, this commerce has improved twenty per cent, while the traffic in German ports has gone up a hundred and twenty-four per cent.

When one reads these reports, it is easy to understand the fear felt by all these English that they will be commercially ousted by Germany, just as, two centuries ago, they themselves ousted the Dutch. They are unanimous in acknowledging the superiority of German methods. Germany carries off the palm by the quality of her economic mobilization. She possesses a magnificent system of commercial, elementary, secondary, and higher schools. Her clerks assimilate the habits and needs of foreign markets. When serving their apprenticeship, they prepare, at the same time, the success of the firms into which they will later enter. "The Germans have conquered South America," writes the Consul at Rio de Janeiro, "by the peculiar study they have made of its requirements." And the Consul at Riga says in his turn, "A German seizes every opportunity of pleasing his customers." To this the Consul at Havre adds : —

The Germans have secured the contract for supplying the industrial school at Elbeuf with all its material. They have laid down all the machinery at a merely nominal price. . . . What was paid was for the sake of form only. . . . They have thus gained the town's good graces. And this gift will be amply requited by their obtaining the future custom of all the pupils leaving this school, who will have been accustomed to the articles, methods, tools, and skill of the Germans.

This economic menace was bound to provoke a chronic state of nervousness, which soon developed into an obsession. The English grew to think that Germany's policy was everywhere aimed against them. And facts frequently justified the deduction. Sometimes, however, they drew unwarranted conclusions from the course of events. As an example, may be quoted what was written, in September, 1897, by an English politician who has been one of the men most intimately associated with the events of the last twenty years. It will show the gradual formation of England's impeachment of Germany.[1]

Up to 1895, he said, our relations with France and Russia, which left much to be desired — Prince Bismarck took good care of that! — and, on the other hand, our old ties of friendship with Austria, and especially with Italy, rallied to the *Triple Alliance*, and consequently to Germany, not only English policy, but English opinion in general. Already, however, before the telegram to President Kruger, the Emperor William's visit to Cowes, in the previous summer, after the general elections of 1895, which restored Lord Salisbury to power, had produced disappointment in Government circles on both sides. An almost open hostility with regard to South Africa was manifested during Sir Edward Malet's last interviews in Berlin, before the Ambassador quitted his post; and the Jameson raid did no more than furnish German policy with the pretext for a *coup de théâtre* which was bound to occur sooner or later.

The *coup* failed in its effect, first because Portugal refused to lend herself to Germany's tactics, and next because greater Powers than Portugal turned a deaf ear to the proposals for a European coalition against England emanating from Wilhelm-

[1] See the *Temps* of September 21, 1907.

strasse.   Moreover, both the Government and the English people
themselves had reacted with a firmness that made Berlin understand the time was not yet come to "administer a correction"
to us.   Germany made a *volte face* and, some few months later,
countenanced the recapture of Dongola by the Anglo-Egyptian
troops.

But the order to march on Dongola was given at the sugges-
tion of Italy, in order that a diversion might be created in her
favour and the Caliph and his dervishes be prevented from
threatening the Italian positions on the Red Sea, just at the
moment when the Italian army in Africa had been almost
wiped out by the disastrous issue of its Abyssinian campaign.
Could the Emperor William do otherwise than back the appeal
addressed to England by King Humbert, his ally as well as our
friend?   Besides, he knew that by urging England to reconquer the Soudan, he would not fail, under then existing circumstances, to aggravate the friction between England and France.

It was for the same reason that, three years later, the Emperor addressed his congratulations to the conquerors of Omdurman, on the very eve of Captain Marchand's arrival at Fashoda.
If the agreement come to between England and Germany with
regard to certain colonial questions in Africa gave us, as has
been asserted, without its being established, *carte blanche* in the
Transvaal, it was only a small instalment compared with the
price exacted at various times by Germany for her complaisance.
Kiao-Tcheou, Samoa, Salaga represent for us so many bribes
we have had to pay in order to secure Berlin's ever malevolent
neutrality.   But we have kept a remembrance of it, as well as
of the tone of contempt assumed towards our army not only by
the German press, but by the German Chancellor himself in
the midst of the Reichstag, during the painful war of the Transvaal.   Nor have we forgotten the discourteous behaviour of
Marshal von Waldersee in China, nor the way in which, immediately after the Chinese agreement of September, 1900, had been
signed between England and Germany, the latter audaciously
misinterpreted its meaning, so as to exclude Manchuria from its
scope, and to claim her sphere of influence in the Yang-Tse
Valley.

And can it be imagined we have forgotten Germany's tactics
during all these years at Constantinople, the opposition now

underhand, now declared, she has always made to our diplomacy in the Armenian question, the Cretan question, and later the Macedonian question? Are we perchance so blind as, without speaking of the Bagdad railway, not to have seen Germany's hand behind Turkey both in the region of Aden and on the Persian Gulf, and also in the construction of the Hedjaz railway, which, last year, caused the Anglo-Turkish dispute with regard to Tabah? Have we not heard the Emperor William proclaim aloud that Germany's future is on the seas. Have we not read the preamble, directly aimed at England, of the great Parliamentary bill for the increase of the German fleet.

It was by their cumulative effect that all these incidents, — the agreements by which Germany has grudgingly accorded us her good graces at a usurious price, as well as the diplomatic shocks, which no agreement has attenuated — have, somewhat late alas! convinced us that it would be much more simple and advantageous for us to come to an understanding, once for all, with France, and even with Russia, than to remain indefinitely under the pressure of Germany's exactions. Lord Salisbury had grown too old in the ancient order of things to take the decisive step, although no English statesman chafed under the German curb with more bitterness than he, during his last years of power. For the Anglo-French *Entente*, new men were needed: King Edward on the throne, and Lord Lansdowne at the Foreign Office. Not that they intended to make the *Entente* against Germany. Their sole aim was to put an end to a situation which Germany had exploited too long with a view to securing the predominant power in Europe. It was a measure not of aggression but defence. However, for Germany, he who is not with her is against her.[1]

In London, therefore, the Franco-English *rapprochement* appeared to be the best means of coping with Germany for the joint good of "Trade" and the "Empire." On the French side, economic interests counselled this *rapprochement*, and political interests were not opposed to it. Taking one year

[1] See the *Temps* of September 21, 1907.

with another, England purchases from us a billion's worth of merchandise. On this account, she is, as was said one day, "the oldest, nearest, richest, and most constant of our colonies." All the articles that we chiefly export (Paris articles, ready-made goods, tissues, fashion articles, worked leather, chemicals, pottery, and metal goods), compete only to an insignificant degree with articles of British production. As, on the other hand, England has large available capital, and is an excellent buyer, capable of appreciating an article of luxury and paying for it, French production is to such an extent complementary of its neighbour's that it might, if it tried, considerably increase its exportation across the Channel.[1] If it has remained thus long stationary, or nearly so (46 millions in 1875, 35 millions in 1885, 47 millions in 1895), the fault is rather that of the sellers than of the things sold. Our merchants persisting in a regrettable routine, considering that the merits of their goods are equal, the requirements of the English market identical, too often believe it unnecessary for them to alter their methods and to reckon with the modern, growing intensity of competition, especially that of Germany. There was consequently room for a development, which could not but gain by the establishment of friendly relations. Such development had been, for several years, regarded with a favourable eye by the commercial associations of the two countries.

[1] See the reports of Mr. Jean Périer, French Commercial Attaché in London, published by the National Office of Foreign Commerce.

On the 14th of September, 1901, the Associated Chambers of British commerce passed a resolution advocating a treaty of Franco-English arbitration, basing their vote on the "immense advantages that would accrue from it to commercial relations between the two countries." In 1903, during a visit of some French members of Parliament to London, Mr. Louis Sinclair, the founder of the Commercial Committee of the House of Commons, expressed the hope that the *rapprochement* might bring about an economic *Entente*. Sir Edward Sassoon said on the same occasion, "Our aim should be to arrive at the one *Entente* which is really stable, that based on material interests." In France, the various Chambers of Commerce had likewise rallied to the same idea. All of them, one after another, passed resolutions, to which several Municipal Councils adhered, calling for the development of the two countries' commercial relations. On this point, there was entire agreement between the traders on both sides of the Channel.[1]

Politically, the repulses even which Great Britain had inflicted on France in Africa — the Niger, the Upper Nile, and Egypt — had exhausted the ancient rivalry. We had nothing more to gain and nothing more to lose. A policy of reconciliation, based on the recognition of accomplished colonial facts, was therefore theoretically possible. At this moment, Mr. Delcassé, being resolved to seek in the Mediterranean, and, more especially in Morocco, compensa-

[1] See Gabriel Louis Jaray's *Franco-English Policy.*

tions for the set-back by which his ministry had
begun and for which it would be unjust to hold him
responsible, rightly thought that a Mediterranean
policy, already facilitated by the *rapprochement*
with Italy, could only be carried out in conjunction
with England. Had he then formed the chimerical
design since attributed to him of isolating Germany?
This is not probable. At any rate, it was legitimate
for him to seek for further political security on the
side of England, and to bestow an additional guarantee on our diplomatic autonomy and through it on
the balance of power in Europe. And the British
Government's inspiring thought with regard to the
balance of power must necessarily have found its
echo in Paris. Last of all, the analogies, sometimes
inexact, which can be discovered between French
and English institutions were, with certain people,
an additional argument in favour of a *rapprochement*.
"We lost a great deal of time with England between
1882 and 1898," said Mr. Deschanel in 1903. In a
few months, this lost time was about to be regained,
and the *Entente Cordiale* sealed.

III

The English King was the initiator of the *rapprochement*. He it was who both conceived and
facilitated it, while still many believed that the
moment was premature.

Edward VII has been both praised and attacked
without stint. Perhaps he deserves neither the

"excess of honour, nor yet the excess of abuse."
Among present sovereigns, he has one superiority,
that of having gained experience in life before
reigning. The existence of leisure imposed on him
by the British Constitution during his mother's
life, a leisure which he freely profited by, enabled
him to form his opinion of men and things by close
personal observation. Madame de Genlis used to
say that princes are the worst-brought-up people
in the world. She meant by this that their education is artificial, and that they grow up without
ever encountering contradiction, which is the leaven
of the critical mind. Such was not the case with
Edward VII. And, doubtless, it is for this reason
that he possesses more consistency of thought, more
tact, and more shrewdness than other sovereigns.
He is not afraid of taking the initiative; and so far
his initiative has been a success. The boldest
example of it was his visit to Paris in 1903. Putting
aside all objections, and being convinced of his
success, he arrived in France, amidst an atmosphere
of uncertainty. When the first platoons of cuiras-
siers rode down the Champs Elysées, embarrassment
and anxiety weighed on the public. The Nationalists had declared their intention of hissing. What
would be the result of a hostile manifestation?
The King, as far as he was concerned, did not believe
in the danger, and he was right. The Parisians
accorded him not an enthusiastic, but, from the
first, a respectful, and soon a genial, reception. The
road was clear. Two months later, Mr. Loubet

paid King Edward a return visit. And, on welcoming his colleague, Mr. Delcassé, to London, Lord Lansdowne said to him: —

"Now we are going to have some conversation."

As a matter of fact, there was conversation both in Paris and in London. Lord Lansdowne, Mr. Delcassé, Mr. Paul Cambon — the French Ambassador in London, — Sir Eldon Gorst, at that time the Egyptian Government's financial adviser, were the chief interlocutors in this dialogue that lasted eight months. On the English side was shown a sincere desire to come to an understanding, but also in details great minuteness and a wary fear of yielding too much; on the French side an equal willingness to come to an arrangement, the best intentions, in fine, but too much southern imaginativeness, and, here and there, carelessness in practical precision. On the 8th of April, 1904, the agreement was signed, and its immediate publication produced a deep impression in Europe.

The arrangement, which comprised a convention relative to Newfoundland and Western Africa, and a declaration concerning Egypt and Morocco, formed a treaty of liquidation and equilibrium. The convention had merely a local importance, and settled ancient disputes, somewhat to England's advantage, with the artificial adjunction of questions of very different nature. On the contrary, the declaration had a general value, and mapped out the main lines of a future policy. As already seen, we had lost in Egypt, from year to year, the bigger share of our advantages, and our dispossession had been practically effected by the Fashoda incident terminating in the treaty of March, 1899. Yet, theoretically, we preserved our liberty to profit by any opportunities that might occur, and to draw Europe's attention to a problem that was not juridically settled. It was, therefore, an appreciable success for England to obtain the assurance that "the Government of the French Republic would not thwart her action in Egypt by asking that a date should be fixed for the British occupation to cease or by taking measures of another kind." The Egyptian Government, that is to say, Great Britain, regained the liberty, besides, to dispose of the savings resulting from the conversion of 1890. And she was freed from the obligation of devoting to the Debt service revenues double the sum annually required. Instead of the Debt Exchequer being compelled, in each financial period, to make a sort of seizure on the totality of the Egyptian revenues, it was the land tax which became the creditors' pledge. In return, France obtained certain guarantees, in particular, that the reimbursement of the Preference Debt should be adjourned from 1905 to 1910; that the 1885 Loan, for which no limit of reimbursement had been specified, could not be reimbursed before the same date; that the Consolidated Debt, three-fifths of which are held in France, could not be either converted or reimbursed before 1912. These were wise precautions, but of very secondary importance compared with the advantages of the highest order secured by Great Britain.

This being so, the agreement concerning Egypt comprised also a reciprocal liberty of action for ourselves in Morocco. One needs only to consult a map to see that France, being supreme in Algeria and Tunis, cannot regard with indifference what takes place in the Moorish Empire. It is a necessity for her that order shall reign there and that no Power shall acquire preponderant influence over the country at her expense.[1] After being for twenty years our most redoubtable adversary in Morocco, England now recognized that "it belonged to France, as having territory contiguous to this country over a great distance, to have the more exclusive charge of its tranquillity and to lend her assistance to it in all the administrative, economic, financial, and military reforms required." She declared besides, "that she would do nothing to thwart French action in these matters." A reciprocal engagement, valid for thirty years, secured to the two contracting parties commercial liberty and equality of treatment both in Egypt and Morocco. Last of all, it was stipulated that the two signataries "should lend each other mutual help diplomatically for the execution of the clauses of the present declaration."

Is it possible to estimate arithmetically the respective advantages assured to the two parties by this double-barrelled arrangement? It is certain that by effacing ourselves in Egypt in England's favour, we did no more than acknowledge the force of actual facts, whilst British diplomacy abandoned

[1] See below, Chapter III.

in Morocco designs to which the future was open. It is no less evident that our adhesion to Great Britain's Egyptian policy confirmed an existing situation and constituted a real profit for her, whereas in Morocco she granted to us virtual advantages, prospects, and possibilities only. France paid cash down, England by draft; and Morocco, as events proved, was not yet the hatched chicken of which one could freely dispose. On the other hand, it must be acknowledged that what we gave up had a greater value for England than for ourselves, and reciprocally. The balance of equity was undeniable; and, on the whole, its effect was a success. The drawing up of the agreement, however, left more than one thing to be desired. The article relating to Egypt was too vague; and the expression, "by taking measures of another kind," was altogether wanting in precision. Moreover, certain eventualities had been overlooked, which it would have been wiser to provide against. This was discovered notably when Mr. Lambert, the French director of the Khedive's School of Law, resigned and was replaced by a young Englishman, Mr. Hill, who had none of the qualifications requisite for presiding over an establishment imbued with our spirit. However, in a general way, the good was greater than the bad; and Mr. Delcassé deserved the praise that was unstintedly bestowed on him.

Furthermore, whatever might be the value of the agreement in its reference to Africa, it drew the

F

attention of the world at large rather by its general significance. The colonial rivalry between France and England had, for centuries, become a common property. It was the postulate of European policy, the favourite instrument of the policy of Germany. By putting an end to this state of things, the Cabinets of London and Paris introduced a new weight into the international balance of power. They mutually freed themselves from preoccupations that had long been a burden; and they guaranteed each other a liberty of action which was equally precious to both. France, in particular, who had not been able to hold Russia back from the Manchurian adventure, found an opportune compensation for the enfeeblement she incurred through the Japanese victories. Preceded by the Franco-Italian agreement and soon followed by the Franco-Spanish one, the Franco-English arrangement procured us, in Western Europe, a moral authority which made us a centre of attraction; and, if it was calculated to expose us to certain difficulties, it rendered us in return capable of solving them. It was, in fact, the second phase of the diplomatic evolution which enabled us to issue progressively from our position of isolation. Of course, there was the fear that it would not be easy, in presence of the Anglo-Japanese Alliance, together with Anglo-Russian hostility and the Russo-Japanese war, to reconcile our necessary alliance with Saint Petersburg and our useful friendship with London. But, at once, without noticing newspaper objections, Russia's official representatives declared that their Government took no umbrage at the Anglo-French *rapprochement*.[1]

Indeed, before long, facts occurred which most happily justified the agreement thus concluded. And here again, it was neither in London nor in Paris that the decisive events happened. The fear of Germany was responsible for the *Entente Cordiale;* and Germany's mistakes transformed and strengthened it. Whatever merit may be assigned to the repeated Franco-English manifestations of sympathy, — King Edward's visits to Paris, the English fleet's welcome at Brest, that of the French fleet at Portsmouth, the Paris Municipal Council's stay in London, the London County Council's reception at our Hôtel de Ville, and, last of all, Mr. Fallières' official visit to London — the strengthening of the *Entente* is not due to these; all such fêtes have been effects, not causes. The cause must be sought in Germany. On the morrow of the signing of the treaty of 1904, Germany affected the most serene indifference. A year later, the Emperor William's journey to Tangier, strikingly showed that his Government had only waited for the Russian defeats to manifest the inimical sentiments they had felt from the very first.[2] During the Moroccan crisis, Franco-English solidarity was cemented by the common peril. The identity of French and British interests affirmed itself by an identity of policy; and, when the Algeciras Conference closed, no one in Europe could fail

[1] See André Tardieu's *Diplomatic Questions of the Year* 1904.
[2] See below, Chapter V.

to see that, for the agreement of liquidation signed two years previously, an *Entente* had been substituted which, though not set down in treaty form, no less counted as a diplomatic security of the highest order.

More recent events have tended only to increase the value of this security. The Russo-Japanese war, which coincided with our Moroccan embarrassment and was partially the cause of it, had made it harder for us to fit in the Russian Alliance with our friendship for England. For a while, when our neutrality dispute with Japan was in its acute stage, and more especially when the Dogger Bank incident happened, it seemed as though France would have to choose between one of two dread alternatives. But Mr. Delcassé, with infinite skill, discovered a remedy in the peril itself; and the meeting in Paris of the International Commission of Inquiry, intrusted with the task of arbitrating between the English and the Russians, was the first step towards the achievement of their reconciliation. A year later, negotiations were entered into between London and Saint Petersburg; and, on the 31st of August, 1907, an Asiatic agreement, with a wider bearing than its actual clauses, was signed between those who had been adversaries for ages and who, in June, 1908, at Revel, set public seal to their recent intimacy.[1] The grand German design of a "Continental League" against England was definitely ruined. Bismarck's trick of using Anglo-Russian hostility to press on

[1] See below, Chapter VI.

France with all the weight of Central Europe was no longer possible. A *Triple Entente* facing the Triple Alliance, gave a new foundation to Europe's balance of power.

IV

This internal evolution of the *Entente Cordiale*, — as also certain public manifestations, such as the toasts in which, in June, 1908, the King of England and the President of the French Republic spoke of "strengthening" the *Entente* and rendering it "permanent," — have, in the most natural manner possible, placed before public opinion in Europe the question of an eventual transformation of the *Entente* into an alliance.   When political questions are dealt with, the mind, as Talleyrand used to say, must take in the future.   It is never too early to scrutinize a probability which unforeseen circumstances might any day oblige those interested in it to change into a reality; and, in so far as opinions vary, it is important to express them.

If language has a meaning, what is intended by strengthening the *Entente Cordiale* is the substitution of a formal treaty for the moral agreement of 1904. At present, France and England are friends, but not allies.   If it be urged that the distinction is a secondary one, in presence of the keenness of mutual sympathy, we must reply that, when the relations of two great Powers are concerned, precision is a duty, and ambiguity a danger.   For the moment, English policy and French policy run parallel; but they are not bound to each other. They joined, four years ago, in negotiating a treaty of liquidation; and this treaty has become the basis of a sincere reconciliation. However, neither on one side nor on the other were pledges given. It may be admitted that, in a time of crisis, such pledges would be spontaneously forthcoming from an identity of interests. But, if this is likely, why not examine the question thoroughly in advance, weigh its pros and cons, and, in fine, estimate the advantages and inconveniences attaching to such "strengthening," which heads of States and the press speak of continually without clearly defining it.

Diplomatically and preventively, the *Entente Cordiale* has justified itself. When it was concluded, its object was negative and limited, and recorded merely a colonial understanding. Very quickly, so quickly indeed that some were surprised, this *Entente* assumed a positive value. Perhaps there would be exaggeration in saying that to it was owing, in 1905, the preservation of peace; for this peace — analogous to that of Fashoda and of a kind such that not many would be needed in a century to deprive its beneficiaries of their right to rank as a great Power— we paid for, we and we alone, with an unprecedented humiliation, and the sacrifice of a Minister of Foreign Affairs, under the threats of a neighbouring country.[1] On the other hand, during the negotiations that followed the crisis, before, at, and after Algeciras, Great Britain supported us with a loyal energy to which the

[1] See Chapter V.

French owe grateful homage. The weight of English approval which our proposals constantly met with throughout, contributed to insure their success. And this visible unity has exercised an attraction so great that, in the next year, following the example of France, Russia concluded with Great Britain a pact of reconciliation which opens to our policy a wide perspective of safety.

Does this mean that a Franco-English alliance would be justified *de plano*? It is certain that one of the gravest objections that would have been raised not long ago against such an alliance has disappeared since our ally, Russia, has become reconciled with Great Britain. France would have been false not only to her pledges, but also to her own interests, if she had allied herself with England while the latter Power was inimical to Russia. That is not, however, the case to-day. And, as far as this is concerned, the way is open. For the English, the French Alliance is desirable. England has always wished to have, in case of difficulties, a Continental ally. The history of the eighteenth century proved this, and that of the nineteenth likewise. It was even possible to say that she got others to fight, and herself entered the lists only at the last. The support of the French Army in a European war in which Great Britain should be engaged, would be of inestimable value to the Cabinet of Saint James. Would England's support, in a European war in which France should be engaged, be of equal value to our own country?

To this question — the gravest that our statesmen have conscientiously to ask themselves — it is
essential that a candid reply should be given. In
the present situation, England's diplomatic coöperation, before a war, would be of infinite service to
us. When once war were begun, this coöperation
would be but of small avail. Great Britain's naval
victories would not hold off a single cannon or
a single man from our frontiers. They would render us none of the services which Russia, and
Russia alone at present, is able to render us. In
a word, a Franco-English alliance would mean for
us, in the military domain, a minimum of profit.
And for things to be different, it would be necessary
for the British Army, thoroughly reformed not only
in its organization, but in its manner of recruitment,
to become capable of taking energetic action on the
Continent, for it to be able to create on land an
effective diversion, for it to be ready to lessen the
shock our own army would have to support; in fine,
it would be necessary for Great Britain to be, as far
as France is concerned, a second Russia.

Unfortunately, the English Army is far from being
in a position to play this rôle. Mr. Haldane, the
Minister of War, has attempted to realize a certain
progress by means of a reform which came into
force on the 31st of March, 1908. But his attempt
would seem to be altogether insufficient. Under the
new scheme, the principle of free enlistment has been
preserved which is the traditional basis of military
organization in England for the active army as well

as for the Reserve forces, including Yeomen and Volunteers. However, the engagement of the Territorials, that is to say, of the two latter categories, will be of a stricter kind. The Volunteers (infantry) used to enlist for any period they wished, and could cancel their engagement at will on condition of giving notice to their colonel a fortnight beforehand. The Yeomen (mounted infantry) were bound for periods of three years, which conferred on their body a relative stability. But for both of these classes, the period of service in times of peace was only of short duration. In times of war, the periods of forced service remained variable. The law of the 2d of August, 1907, completed by ulterior regulations, in particular by the Special Navy orders of the 18th and 20th of March, 1908, prescribes for both infantry and cavalry a four years' period of service. In order to cancel the engagement, three months' notice must be given; and, in addition, the soldier that breaks his bargain must pay a fine, and must bring back his arms and outfit to the depôt of the battalion or squadron. The new system, therefore, is stricter than the old.

And its stringency shows itself still more clearly, if the provisions are considered that determine under the new law the activity of the Territorial Army. This army can, as a matter of fact, be called out on active service, and the Territorial soldier be then kept for a whole year on duty. The object is evidently, not only to amalgamate the two species of auxiliary forces, which, to use Mr. Haldane's expres-

sion, had grown up, anyhow, like mushrooms, but
further to give to this amalgam a military value and
make out of these incoherent elements a compact,
organic whole, an army in the modern sense of the
word. For that, these battalions must be disci-
plined, instructed, and properly trained in their respective regiments, brigades, and divisions; a field
artillery must be given them which the auxiliary
forces did not possess; engineering troops, which
formerly were also lacking; and behind these must
be created troops for foraging and revictualling —
all that provides for the nourishment of an army, all
that constitutes the framework without which there
are neither legs for marching nor arms for fighting.
County associations, local staffs, are commissioned
to see to this organization.

Thus remodelled, the new Territorial Army would
have the sole charge, in the case of a war with a
European Power, to assure the defence of the English metropolis. For Mr. Haldane has decided —
and this is the second characteristic feature of the
reform — that the Militia shall henceforward be
required, in time of war, to join the active line regiments and to coöperate, if need be, with them in a
campaign abroad. Then, it would be the remodelled Territorial Army which would take the place of
the old Militia for the defence of the Metropolis, the
Militia becoming a "special reserve force," the battalions of which will encircle the active battalions of
the line, in order to supply them with additional men
during a war in the enemy's country. Thus they will

become the headquarters of the regiments composing the expeditionary force. With this end in view, the personal obligations of militiamen are to be rendered more rigorous — six months' effective services in the year following the enlistment, and longer in each of the other years, with a fortnight's training and six days' rifle practice. The Militia, under its new constitution, will yield a hundred and one battalions, seventy-four of which will fill up the gaps occurring in the active battalions serving abroad, the twenty-seven others being employed as foraging, garrison, and auxiliary service troops. Mr. Haldane hopes to have in this way a body of 166,000 men capable of disembarking on an enemy's shore, and a home army of 315,000.

All this reads very well on paper; but the question is how far it is realizable. Still now, as in the past, what the English Army lacks is a proper system of recruitment; and recruitment is the muscle of war, just as money is its nerve strength. Both Yeomen and Volunteers were given till the 15th of June, 1908, to accept or refuse the new order of things; and it turns out that enlistments have been appreciably fewer than was expected. On the other hand, grave difficulties crop up, when the question of artillery is considered. The Volunteers have in the Yeomen a kind of Territorial cavalry. But they must have cannons. And Mr. Haldane has asked for the authorization to form for this purpose a hundred and eighty-two field batteries. In the House of Lords, such competent authorities as Lord Rob-

erts, Lord Denbigh, and Lord Grenfell have sharply
criticised the project, which can only be carried out
by dismissing thirty-three active batteries, that is to
say, by bringing about an important diminution in
the forces of first line.   Writing on this subject, the
Army and Navy Gazette says: "The active army has
been reduced and is threatened with fresh reductions; and its reserve force will itself decrease,
through the operation of the same cause.   The Militia has been destroyed, and no one can say to what
extent it will be replaced by the special reserve force.
The Volunteers have disappeared to the extent of
two-thirds of their numbers, and are replaced to the
extent of a third only by Territorials.   The Royal
Artillery force, through the effect of an innovation
that is nothing less than criminal, is about to lose a
part of its effective units.   We regret to see that the
Minister is refractory to every argument brought
forward by the most enlightened authorities in both
Army and nation."   How is it possible to ignore Mr.
Haldane's own avowal that the English Army ought
to have eight thousand officers more than it possesses
at the present time?

Such being the state of affairs, it is only prudent
to conclude that, in a Continental war, Great Britain's assistance would have but mediocre value;
prudent not to abandon one's self to dangerous illusions.   The polemics that were carried on in the
month of June, revealed that there are two contradictory currents of opinion in England.   One,
which was expressed in a remarkable article that

appeared in the *National Review*, is favourable to
an increase of the British Army. "An Anglo-
French alliance," said the writer, "would be without profit for France as long as England cannot
offer her the assistance of a large army in Lorraine."
The other current, which manifestly represents the
majority, is opposed to an alliance and to the thorough military reform which, from our point of view,
would be its *sine qua non*. Many English people,
it is true, seem to think that, in case of war, the
alliance would come about of its own accord. But
it is just against such a way that one ought to protest. International improvisations are perilous.
Should the day come when, for Mr. Haldane's inade-
quate scheme, the English authorities would decide
to substitute a more serious programme and to provide their country with a modern army, should the
day come when they would recollect that Napoleon
succumbed, not at Trafalgar, but at Waterloo, then
clear-sighted Frenchmen might be partisans of an
alliance that would complete and widen the system
of pacific defence, sealed in 1891, by the Franco-
Russian Alliance, and the political risks of which
would be compensated for by military advantages.
Until then, on the contrary, there can be no question between France and England of pledges for the
future and military coöperation. And if, while
things remain as they are, an Anglo-German war
should break out, our country's sole duty would be
to safeguard, with all her energy, her diplomatic and
military autonomy.

Here comes in, it is true, the too famous hostage
theory: Germany, while at war with England, attacking France in order to have guarantees on the
Continent. Once more, with regard to this, a clear
understanding is necessary. The hostage theory
may well have been menacing, at a time when,
France being disorganized and Russia vanquished,
neither Power was able to make use of the alliance
between them. This time has gone by. If Germany
were to attack France now, she would set in action
the chief clause of the military convention signed
between France and Russia in 1892, and would
have on her back not only the French but the Russian Army, too. Under these circumstances, the
so-called guarantee to be taken against Great Britain would risk being a most unprofitable one. The
hostage theory to-day is a mere scarecrow, at which
we can afford to smile, on condition of remaining
able, in accordance with Russia, to energetically
enforce our armed neutrality.

That which our country needs to do is to regard
the English *Entente* with a matter-of-fact mind, and
while having a practical regard for her own interests.
This *Entente* has a great political value, not a military one, and we must act in accordance. Having,
during the last thirty-eight years, made no war on
account of Alsace-Lorraine, we must not expose
ourselves to make it for others. In a word, France
must be decided to reject improvised combinations
which would drag her from peace into a conflict
wherein all the risks would be for her. These res-

ervations are neither offensive nor superfluous,
since they are inspired by care for French interests
and by the experience of the past. Already, when
the practical side of the Russian Alliance was in
question, some of our fellow-countrymen claimed
that it should be withheld from discussion, and dealt
with by an act of faith. To regard the holy ark with
a critical, independent eye, was deemed sacrilegious
audacity. What did we gain by such discretion?
And what did the Russians gain by it? Instead of
reminding our Allies of their duties towards us —
which, in the case at issue, were one with their duties towards themselves — we docilely accepted the
deviation of the Alliance; we allowed the money,
Army, and Navy of Russia to desert Europe for Asia.
Under our approval, the Saint Petersburg Government, between 1895 and 1902, turned more and
more in the direction of the Far East. Continually
deceived in their hopes, they incurred thus the disasters of Mukden and Tsusima, without our doing
anything to restrain them. And, a few weeks after,
we learned to our cost, both at Tangier and in Paris,
what these defeats meant to us.

These things must be borne in mind in our relations with England. As a Continental Power,
France needs allies who, in case of war, are capable
of helping her on the Continent. Good business
makes good friends, and, still more, good allies. If,
in the interests of the world's peace, the Anglo-
French *Entente*, the foundations of which are already
laid, is one day to become permanent and "stronger,"

if, in other words, a treaty is destined to confer on it the form of a contract, it is only right that this treaty, negotiated in a fair spirit, should impose on each the sacrifices required, — on France and Russia an enlightened attention to their naval power, on which Great Britain must be able to count, and on Great Britain a thorough reform of her land forces, whose development both France and Russia are entitled to expect.

Until then, let us maintain a reserved attitude. Friends, but not allies; such is the necessary and sufficient programme, the only one calculated to ward off alike the dangers that might come from our adversaries and those that would risk being caused by our friendships.

CHAPTER III

FRANCE AND THE MEDITERRANEAN UNDERSTANDINGS

I

IN the thought of the French Government, the Franco-English *rapprochement* was not only a useful measure of general interest. It appeared to them, also, as the necessary instrument of the Mediterranean policy dictated to them by their traditions and future interests.

To quote Gambetta's saying, the configuration
of our coasts and our establishment of French rule
in Algeria have made the Mediterranean, and the
Western Mediterranean especially, our "scene of
action." Historically, France has had a preponderant rôle in the three events dominating the
modern history of the Mediterranean: the unifica-
tion of Italy, the opening of the Suez Canal, and
the Europeanization of North Africa. Geographically, she is the only Power who, over a long extent
of coast, borders on both sides of the Latin Sea.
Politically, her successes in Algiers and Tunis, her
repulses in Egypt and on the Continent, have concentrated her activity on the west basin of the
Mediterranean, which is peculiarly accessible to
her commerce and her fleets, and is the route to her
African and Asiatic colonies. But it places France
in presence of three Powers with whom she has to
count. One of them, Great Britain, through Gibraltar, Malta, and Egypt, holds the two Gates of
the Central Sea. The two others, Italy and Spain,
by their situation itself, have interests of the same
kind as France has; and, from this fact, may, in
pursuit of such interests, come into conflict with
our own country. The agreement of the 8th of
April, 1904, liquidated the Anglo-French quarrel.
How did the reconciliation of France with Rome
and Madrid come about?

If nothing in the past had given any reason to
hope for a *rapprochement* between France and England, that between France and Italy was no less

unlikely. True, we had rendered the Italians sig-
nal services at the time when they achieved their
unity; but Napoleon III's mistakes, his pretension to check at his will the national movement that he had let loose, Rouher's "Never," and,
last of all, Victor Emmanuel's utilitarian policy in
1870, had separated the two peoples, after their
bond of union had apparently been sealed on the
battle-fields of Magenta and Solferino. Moreover,
young Italy was indulging in dreams of grandeur;
and it was in the Mediterranean, that is to say, at
our expense, that she was hoping to realize them.
As early as 1838, Mazzini had declared: "Northern
Africa is Italy's inheritance." And to Mazzini it
was that Bismarck wrote in 1866: "Italy and France
cannot associate to their mutual advantage in the
Mediterranean. This sea is an inheritance that
cannot be divided between two kindred nations.
The empire of the Mediterranean belongs indis-
putably to Italy, who possesses in this sea coasts
twice as extensive as those of France. . . . The
empire of the Mediterranean must be Italy's constant thought, the aim of her ministers, the fundamental policy of the Florence Cabinet." In 1870,
not content with taking Rome, many Italians had
the idea of occupying either Corsica or Tunis. A
few years later, Fregosa, in his book entitled, *Il pri-
mato Italiano*, claimed Egypt, Tripoli, Tunis, and
Algeria as Italy's natural colonies.[1] The Policy of

[1] See, in reference to this, René Pinon's *Empire of the Mediterranean*.

the Consulta justified Thiers' saying that "Italy's gratitude would last just as long as her weakness." [1]

These tendencies Bismarck, with his superior skill, managed to excite, foster, and utilize. The clericalism of the National Assembly, the maintenance of a French guardship at Civita Vecchia, the petition of our bishops for the reëstablishment of the Pope's temporal power, and the Duc de Broglie's ministry, everything was taken advantage of by him for the purpose of keeping Italy in a state of alarm. The Tunis affair served to complete the Rome Cabinet's distrust and fear of us. To the laurels which Signor Maccio, the Italian Consul, hoped to gather in the Regency, the expedition of General Forgemol replied with the consent of Europe in 1881. Hatred of France was rampant. Revenge was sought at any price. The moment awaited by Bismarck arrived. Strengthened by the alliance concluded with Austria in 1879, he had no need to solicit Italy to join the coalition. She offered of her own accord. She abandoned herself. The Triple Alliance was concluded, and Italy's armaments at once gave it an aggressive character. Crispinism was the order of the day. From 1881

[1] It is right to add here that in a speech pronounced on the 3d of May, 1894, Baron Blanc, Minister of Foreign Affairs, attempted to clear his country from this charge. According to him, it was out of gratitude towards France that Italy had not anticipated her in Tunis and did not join with England's action in Egypt. This somewhat singular theory, as is remarked in the book, *France and Italy*, written by Mr. Billot, our late Ambassador at Rome, proves the ingeniousness of Baron Blanc's mind — and nothing more.

to 1896, it weighed on Franco-Italian relations. In the *Triplice*, Crispi was the instigating agent whom Bismarck was able to restrain or let loose, just as he pleased. Franco-Italian relations were considerably more strained than those between France and Germany. To act against France rather than on behalf of Italy, such was the line of conduct instinctively followed at Rome, whether in Europe or out of Europe; but, as was soon seen, at the expense of Italy's interests, both political and economic.

During this period, numerous were the disagreeable incidents that occurred between the two countries. In the month of December, 1887, the Florence police, cynically backed up by Crispi, broke open the archives of our Consulate. In the following year, the military commandant at Massowah, acting on his own authority, abolished the capitulations, under the benefit of which, the French residing there had lived for more than twenty years. In February, 1888, the altogether improbable report was circulated that the French fleet was about to attack Spezzia. On the 2d of October, 1891, a French pilgrim having written *Vive le Pape* on the register lying in the Pantheon near Victor Emmanuel's tomb, there was a formidable outburst of anti-French feeling throughout the country. In August, 1893, the Prince of Naples was present at the German military manœuvres in Lorraine; and, in the same month, some Italians having been killed at Aigues Mortes in a quarrel with French workmen,

the Palais-Farnèse, which was the residence of our
Embassy, was attacked by the mob. In September,
1894, the Italian authorities of the frontier
made several arrests of French officers, while in the
December following, a whole series of expulsions
of French journalists who had been long established
in Rome, was carried out. Now and again, it is
true, there were Franco-Italian fêtes celebrated
and exchanges of good-will in one place or another:
the visit of an Italian squadron to Toulon, in
April, 1890; the inauguration at Nice of Garibal-
di's monument, in October, 1891; the visit of a
French squadron to Genoa, in September, 1892;
manifestations of sympathy, when President Carnot
was assassinated, in June, 1894; the unveiling at
Magenta of MacMahon's statue, in June, 1895.
True, also, between two armament projects, Crispi
affirmed his attachment to peace and his sentiments of friendship towards France. None the
less, the tension was great, and Italian policy was
responsible for this. Add to these things the clash
of interests embittered by our protectionism and
the rupture of commercial relations between the
two countries; and it will be seen how fragile was
a peace that was at the mercy of every little alarm.[1]

On the 5th of May, Crispi's megalomania exposed
his country to defeat at the hands of the Abyssini-
ans. The morrows of defeat are favourable to
reflection. Italy reflected. Her grievances in the
Mediterranean had induced her to throw in her lot

[1] See Billot's *France and Italy*.

with the Triple Alliance. However, her Mediterranean policy had not secured by it the guarantees
sought, Bismarck, in 1882, granting nothing to
Mancini on this score. In 1886, Robilant, the
Minister of Foreign Affairs, wrote: "I am quite
decided not to take the initiative in meeting the
Chancellor with a view to further negotiations. In
1882, we seemed rather to be begging the Alliance
than to be negotiating it; and, in concluding it, we
exposed ourselves to a Continental war without
securing our guarantees against a Naval war." By
such a policy, what had Italy gained? With regard
to Germany, a subaltern position; with regard to
France, a precarious one, and, as a consequence,
armaments that heavily burdened her budget. Her
extraordinary credits ran up: 127 millions in 1882,
212 millions in 1885, 146 millions in 1886; and,
finally, in the budget of 1894–1895, a deficit of 180
millions. The denunciation of the Commercial
Treaty with France had been ruinous to Italian
agriculture and industry. Within two years Italian exports to France had fallen 61 per cent.
More than 700 million francs had been withdrawn
in one year by French capitalists from Italian
undertakings in which they were invested. The
Exchange rose to 123. As General Corsi wrote:
"The economic consequences of the alliance with
Germany were disastrous." And many people, considering the state of affairs, began to repeat Robilant's words: "Italy is decidedly tired of this barren
Alliance; and I am loath to oblige her to persevere

in it. For, I am too deeply conscious that, as far as we are concerned, it will always be void of results." At least, there was good reason to correct its exclusive, onerous, and burdensome character by a return to a policy of equilibrium.[1]

The logical issue from this situation was through a *rapprochement* between France and Italy; and circumstances, more than any personal good-will, were the active cause of the reconciliation. On the 28th of September, 1896, Italy gave us a first pledge — by accepting a revision of the Tunisian treaties, which implied an official recognition of our situation in the Regency. On the 1st of October, a Franco-Italian treaty of navigation was substituted for the one which had expired in 1886. Last of all, on the 21st of November, 1898, was signed the Treaty of Commerce which had long been desired in Rome. The Italian commercial balance sheet at once showed an increase of 100 millions in imports and of 200 millions in exports. Our French banks, the Paris Comptoir d'Escompte and the Banque de Paris, — intervening just when the German economic crisis of 1900 put an end to the financial aid that had previously been obtained at Berlin, — saved the Rome market from a veritable disaster. "But for the 100 millions of the Public Debt purchased in 1901 by the Paris Market, Italy would in that year have been unable to obtain her economic equilibrium; and the exchange on foreign countries, instead of disappearing gradually, would have advanced to pre-

[1] See Luigi Chiala's *Pagine di Storia contemporanea.*

mium rates."[1] At this juncture, Italy was induced to draw nearer to France by the tightness of her economic situation; and the Italians themselves are the first to acknowledge it, as the following quotation proves: —

The German economic crisis rendered it necessary that Italy should seek for a political *rapprochement* with France. Italy would have been forced (in any case) to inaugurate a policy altogether friendly to France. If, through a political blunder, such as the visit of the Prince of Naples to Metz, the patriotic sentiments of the French had been wounded and the Paris market had again begun to sell Italian Consols, Italy would have been obliged sooner or later to reimburse all the French money invested in them, the exchange would again have advanced to its highest rates; Consols would have declined to their lowest ebb; and Italy would have found herself in presence of an economic crisis like the one she had such a terrible experience of in 1893. The powerlessness shown by the German money market to act as Italy's banker, the need of the latter young country's continuing her economic development, and having the aid of other nations richer than herself, together with the fact that the Paris money market has once more assumed the rôle of banker to Italy, impose on the Government a policy which shall be in perfect accord with that of France.[2]

It is therefore allowable to think that commercial and financial interests on Italy's side would have sufficed to determine the *rapprochement*, while securing to France political advantages that were equivalent. Such was not the opinion of Mr. Delcassé, who, when commercial relations were resumed, seized the opportunity in order to enter into diplomatic negotiations with the Cabinet at Rome. In

[1] See G. M. Fiamingo's book, *The Financial Reasons for the Franco-Italian Friendship.*
[2] See G. M. Fiamingo's book, above.

the month of April, 1901, the Italian fleet, under the
orders of the Duke of Genoa, came to pay an official
visit to President Loubet at Toulon. In the same
year, in consequence of an exchange of views with
Paris, Signor Prinetti, the Italian Minister of
Foreign Affairs, announced that, to his knowledge,
"France had no intention, in the regions bordering
on the *vilayet* of Tripoli, to go beyond the limits
fixed by the Convention of the 21st of March, 1899,
nor yet to interfere with the Caravans." A few
days later, in an interview, Mr. Delcassé stated that,
in return for this assurance, Italy had promised to
do nothing that might hamper French policy in
Morocco. As a matter of fact, this was the substance of the Notes exchanged, in December, 1900,
between the Governments. In 1902, on the renewal
of the Triple Alliance, Mr. Delcassé explained in
Parliament "that the legitimate aspirations of
both nations clashed nowhere"; and he added, "that
neither directly nor indirectly was Italy's policy
aimed against France by reason of her alliances.
They could not, in any case, imply a threat against
us whether in diplomatic forms, protocols, or international military stipulations. In no case and
under no form, could Italy become either the instrument or the auxiliary of an aggression against our
country."

What was the value of this *rapprochement?* What
was its scope? In a general point of view, that is to
say, the European, it made no change in the terms
of existing treaties. However closely Mr. Delcassé's

declarations are examined, there is only one affirmation to be extracted from them; to wit, that the engagements imposed on Italy by the Triple Alliance have not an offensive, but a purely defensive, character, and that, in the case of an attack on France, Italy would not be associated with it. But it does not seem that the constitutive clauses of the Triple Alliance ever had any stipulation of the kind. What gave them their aggressive character was not their wording, but the bias exhibited by Italy in their interpretation. And it was the alteration of this bias which constituted an important *fait nouveau* in the international order. When Bismarck used to speak of "exhausting our life's blood," Italy was the Power he intended should play the provocative agent's rôle. It was through Italy that the *Triplice* was able to become offensive in its action. Without modifying the text that sealed this Alliance, the Franco-Italian *rapprochement* modified therefore its nature. Since the *rapprochement*, the Triple Alliance has lost its edge. It is less threatening militarily, more peaceable politically. To Germany, if attacked by France, it leaves the support of the Italian Army; but for an attack on France there is no longer the assistance of Italian provocations.

This evolution assumes still greater precision, if, instead of considering the friendly understanding between Rome and Paris by itself, we place it as a function of the Franco-English *rapprochement*. Between 1882 and 1900, Italy was not only Ger-

many's ally. She was also bound to Great Britain
by engagements, the nature of which was not clearly
declared, but the existence of which was not doubtful. In February, 1887, Depretis said, "Our situation is now secure both on sea and on land." On the
29th of June, the Marquis di Rudini, who held the
double office of Premier and Minister of Foreign
Affairs, declared in his turn: —

What Italy perseveringly and tenaciously wishes is peace,
because she believes it is necessary for the development of her
institutions and the improvement of her economic conditions.

But, on the other hand, Italy also tenaciously wishes for the
maintenance of the balance of power in Europe, the preservation of the *statu quo* in the Mediterranean especially.

With a view to realizing these designs, the Government has
not waited until to-day, in seeking to come to understandings
and to conclude agreements with the Powers that are in the
same order of ideas and whose interests are bound up together.

An exchange of opinions took place only a few years ago with
England, followed by declarations on the part of Sir James Fer-
gusson in the English Parliament; and there remains but little
for me to add on the subject.

His language was strictly conformable to the facts of the
case. Both Italy and England purpose to maintain peace while
preserving the *statu quo*. I may say, moreover, that I perceive
no questions, respecting which, the views of Italy are not in
accordance with those of England, seeing that their interests
are identical.

Last of all, on the 17th of March, 1896, the Marquis
di Rudini repeated in his ministerial statement that
the country's traditional friendship with England
completed Italy's system of alliances. As long as
England was at loggerheads with France, her intimate relations with Rome, — "her Alliance of

Sentiment," to use the Duke of Sermoneta's expression, — was not, as may be imagined, of a nature
to improve Franco-Italian relations. And, on the
contrary, the Franco-English *rapprochement*, concluded in 1894, at once added value to the Franco-
Italian understanding. It was, so to speak, its
moral security, increasing its diplomatic efficacy in
the cause of peace.

As for the agreements assuring reciprocal abstention in Morocco and the *Tripolitaine* respectively,
they were in harmony with the interests of the two
countries. It will be seen further on, why France
was compelled to intervene in Morocco. And, in
sooth, to quote a pertinent remark, "the key of the
Moorish Empire was not to be sought in Rome."
But still Italy's good-will with regard to projects as
yet ill-defined might one day be useful. On the other
hand, no essential interests required the presence
of the Italians at Tripoli. What they desired, after
their Ethiopian fiasco, was more especially the
satisfaction of their *amour-propre*. The *Tripolitaine* does not possess the first-class value recently
attributed to it by Rohlfs when he wrote: "The
Power that holds Tripoli will be master of the
Sudan: Tunis as an acquisition is not worth the
tenth of Tripoli." Indeed, no one, even at Rome,
nourishes any illusions with regard to the possibilities of profit in the Tripolitan affair. The Sultan
has sovereignty over the *vilayet*, and would only
abandon it in obedience to armed force. As an
Italian Minister once said: "It is proper that our

designs on Tripoli should preserve a strictly platonic
character." Even with this character, certain persons in France have expressed the opinion that it
was imprudent to admit the hypothesis of an Italian
installation at the gates of Tunis. However, while
granting that the *rapprochement* with Rome might
have been negotiated on better terms, it may be
reasonably presumed that such fears are purely
chimerical.

Being convenient in Africa and useful in Europe,
the Franco-Italian agreement, coupled with the
Franco-English one, deserves in itself nothing but
approbation. But the way in which we have made
use of it is undoubtedly less worthy of praise.
Thus, for instance, it was imprudent to compromise
our relations with the Holy See by President Loubet's
visit to Rome, and thus to prepare the rupture of
the Concordat. It was for us to understand our
interests better; and no reproach can be made
against Italy by reason of our mistake. Similarly,
Italy has certainly benefited through the weakening
of our situation in the Far East; and the agreement
of January, 1907, was a seal set upon this change to
her advantage. But here again, we are alone to
blame, for not seeing that, by breaking with the
Vatican, we should sooner or later lose the profit
accruing to us by the exercise of our Catholic protectorate in the Levant. The events that have
occurred since 1902, have allowed us to estimate
the price of our good relations with Italy. What
would have happened notably if the Italy of 1905

had been in the same frame of mind with regard to
us as the Italy of 1889? The policy which had
sought for the *rapprochement*, and realized it, was
good and wise in its principle. The errors made in
applying it cannot induce us to forget that.

II

The Franco-Spanish *rapprochement* was the natural
complement of the reconciliation between France
and England and of that between France and Italy.
It was necessarily inspired by the same principle,
and necessarily served the same policy. But it
could not assume the same form.

The Cuban war and the loss of her colonies compelled Spain to fall back on herself. This admirable
country, which a defective administration, content
to exploit the colonial farm, had for centuries
permitted to lie fallow, understood from the lesson
of her defeat that her future would depend on her
energy. To quote Mr. Victor Bérard's just expression, Spain is at once a farm and a workshop. To
this farm and to this workshop, what is lacking?
Men, money, capital.

The peasant has no capital to buy the machinery and tools,
for want of which, he is unable to stand against foreign competition. The husbandman has not the capital needed to reëstablish the irrigation works which once transformed the whole
of Arabian Spain into a garden. The ironmaster, the miner, the
manufacturer, the tradesman, the commission agent, have found
on the spot a certain amount of capital which had come back
from Cuba or the Philippine Islands and which has enabled
them to set going a large number of businesses that to-day are

thriving. . . . But what they want is ten or twenty times as much money. Spanish industry finds lenders only at seven or eight per cent. And if, after considering private individuals, you come to look at the State, what loans would the latter have to negotiate if it were only to undertake the repair and upkeep of what remains of the national manufacturing appliances and other machinery or the development of that part which is in process of formation! Castile and Aragon demand the remaking of the canals given them by Charles V. Cadiz, Carthagena, Tarragona, Vigo, beg for docks and dykes. Spain throughout needs railways. . . . And, above all, the entire country requires a restored coinage, finances that are sound. . . . Public finance must first be placed on a good footing, if private finance is to be improved.[1]

When once in possession of herself, and turned towards economic action, Spain is too proud not to rely on her future. This future is no longer to be sought beyond the seas. She sees it quite near to her, within her reach, in the Morocco that she herself resembles by the situation of her mountains and the aspect of her soil. As the Marquis de Segonzac[2] has demonstrated, Morocco, more than any other portion of Africa, is like Spain in race, history, and civilization. There is striking similarity between the Sierra Nevada and the Rif mountains. The Straits of Gibraltar are a mere accidental break. They do not constitute a frontier, and have never separated anything, either geographically or historically. The Moors still dream of the palaces of Granada. And as for the Spaniards, ever since Isabella the Catholic assigned them in her will and testament the task of pursuing the

---

[1] Victor Bérard's book, *The Moroccan Affair.*
[2] See Marquis de Segonzac's book, *Travels in Morocco.*

Mussulmans on to the African shore, they have considered Morocco as being their peculiar property, over which they claim "historic rights."

To tell the truth, the realization of these rights has so far been of a mediocre kind. In 1688, Spain obtained the cession of Ceuta. At the time of the 1720 expedition, and more especially on the occasion of that of 1859, which ended in the capture of Tetoan, together with the payment of a war indemnity and the extension of the Ceuta territory, she attempted to establish herself firmly on Moorish soil; but the result was negative, or nearly so. What Spain acquired, to wit, her penal settlement, was purely factitious, a mere administrative abstraction, nothing more. Ceuta, which has no commercial activity, occupies a position of strategic value, but is not seriously fortified. Peñon de Velas, Alhucemas, the Isle of Alboran, Peregil, Ifni, and the Zaffarine Isles, serve as hulks — when they serve for anything at all. Melilla alone, since it has been a free port, has carried on a certain trade; but the countries that chiefly benefit by it are France and England. The penal settlement costs 2,500,000 pesetas annually. The trade, which amounts to about two millions, yields to Spain a sum of about 400,000 pesetas; so that the excess of expenditure over receipts is more than two millions. Between the Spanish residents and the native population there is no intermingling. The Moors do not allow the Europeans to issue from their fortress. In most of the penal settlements everything comes

H

from Spain, even their soft water. Clinging for
centuries to a few islets and peninsulas of the coast,
the Spanish have drawn no profit from them, either
to increase their territory, or even to secure its being
respected. During this long domination, they have
gained only the ineradicable hate of neighbouring
tribes. Such precarious possession of a few rocks
confers on them no more rights over the bulk of the
country, than sticking their nests in windows gives
to swallows the ownership of a house.

In order to work for their economic development,
as also in order to give effect to their aspirations
in Morocco, the Spanish need help. And such help,
France, better than any other nation, is in a position
to afford them. The support of French capital can
be the leaven which shall cause the unexploited resources of the peninsula to germinate. As for
Morocco, what Señor Silvela said in 1901 is true:
"The present situation of the country, closed to
commerce, to civilization, to any increase of population, to the working of its mines, to the consumption
and exchange of productions, is not a source of profit
or wealth, but rather of poverty, sterility, and stag-
nation for Spain. . . . It is in an understanding
with France that we shall find the surest aid, not
indeed for making war but for an equitable and
reasonable division of interests." Although this
idea of sharing, which has a very considerable number
of adherents in Spain, did not correspond with the
views of French policy, Señor Silvela's language
deserved to be taken note of, as indicating a dispo-

sition that, one day or another, we might find it advantageous to encourage.

As a matter of fact, during the last twenty years of the nineteenth century, Spain was far from showing herself favourable to France. Rather towards Berlin than towards Paris it was that her sympathies went. The second marriage of Alfonso XII with an Austrian princess (1879) harmonized with the country's desire to enter into closer relations with the Triple Alliance. Four years later, the King paid a visit to Germany, where William I appointed him Colonel in a Prussian regiment garrisoned at Strasburg. And, a few days later, on his arrival in Paris, Alfonso XII was greeted in the Rue de Rivoli with hisses and groans. In the month of November following, when the Crown Prince proceeded to Madrid to return the Spanish King's visit, all the European press, whether rightly or wrongly, spoke of an alliance between Germany and Spain. True, in 1885, the conflict which broke out over the Caroline Islands, produced throughout Spain a strong feeling of irritation; but, at the death of Alfonso XII in 1886, calm was restored, and the German leanings of the Government in Madrid seemed less doubtful. The minority of Alfonso XIII and his mother's regency were a period of quiet reflection, which was at last disturbed so tragically by the war with the United States (1898). On that occasion, the friendliness towards Spain shown by the French newspapers, and the clever mediation of Mr. Jules Cambon, French Ambassador at

Washington, during the negotiations for peace, effected a *rapprochement* between Madrid and Paris. Although an Austrian, the Queen-Mother, with rare clear-sightedness, understood that Spain could not, without peril to herself, adhere to a political system which would have risked bringing her into opposition against France.

"No country can do our dynasty as much harm or as much good as France," she said one day to Mr. Loubet.

Her prudent and circumspect diplomacy, admirably seconded by Señor de Leon y Castillo, her Ambassador at Paris, succeeded in keeping the future free for a policy which her son, a young man of intelligent, charming, and liberal mind and a friend to our country, resolutely guided, as soon as he came of age, towards a friendship with France.

A Franco-Spanish understanding relative to Morocco encountered, notwithstanding, difficulties that were serious. Certain Spaniards, who though not numerous, made a great deal of stir, had retained a hatred of France. Men like Señor Villanueva, who, when he was at the head of the Admiralty in 1895, resigned rather than accept the Grand Officer's grade in the Legion of Honour, were full of distrust and prejudice with regard to us. As far as Morocco was concerned, the very largeness of their desires rendered them hostile to all precision: for, to define is to limit. Obsessed by the hope of Moroccan profits that were still undivided, they considered any other foreign action than their own as a menace, any agreement with a foreign Power, and especially with France, as prejudicial, France being supreme in Algeria. This explains why, between 1899 and 1904, Spanish policy underwent fluctuations, the main lines of which, if not the details, are sufficiently well known. There were at first, in 1902, preliminary negotiations with Paris, which, while going pretty far, did not issue in the treaty of which an apocryphal text was published. What would seem to have been discussed was a method of sharing, as to which no agreement could be reached. Next there was a double and parallel exchange of views with Great Britain and Germany, which doubtless took its rise in the sale to Germany of what was left of the Spanish colonies in the Pacific, — the Caroline and Marianne isles. Nothing came of this, either. Things went on so till 1904, when, on the 8th of April, Madrid learned that France and England had just come to an understanding on the question of Morocco.

The news of this understanding caused a disagreeable impression in Spain; and the feeling was that there had been too much waiting on events. France, it was thought, being henceforth in agreement with England, would show herself less conciliatory than in the past. However, these two Powers had taken the precaution to put into the statement of their arrangement a clause proving their friendly intentions with regard to Spain. "The two Governments," said Article 8, "basing themselves on their amicable sentiments towards Spain, take into special account the interests she has acquired from her geo-

graphic position and her territorial possessions on the
Moroccan coast of the Mediterranean, with respect
to which subject, the French Government will ar-
range with that of Spain." In accordance with this
pledge, Mr. Delcassé at once entered into negotiations with Señor de Leon y Castillo, the Spanish
Ambassador, their exchange of views continuing
throughout the summer of 1904. Now and again,
they found it difficult to reconcile the claims of their
respective countries; but finally a convention was
agreed upon, and duly announced in the press. Its
terms were as follows: —

> The Government of the French Republic and that of his
> Majesty, the King of Spain.
> Having agreed to determine the extent and the guarantee of
> the interests belonging to France by reason of her Algerian pos-
> sessions and to Spain by reason of her possessions on the coasts
> of Morocco.
> And the Government of his Majesty, the King of Spain, hav-
> ing in consequence given their adhesion to the Franco-English
> declaration of the 8th of April relative to Morocco and Egypt,
> communication of which had been made to them by the Govern-
> ment of the French Republic.
> Declare that they remain firmly attached to the integrity of
> the Moroccan Empire under the sovereignty of the Sultan.

This document was fairly vague. On reading it
and re-reading it, one experienced a feeling that the
two Governments had kept the essential part of it
to themselves. Undoubtedly, Spain, by adhering
to the Franco-English declaration, affirmed, together
with the two signataries of the declaration, her attachment to the integrity of Morocco and to the
sovereignty of the Sultan. She also recognized that

"it belonged to France, more peculiarly as a border
Power having a long contiguous frontier, to see that
this country remained tranquil and to lend her assistance, with a view to all the economic and financial
administrative reforms required." She also declared herself equally decided "not to hamper France
in what might be done for this purpose, and to afford her the help of Spain's diplomacy for the execution of the clauses of the present declaration."
But if France obtained this precious adhesion from
Spain, it was "in consequence" of something else.
This something was the determination of "the extent of Spain's rights and the guarantee of her interests resulting from her possessing territory on the
coasts of Morocco." In other words, Spain's adhesion corresponded to concessions from France. And
it was just on the chapter of such concessions con-
taining the essence of the agreement that nothing
was openly said. What were these secret clauses?
What rights — new ones evidently — had we ceded
to Spain? How and in what measure had the extent of these rights been fixed? How and under
what form had the guarantee of such interests been
established? These questions were left without answer.

In reality, the privileged political position of
France with regard to Morocco was acknowledged by
Spain. But France consented to certain restrictions
in the exercise of her privilege, and these restrictions
were in favour of Spain. She associated Spain with
herself in her designs of peaceful penetration within

the part of Morocco where such penetration had the greatest advantage for Spaniards. However, in this same part, any action of Spain, during a limited time, was subordinated to previous arrangement with France, whereas, on her own ground, France was obliged only to notify Spain of her initiatives. There was no question of divided shares, but merely of an economic coöperation, as also of the contingency of concerted measures, with a view to the maintenance of order in case of serious disturbance breaking out. It was a complicated combination, which, in the year following, had to be rendered more precise in certain of its terms by a supplementary agreement (September, 1905).[1] Moreover, it recorded, unlike the Franco-English and Franco-Italian arrangements, a sort of purchase-out in favour of France; and, on the other hand, coupled Spanish projects with French. It was positive instead of being negative.

A few months earlier, this political agreement had been preceded by an economic understanding, which in the future is destined to bear the best fruits, to wit, the treaty relative to the Trans-Pyrenean railways. There is no journey more uselessly long than that from Paris to Cadiz. A plan for remedying this state of things had been long under consideration; and a Franco-Spanish convention on the subject was signed in 1885. After a series of preliminary negotiations and preparatory surveys superintended on the French side by Mr. Mille, Civil Engineer-in-

[1] See our book, *Diplomatic Questions of the Year* 1904.

Chief, two lines were mapped out, one running from Oloron to Jaca through the Canfranc pass, the other from Saint Girons to Lerida through the Salau pass. It had been decided by the two Commissaries that the two lines should be made on the same level. Everything, therefore, was apparently settled, when an article was published to the effect that the two Governments were to come to an understanding as to the date on which the convention should be submitted for Parliamentary approval. This was equivalent to an indefinite postponement. The convention was never brought before the Chambers. The ratification was never accorded. From that time forward there were frequent attempts to take up the matter again, but always without anything definite being done. In 1904, however, a step forward was taken. To the two lines first planned, a third was proposed from Ax-les-Thermes to Ripoll, shortening the journey from Toulouse to Barcelona by three hours. A treaty embodying the new scheme was signed on the 18th of August, 1904, and was completed by an additional act in February, 1905. This was a first definite effort towards economic coöperation between the two countries. It would be advantageous to have others following.

The thought may occur that in the case of the Franco-Spanish *rapprochement*, as in that of the Franco-Italian, less onerous conditions might have been secured. However, Spain, with her haughty temperament, would not have accepted the Moroccan developments of our Mediterranean policy, unless

satisfaction had been granted to her historic claims.
By refusing her this satisfaction, we should have
aroused her hostility. And either in Europe, in the
event of a war, or else in Morocco itself, such hostility might have become dangerous. On the contrary,
the agreement thus opportunely concluded was a
guarantee for the future, which was further strengthened by Great Britain's intervention. As a matter
of fact, it is not too much to say that the Franco-
English *Entente* was the determining cause of Spain's
throwing in her lot with Europe's Western Powers.
The marriage of Alfonso XIII with a princess of the
English Royal Family, his interviews with Edward
VII, his visits to London and Paris, confirmed this
trend of Spanish policy, which indeed was in accordance with his personal preferences, since he has no
leanings towards Germany. From his stay at Berlin he brought back a disagreeable impression. It
seemed to him as though attempts were being made
to astonish and daunt him; and the result was that
he was annoyed. His presence on the throne, therefore, is the pledge that a policy will be followed
which, if partially caused by a somewhat naïve Pan-
Latinism, none the less corresponds, in its existing
form, to the practical interests of those that it binds
together.

III

On the 5th of November, 1881, when explaining
to the Chamber his Tunisian policy, Jules Ferry said:
"The Tunisian question is as old as the Algerian one.

It is contemporaneous with it. Can any good Frenchman support the idea of leaving to any but a weak,
friendly, or subordinate Power the possession of a
territory which, in the full acceptation of the term,
is the key of our house?" The necessity thus clearly
recognized by the greatest statesman of the Third
Republic, was bound to become the inspiring principle of our policy from the moment when, after the
Algerian and Tunisian questions, that of Morocco
arose.

Situated at the extreme western end of Africa,
Morocco has remained down to our own day as a
wreck of antiquity. During the past century, all
the various Mussulman countries have more or less
adopted our European civilization. Morocco alone
has continued a closed country, rigidly preserving
her peculiar exclusiveness. In no other spot is religious life so intense as in the *Maghreb el Aksa*. In
no other clime is the national life feebler. It has
been truly said that Morocco is not an empire falling
to decay, but an empire in process of birth, an empire which has not succeeded in imposing a State
unity on the independent tribes that theoretically it
governs. The nature of its soil favours such independence, which manifests itself more or less strongly
according as the reigning Sultan is more or less capable of exercising his authority, but which so far has
never been subdued. Morocco is divided into two
portions, each varying with the reach of the central
Power. The *Bled el Maghzen,* in a general way, com-
prises the populations of the plain, who yield obedi-

ence to functionaries appointed by the Sultan and consent to pay a tax, which, however, is irregularly collected. The *Bled es Siba* acknowledges the Sultan's authority only when imposed by means of an expedition. However, what at one moment belongs to the *Maghzen* country may very well belong to the *Siba* country at another. For the last ten centuries, it has been the lot of Moroccan Sultans to have continually to conquer their subjects, and the special occupation of the subjects has been that of disobeying their sovereigns. To tell the truth, the notion of sovereignty does not exist. Where there is no hierarchy, it is impossible that there should be any moral notion attaching to revolt. Morocco is a country of feudal and theocratic anarchy; and the disturbances that have occurred there in recent times are merely a fresh manifestation of tendencies that have long existed. It is Europe alone which, first through mental assimilation, and subsequently through political interests, has created the unity of Morocco. In such unity there has never been either reality or totality. What does exist is a Moorish Empire, with which other Powers treat; but inside the empire one finds merely tribes who, in battles or else in incessant negotiations, seek their personal profit only.

The Sultan Muley Hassan, who reigned from 1873 to 1894, was an energetic man who had strengthened his power by making war throughout his reign. When he died, still fighting, in the course of an expedition in the Tedla, near the Oued el Abid, he was succeeded by his son Muley Abd el Aziz, who, at the time, was sixteen years of age. The Chamberlain of the dead monarch, Si Ahmed Ben Mouça, caused the young man to be proclaimed *Emir el-Muminin*, that is to say, Commander of the Faithful. Then, thrusting into the background the person of him whom he had just proclaimed Sultan, he seized on the Government, which he exercised alone. Between 1894 and 1900, he was the sole ruler of the Empire. "Gifted with dauntless will, an untiring worker, eager for power and wealth,"[1] he dispensed the Sultan from exercising his king-craft, giving him people to entertain him instead of teaching him how to reign. Abd el Aziz acquired nothing of that virile teaching suitable for scholars destined to a throne. When Si Ahmed died, he had completed his twenty-second year; but was completely lacking in maturity of mind, in method, and in consistency. After Si Ahmed's disappear-ance, rival influences sought to monopolize the Government. There was that of the Sultan's mother, that of Si el Hadj el Mokhtar ben Ahmed, who was the secretary and successor of the deceased vizier, and, last of all, that of Si el Mehdi el Menebhi, who was Minister of War. This third influence soon contrived to supplant the others. In the month of April, 1901, Si Fedul Garnit was installed as Grand Vizier. But, under cover of his name, it was Menebhi who reigned and held the chief power until his disgrace placed the Sultan in other hands.

[1] See Dr. F. Weisgerber's book, *Three Months' Campaigning in Morocco.*

By his qualities as by his failings, Abd el Aziz was utterly unfitted for the task of consolidating an authority that was tottering to its fall. This tall young man, of sallow complexion, with straggling beard just beginning to grow, and a tendency to stoutness and a certain awkwardness and timidity, remained until he was thirty in this boyish stage. He is good-hearted and quick of intelligence, but possesses neither patience nor energy. His mind is an open one, and more liberally inclined than that of most of his subjects. He is favourable to reform and progress, and has a friendly feeling towards Europe, on occasion showing it. However, in all this there is no system nor. method, nothing that resembles a policy. What Abd el Aziz likes best in European civilization are its eccentricities. Every one has heard of his useless acquisitions, made at the instigation of unscrupulous advisers, to the detriment of his budget. Billiard-tables, motor-cars, cabs, uniforms, toy railways, balloons, cinematographs, ice machines, serving for a day and neglected on the morrow, have filled his palace and emptied his purse. Such frivolous amusements have shocked native sentiment. And Abd el Aziz has been, in a large measure, the destroyer of his own authority. Even his good intentions have, by his own fault, turned against him. In 1901, he tried to reform the system of taxation, which, to tell the truth, was iniquitous. But he suppressed the ancient taxes before settling what could be put in their place. The Moroccans have profited by the change, but have obstinately resisted the new system; so that since 1901, the Moorish Exchequer has had no regular revenues to draw on except the Customs. Similarly, it is the Sultan's blunders which have encouraged successive revolts, first that of the Roghi Bou-Hamara, then the one, at present victorious, of Muley Hafid.[1]

And yet Morocco is a rich country. "Well watered by the rains which are attracted by its high mountains from the ocean, irrigated in its driest parts by the waters of the ouadi which flow down from the summits of Atlas, both its climate and its situation make it a country more favoured by nature than either Algeria or Tunis. To the east, the basin of the Moulouya is barely more than a continuation of the *Oranie*. At the foot of the mountains, the oases of the Tafilat and the Oued Draa share in the geographic conditions of the Sahara and resemble our finest oases of Southern Algeria. But to the west, along the ocean, from Tangier to Atlas, a long strip of land stretches, between fifty and a hundred kilometres in breadth, composed of black soil which, if ploughed by European settlers, and if peace with an equitable system of taxation were assured by a regular government, might become a rich cereal-growing country. Between this coast-zone and the mountains, extend grassy steppes capable of supporting herds of cattle and horses, and also of being here and there transformed by irrigation. On the mountain plateaus, in the raised

[1] See Eugène Aubin's book, *The Morocco of To-day*.

valleys, where rain is abundant, the olive, vine, and other fruit trees of the Mediterranean grow almost without any cultivation. More towards the south, between the two terminal branches of Atlas, the Sous Valley displays its orchards and its fields. If to this be added that a geological survey of the Maghreb region and various traces found by travellers encourage the belief that coal and different metals are hidden beneath the surface of the soil, . . . one has less surprise in remembering that, according to Diodorus, the Phœnicians once established on the African coast, beyond the pillars of Hercules, three hundred factories from which they derived wealth of all kinds."

It was only natural that France, being supreme in Algeria, should bethink herself of the future possibilities she saw offered to her in Morocco. Between Algeria and the Moorish Empire, there really exists no natural boundary. The Berber countries form one whole. Mountains and valleys cross the frontier; and the races are also similar, while religious and family organization is identical throughout. Moreover, the economic consequences of this situation have been felt ever since a remote past, as the following tables will show: —

1. PERCENTAGE OF FOREIGN TRADE WITH MOROCCO

	1902	1903	1904	1905	1906	1907
France and Algeria .	31.1	37.7	30.	46.3	50.42	43.34
England	41.6	41.1	40.1	29.5	28.78	33.05
Germany	9.01	9.6	11.1	9.9	8.41	12.98
Spain	8.4	7.2	7.7	4.02	4.56	4.10

2. MOROCCAN COMMERCE WITH OTHER POWERS.

(in millions of francs)

	1902	1903	1904	1905	1906	1907
Aggregate trade	103,347	109,493	97,689	78,642	84,526	76,928
France and Algeria . .	32,900	34,813	29,413	36,467	42,613	34,883
England . .	43,011	45,036	39,266	23,240	24,332	25,428
Germany . .	9,317	10,522	10,900	7,832	7,114	9,983
Spain . . .	8,723	7,903	7,602	3,163	3,861	3,116

In the commercial relations of France and Morocco, there are two characteristic reciprocal needs. France in Africa requires Moroccan labour; and Morocco requires French merchandise. Our trade with the Moorish Empire consists more and more in sending our products there. To a greater extent, therefore, than any other Power, France must desire to see order established over its length and breadth. She must desire this also on behalf of her citizens who are settled in the country. The number of French firms that have established themselves in Morocco is not far short of three hundred. The capital invested in trade there, exclusive of navigation companies, is about thirty million francs. For the most part, the French tradespeople residing in the Empire are modest workers, small folk who have emigrated to get a living, — market-gardeners, bakers, restaurant-keepers, grocers, bricklayers, mechanics, — who, by dint of toiling hard, earn on the Moroccan soil enough to furnish themselves with subsistence. The duty of the French Government as regards their protection cannot therefore be disputed.

I

Moreover, political interest, still more imperious than economic interest, compels France to occupy herself with Moroccan affairs. Enough has already been said to show how radical the anarchy is which prevails throughout the land. On account of Morocco's proximity to Algeria, and the geographic, ethnographic, and religious unity of the two countries, such anarchy is a constant menace to our colony's tranquillity. All the various Algerian agitators, Abd el Kader, Ulad Sidi Cheikh, Bou Amama, have used Morocco as an operating base against us. Order in Morocco is consequently necessary for order to reign in Algeria. *A fortiori*, we ought to have the assurance that this already redoubtable spontaneous anarchy shall not be aggravated by European instigation, using it and keeping it up against us.

Thus is determined the necessary policy which is imposed on the French Government. They desire that order shall reign in Morocco. They desire further that no European Power shall acquire there a preponderant influence which might threaten to compromise our situation in Africa, and in the Mediterranean, and, as a consequence, our situation in Europe. The defence of this double interest — with the maintenance of order as its positive portion and the exclusion of foreign influence as its negative one — such, with regard to Morocco, must be the rule of French action.

During many years, our action in the country was uncertain in its aim and fluctuating in its

methods. On the morrow of the conquest of Algiers, the battle of Isly, the bombardment of Tangier and of Mogador, demonstrated our military
power to the Moroccans. But this work of repression was not politically utilized. The Treaty of
Lalla-Marnia of 1845, indeed, revealed the Government's hesitations by the lack of precision in its
clauses. In proportion as Oran was more thickly
colonized, the inconveniences resulting were increasingly felt. Continual aggressions, which caused
long controversies, troubled the security of our
dependent population. And the claims that our
Ministers in Tangier were each year called upon to
defend, produced no other effect than that of giving
the Moorish Power, though without the least practical efficacy on our frontiers, an artificial existence.
By virtue of our "right of pursuit," inscribed in the
Treaty of 1845, and in agreement with the Maghzen,
France sent several punitive expeditions into Moroccan territory, that of General de Wimpffen in 1870,
those of 1881 and 1882, owing to the revolt of Bou
Amama. For nearly half a century, however, she
confined herself to isolated measures without seeking
to reach the evil in its source and to prepare a lasting remedy. Not until 1900, and then only after
successive rebounds and under the pressure of
circumstances, did the French Government, by
deciding to occupy the Touat region, take the pre-
cautionary measures requisite for the defence of our
southern frontier. A year later, Mr. Revoil, the
Governor-General of Algeria, being convinced that

this occupation would be without lasting effect, if conquest were not followed by organization, entered into negotiations with the Moroccan Government which resulted in the Treaty of the 20th of July, 1901, this latter becoming thenceforward the basis of our policy.

The agreement — which, as indicated in the wording of its preamble, was intended to "consolidate the bonds of friendship existing between the two Governments and to develop their reciprocal good relations by establishing them, on the one hand, on the guarantee of the Moorish Empire's integrity, and, on the other, on the improvement of the frontier situation, in which both were immediately interested, by all such detailed arrangements as the said frontier situation might necessitate" — instituted a veritable coöperation between the two neighbouring Governments. Without seeking to fix an absolutely immovable boundary line amidst limitless sands and wandering tribes, an exchange of good offices was provided for, both as regards police, and the regulation of trade and Customs. A Franco-Moroccan Commission proceeded to the place; and, in order to facilitate its labours, a second agreement was signed at Algiers on the 20th of April, 1902, "with a view to securing permanent peace, safety, and commercial progress." The first article said: "The Moorish Government engage, by all possible means, throughout the extent of their territory from the mouth of the Oued Kiss to Figuig, to consolidate the authority of their Maghzen such as it has been exer-

cised over the Moroccan tribes since the Treaty of
1845. The French Government, by reason of their
frontier situation, will lend their aid to this task
in any and every case of need. The French Government will establish their authority and a condition
of peace throughout the Sahara regions, and the
neighbouring Moroccan Government will help in this
by every means in their power." It was further
stipulated that a triple line of markets, — French,
mixed, and Moroccan, — with a corresponding collection of dues, should be created between Morocco
and Algeria. The French Government pledged
themselves to pay the Maghzen each year a sum
equivalent to the Customs duties accruing from the
merchandise entering Algeria from Morocco between
Figuig and the Teniet es Sassi. A supplementary
agreement, dated the 7th of May, 1902, rendered
more precise certain of the clauses in the previous
arrangement. And the policy, as thus defined,
was forthwith put into execution.

In carrying out this work, France gave proofs of
her generosity and friendliness, placing instructors
at the Sultan's disposal for his troops at Figuig,
Oudjda, and Adjeroud (July, 1902), enabling him to
negotiate a loan (October, 1902), not holding him
responsible for the sanguinary outbreaks at Taghit
(August, 1903), and at El Moungar (September,
1903), nor yet for the attack made at Zenaga by the
people of Figuig against Mr. Jonnart, the Governor-
General of Algeria (June, 1903). In spite of certain
fluctuations due to Algerian influences and to

General O'Connor's imprudent language, the coöperation continued. As Mr. Delcassé wrote: "The anarchy with which the Moorish Empire had to contend did not allow us to visit upon its monarch the responsibility for acts from which we had to suffer." We therefore permitted free entry, into the Algerian territory, of the money, weapons, ammunition, and even troops which the Maghzen needed in order to cope with the Roghi (June, 1903). We further placed at his service a member of our military mission, Captain Larras, for the organizing of the expedition against Oudjda (July, 1903). We gave him two pieces of artillery with their material and men (August, 1903). Captain Martin, another French officer, was commissioned to instruct the Moroccan troops on the frontier (September, 1903). The Algerian Lieutenant Ben Sedira, with his cannon "carrying dread everywhere," assured the success of the *mahalla* directed against Taza (October–November, 1903). Thus, the Maghzen was able to appreciate at the same time the necessity and efficacy of our assistance. And under the excellent superintendence of General Lyautey, who, in the autumn of 1903, was appointed to the command of the subdivision of Ain-Sefra, there was a commencement of peace on the frontier, which a few months before had been in such a serious state of disturbance.[1]

Although this pacification was important, it was not, however, adequate, considering the double interest that inspired our Moroccan policy. It was not

[1] See the Yellow Book (1901–1905).

only on our borders but through the whole of the Moorish territory that, both commercially and politically, we needed the restoration of order. Our policy of reform and coöperation was intended to be applied over the entire length and breadth of the Empire. In order to prevent the establishment of any influence hostile to ours, it was necessary for us to make our action felt at Fez. On the 8th of April, 1904, the Franco-English agreement secured us the renunciation of Great Britain, up to then our most redoubtable adversary. We had been guaranteed a similar renunciation of Italy several years before. Spain's adhesion was to be secured six months later. By a grievous error, Mr. Delcassé lost a great deal of time before he bethought himself of drawing the necessary conclusions from this new situation. Not before the 16th of May did Mr. Saint-René Taillandier, our Minister at Tangier, furnish Ben Sliman with explanations concerning the Franco-English Treaty; and, only in January, 1905, when nine months had been lost, did he go to see the Sultan at Fez. However, in spite of this grave mistake, some useful measures were taken. On the 27th of May, 1904, Captain Fournier, a Frenchman, was intrusted by the Sultan with the organization of the police at Tangier. On the 12th of June, an association of French Banks granted the Sultan a loan of sixty-two and a half millions, guaranteed by the Customs duties, the lenders having the option of checking the receipts in the eight ports open to commerce, and furthermore a previous deduction and prefer-

ence rights on future loans.   The creation of a State
Bank through our agency was also planned.   In
May, 1904, at the Maghzen's request, we lent our
diplomatic assistance for the purpose of delivering,
from the hands of the brigand Raisuli, Mr. Perdic-
caris, an American, and Mr. Varley, an Englishman,
who had been captured and detained by him.   Notwithstanding the reservations formulated by Ben
Sliman as to the Franco-English agreement, especially respecting its "difficult points," and those of
its terms that "might offer ambiguities and lead to
something contrary to what was aimed at" we were,
therefore, justified in believing that the programme
of reforms elaborated — too slowly — by the Minister of Foreign Affairs and the Tangier Legation,
would be considered at Fez as the logical development of the amicable policy which Ben Sliman himself, in July, 1904, had defined when saying: "His
Majesty knows that the most powerful motive of
your insistence is the community of interests possessed by the Governments of the two neighbouring
countries and also the community of harm that they
are exposed to suffer."

There was nothing extraordinary about the programme of reforms.   It was based on three guiding
principles: Morocco's integrity, the Sultan's sovereignty, commercial liberty.   It continued the
work that had been begun, — police, trade, civilization.   There was no design of conquest, or of protectorate, or of monopoly.   Conquest would have
cost too dear.   A protectorate would have served no

purpose in face of the exclusiveness of the tribes. Monopolization would have been contrary to international treaties. To create police forces with Moroccan natives and Algerian instructors in all the principal towns; to restore finances by means of a more honest collection of taxes, a genuine checking of expenses, and the repression of smuggling; to increase the carrying trade by public works wisely planned and the construction of ports, bridges, and roads — all this by contract law; to multiply hospitals, schools, educational and charitable institutions, — such was the tenor of the programme, which, if realized with the unique means of action conferred on us by Algeria, and with the clear-sighted sympathy of Europe, herself destined to benefit by it, would, within a short time, have been able to change the face of the Moorish Empire. As Mr. Delcassé wrote: "Far from diminishing the Sultan's authority, we were peculiarly anxious to enhance his prestige." And with reason, the Foreign Minister added: "It will be in his name that the agents we may have to place at his disposal will exercise their functions, carefully applying themselves, in accordance with our wishes, to ingratiate themselves with the population, not to offend their feelings, but to respect their beliefs, their customs, and their organization. In return, we expect the Makhzen, while appreciating our efforts, to do his best sincerely to second them. And, thus, an era of peace and prosperity will soon dawn upon Morocco."

A few weeks later, all this appearance of promise

had vanished. At the instigation of Germany, the Maghzen and the Sultan separated themselves bruskly from the policy of coöperation. The Moroccan problem passed from the African into the European domain. The solution, which had been rendered possible through the development of our alliances and friendships, was handed over to a diplomatic *mêlée* — a veritable conflict of alliances, the consequences of which were to weigh heavily on the world, while the causes leading up to them must be sought in the history of the past twenty years.

CHAPTER IV

FRANCE AND THE TRIPLE ALLIANCE

I

FRANCE has not developed her alliances and friendships with nothing in the way of opposition to face her. When our diplomacy began to incline towards Russia, about the year 1889, the Triple Alliance, initiated in 1879 by the bond between Austria and Germany, and completed by Italy's joining the combination, in 1882, dominated Europe without any-

thing to counterbalance it. Fifteen years later, this
same Triple Alliance subsisted over against the har-
monious edifice of agreements, the completion of
which once more enabled us to make our diplomacy
actively felt. A study, therefore, of the relations
between France and the Triple Alliance is necessary
for the right comprehension of our conduct and our
interests.

On the 10th of May, 1875, the Czar, Alexander II,
arrived in Berlin. For several weeks, Europe had
been living in the dread of a crisis. A sensational
article published by Mr. de Blowitz in the *Times* on
the 6th of the same month, and giving a summary
of what had recently appeared in the German press,
predicted that a war was on the point of breaking
out. What the German writers said was in substance this: "To finish once for all with France is
not merely opportune. It is a duty Germany owes
to herself and to humanity. Europe will never be
tranquil as long as a struggle is possible; and there
will be this possibility of a struggle as long as the
blunder made by the Treaty of Frankfort remains
unrepaired. For it leaves France in a position to
survive and recommence the duel. Germany is
troubled by the consciousness of having only half-
crushed her enemy and of being able to defend
herself only by sleeping with one eye open." This
accurate and striking recapitulation of articles that
could be read every day in the Trans-Rhenish press,
aroused, according to Lord Derby's expression, "universal indignation." Sympathy for France, van-

quished but dignified in her defeat; and, what was more, the fear of a definitive rupture of the balance of power in Europe, facilitated the task of the Duc de Decazes, who was resolved on "exciting" the Powers.

To General Le Flô, the French Ambassador, the Czar had made a promise that he would intervene; and between the Czar and the British Government there was an entire agreement on the subject. In vain Bismarck had the following statement inserted in the *North German Gazette:* "The language of the European press is all the more unintelligible, as absolutely nothing has occurred which is of a nature to trouble the relations existing between the French and the German Government." In vain, he denounced the "hypocritical league composed of ultra-montane-revenge politicians and Exchange bears." No one believed him. On the 12th of May, Alexander II said to Viscount de Gontaut-Biron, the French Ambassador, in an interview he had with him while at Berlin: "Peace is necessary to the world. We each have enough to do at home. Rely on me, and make yourself easy. Tell Marshal Mac-Mahon how much I esteem him and how sincerely I wish that his Government may be strengthened. I hope that our relations will become more and more cordial. We have interests in common. We must remain friends." On the 14th of May, Gortchakoff addressed a telegraphic circular to the various Russian Ambassadors, announcing that "the maintenance of peace was assured." Bismarck, in his anger, overwhelmed the Russian Chancellor with his sarcasms: "Why not," said he, "coin five-franc pieces with this motto: 'Gortchakoff protect France.' Or else, why not organize at the German Embassy in Paris a theatre where, with the same device, he might appear before French society in the rôle of a guardian angel, in a white robe, with wings, amidst a display of Greek fire." Whatever may have been his real intentions, Bismarck was none the less caught in his own trap. Russia and England spoiled his game. If he did not desire war, he had allowed or caused the contrary to be believed. In either case, the issue was the same: a discomfiture. "Whether it had been his wish or not to enlighten himself as to the sentiment of the Powers, he knew now what he had to expect. The Franco-Russian *rapprochement* had appeared as a combination eventually realizable, in the course of this press campaign so brutally entered upon, so ingeniously magnified, and so happily closed." [1]

Thence was born the Triple Alliance. From the moment of this alarm, which he himself had been responsible for, Bismarck was obsessed, as Count Schouvaloff put it, with the "coalition nightmare." He saw only one way of warding off the fancied danger; namely, to take the initiative, and on the German victories establish a league so strong and so wide-reaching that France would be for a long time condemned to isolation. The Alliance of the Three Emperors proposed in 1872, which indeed was to

[1] Hanotaux' *History of Contemporary France*, Volume III.

have been rather an understanding than an alliance, appeared to be impracticable on account of Eastern difficulties. At Germany's instigation, Austria was nourishing hopes of revenge in the East. Russia lived only for her policy in the Balkans. Between Vienna and Saint Petersburg there was bound to be conflict. A choice had to be made. Bismarck did not hesitate; and, in spite of the Emperor William, he chose the good-will of Vienna. Already, in 1878, he had refused to give any pledges to the Czar against the hypothesis of an Austro-Russian war.[1] His pretension to play the rôle of the "honest intermediary" expressed nothing more than his determination to remain neutral. At the Congress of Berlin, his attitude was explicable only by the choice he had made of Vienna in preference to Russia through his hatred of Gortchakoff. Three months later, the Russian Chancellor quitted Germany, saying that the Congress had been "the darkest episode in his career." Alexander II declared that "Bismarck had forgotten his promises in 1870." The Russian newspapers raged against the German policy. Troops were massed on the frontier of Poland. Uneasy at the Russian movements in the East, Francis-Joseph asked for protection. On the 7th of October, 1879, the Austro-German Treaty was signed, in spite of the Emperor William's reluctance. Austria's abrogation of Article 5 in the Treaty of Prague, and Bismarck's assurances of political help to Count Andrassy, with regard to the occupation of

[1] See Bismarck's *Thoughts and Souvenirs*, Volume II.

Novi-Bazar, were the first indications of the *rapprochement*. Within less than a year, an alliance was substituted for it. The Treaty, which was published by the two signataries in 1888, was drawn up as follows: —

Considering that their Majesties, the Emperor of Austria and King of Hungary and the Emperor of Germany and King of Prussia must esteem it to be their unavoidable duty as sovereigns to watch under all circumstances over the safety of their Empires and the tranquillity of their peoples;

Considering that the two Monarchs will be able, by a solid alliance of the two Empires, in the kind of that which previously existed, more easily to accomplish this duty, as also more efficaciously;

Considering, in fine, that an intimate agreement between Austro-Hungary and Germany can threaten no one, but is rather calculated to consolidate European peace as created by the stipulations of the Treaty of Berlin;

Their Majesties, the Emperor of Austria and King of Hungary and the Emperor of Germany and King of Prussia, promising each other solemnly never to give any aggressive tendency whatsoever to their purely defensive agreement, have resolved to conclude a reciprocal alliance of peace and protection;

In this aim, their Majesties have appointed as their plenipotentiaries:

For his Majesty the Emperor of Austria and King of Hungary, his real Privy Councillor, the Minister of the Imperial House, as also for Foreign Affairs, Lieutenant Julius, Count Andrassy, etc.;

For his Majesty the Emperor of Germany, his Ambassador and plenipotentiary extraordinary, Lieutenant-General Prince Henry VII of Reuss, etc.;

Who have both entered into relations with each other to-day in Vienna, and, after showing each other their powers duly recognized as good and sufficient, have settled what follows: —

Article I. — If, contrarily to what may be hoped and contrarily to the sincere wishes of the two high contracting parties, one of the two Empires were to be attacked by Russia, the two high contracting parties are bound to lend each other reciprocal aid with the whole of their imperial military power, and, subsequently, to conclude no peace except conjointly and in agreement.

Article II. — If one of the two high contracting parties were to be attacked by another Power, the other high contracting party binds itself, by the present act, not only not to uphold the aggressor against its high Ally, but at the least, to observe a benevolent neutrality with regard to the contracting party aforesaid.

If, however, in the case previously mentioned, the Power attacking were to be upheld by Russia, whether by way of active coöperation or by military measures that should threaten the Power attacked, then the obligation of reciprocal assistance with entire military forces — obligation stipulated in Article I of this Treaty — would immediately become executory, and the military operations of the two high contracting parties would also, in such circumstances, be conducted jointly until the conclusion of peace.

Article III. — This Treaty, in conformity with its pacific character and to avoid all false interpretation, will be held secret by all the high contracting parties.

It may only be communicated to a Third Power with the knowledge of the two parties and after a special agreement between them.

Considering the intentions expressed by the Emperor Alexander at the Alexandrowo interview, the two contracting parties nourish the hope that Russia's preparations will not, in reality, become threatening to them; for this reason, there is at present no motive for communication.

But, if, against all expectation, this hope should be rendered vain, the two contracting parties would recognize that it was a duty of loyalty to inform the Emperor Alexander, at least confidentially, that they must deem any attack directed against one of them as being directed against both.

To testify which, the plenipotentiaries have signed this Treaty with their own hand and have affixed their seals thereto.

Made at Vienna, on the 7th of October, 1879.

Signed :   ANDRASSY.

PRINCE HENRY VII OF REUSS.

K

This defensive Alliance was especially aimed at
Russia, and, subsidiarily, against France. Militarily, it constituted a guarantee against one or the
other of these two Powers. Politically, it consolidated the triumph of 1871. But in order to hold
Europe in check and to impose on her, in peace,
the German supremacy, as also to avoid surprises
such as that of 1875, it was not altogether adequate.
A wider foundation was needed for the hegemony
which Bismarck claimed to exercise from Berlin
over the rest of the world. With a view to supply
this breadth of base, an invitation was given to Italy
in 1882. Mention has already been made of the
grievances that irritated her against France. She
was only too willing. Bismarck had merely to
beckon to her. In the autumn of 1873, Victor
Emmanuel had paid a visit first to Vienna, then to
Berlin; and, from that date, journalists and other
political writers, such as Colonel Marselli, had
preached the German Alliance. In 1875, the Emperor of Austria went to Venice, and the Emperor
of Germany to Milan. And the triumphal reception
accorded, at once to William I and to Marshal von
Moltke, was rightly judged to foreshadow a political
understanding. The Tunis affair did the rest. In
October, 1881, King Humbert, accompanied by de
Depretis and Mancini, made a journey to Vienna;
and, at the end of December, his Ambassadors
informed the Governments of Germany and Austro-
Hungary that he was ready to give his adhesion
to the defensive pact of 1879, on the basis of a

reciprocal territorial guarantee. In February, 1882, negotiations were begun at Vienna between Count Kalnoky, the Prince of Reuss and Comte de Robilant. On the 20th of May, 1882, the Triple Alliance was concluded. Its text was not published. But the tenor may be guessed by that of the Austro-German Treaty, to which Italy merely acceded. The pact was concluded for five years and, failing a formal renewal, was to expire on the 20th of May, 1887. As every one knows, the Triple Alliance has never, since then, ceased being in force. Quinquennial renewals took place in March, 1887, and June, 1891. At the latter date, it was stipulated that the Alliance should be prolonged for twelve years with the option of denunciation at the end of the first six years. The three contracting parties not having made use of such option, the third renewal, for a period of twelve or six years, was signed at Berlin on the 28th of June, 1902.

The conclusion of the Triple Alliance corresponded to the desire expressed by Bismarck when he wrote: "We had made victorious wars on two great European Powers. It was essential that we should remove one of these two powerful adversaries that we had vanquished on the battle-field from the temptation to make alliances with others for the purpose of obtaining revenge. We could not address ourselves to France. Any one acquainted with the history and character of the Gallic nation had no difficulty in understanding why." [1] The Austrian

[1] *Thoughts and Souvenirs*, Volume II.

Alliance, which he had always desired, gave him satisfaction. As for the Italians, of whom he said in 1880, "The Italians are like those crows that feed on carrion and hover around battle-fields until something is left for them to eat," [1] he accepted them with a touch of disdain, as a sort of political instrument, and still more as affording by their connection with Austria and Germany an additional guarantee for Austria. Germany thus found herself at the head of a coalition disposing of more than two million men on a war footing, and barring Central Europe from the North Sea to the Mediterranean with a line of alliances of which she was the guiding hand. She was the dictator of peace — a peace which she both imposed and guaranteed. "The force of Germany was protected by a belt of two bulwarks: against France, there was the Italian alliance; against Russia, that with Austria. Within this double dyke, where she was invulnerable, she remained free for making an attack. Defensive in its appearance, this grouping of forces allowed Germany to act on the world at will. This it is which, since that time, has been called the German hegemony." [2]

In face of such a combination, France, by herself, was paralyzed. True, the Republic had not permitted her to sink "gradually or by sudden drops" [3] to the degree Bismarck hoped. Her army was in

---

[1] Maurice Busch's *Memoirs*, Volume II.
[2] Charles Andler's *Prince Bismarck*.
[3] Bismarck's *Thoughts and Souvenirs*, Volume II.

process of reorganization. In Jules Ferry she possessed a firm, clear-sighted statesman. She had just proved in Tunis that she was capable of willing and executing. However, diplomatically, she was, none the less, reduced to impotence. Russia was not ready for an action in common. Great Britain, who had been favourable at the Congress of Berlin, was already veering round. She was displeased with France on account of the latter's hesitating attitude during the negotiations respecting the frontiers of Greece. She experienced both surprise and irritation on discovering what advantage had been taken in Tunis of Lord Salisbury's encouraging language. She foresaw also that her own action in Egypt would, for a long time to come, place her in opposition to the Cabinet of Paris. And, as a matter of fact, from the month of July, 1883, Anglo-French relations assumed that character of unfriendly coolness which they were destined to keep for the next twenty years. Spain, as previously shown, inclined towards the Triple Alliance.[1] And through the medium of Italy, Bismarck was able to influence London. Nothing, therefore, thwarted German preponderance. In order to maintain and strengthen it, there was no need to make war. A state of peace sufficed. And to secure such peace, not even the adhesion of the nation vanquished in 1871 was necessary.

[1] See above, Chapter III.

II

For the purpose of maintaining this situation, Bismarck could unreservedly rely on his Allies. Until his fall in 1890, he used them at his will, with perfect security. By the very reason of her hostility let loose against France, Italy was a puppet in the hands of Berlin. Having to procure forgiveness for his own "*red*" past, Crispi displayed great zeal. As soon as he came into power, he hastened to Friedrichsruhe in order to receive his instructions. And a military convention was the outcome of this journey. Under Kalnoky, Austria was no less docile. The "dog of the Empire," as Beust [1] called him, was forever on the road between Varzin and Friedrichsruhe. There were interviews in abundance, in 1884, in 1885, in 1886, in 1888. The Emperor William, completely reconciled to the Austrian Alliance, had no need to stimulate Francis Joseph's fidelity in their long chats at Gastein or Ischl. In March, 1887, the *Triplice* was renewed on the same terms as those made five years earlier, without Comte de Robilant's obtaining anything else through his velleities of independence besides the Grand Cross of the Black Eagle.

It was less easy to deal with Russia. But Bismarck was not a man to be discouraged by difficulties. He, therefore, played his game — and played it with full success. The grievances of 1878 had deeply affected the Czar, Alexander III, who,

[1] See Count von Beust's *Memoirs*.

moreover, had a dread of revolution; and Germany seemed to him to be the last rampart of the Monarchy. Granted, all the "Slavists," including Ignatieff and Skobeleff, did not pardon the Germans, and continued to preserve their antipathy. Granted, there were commercial and fiscal difficulties with Germany, while the two countries' systematic armaments aroused on either side an amount of distrust and ill-humour. Yet, for all this, Bismarck's will enabled him to find instruments, and he left nothing untried to ingratiate himself with Russia. No sooner was Prince Orloff appointed Ambassador at Berlin (February, 1884) than all the newspapers of the Chancellor extolled this "token of *rapprochement*." Six days afterwards, the Grand Duke Michael arrived for the celebration of the Emperor William's seventieth birthday, in his quality of Knight of Saint George. On the 16th of May following, Prince William went to Saint Petersburg to take part in the fêtes given on the occasion of the coming of age of the Czarevitch; and, across the frontier, there was a fraternizing of German and Russian officers (June, 1884). In July, at Russia's request, Bismarck expelled from Berlin all persons residing in the German capital who were held to be suspects by the Czar's Government. Last of all, on the 14th of September, the Three Emperors, of Germany, Russia, and Austria, met at Skiernevice in a solemn interview. This interview did no more than reveal to the world at large an agreement that had been made six months previously.

As a matter of fact, on the 21st of March, Bismarck,
at length attaining his desire, had completed the
Triple Alliance by the signing between two of its
parties and the Russian Government of a secret
understanding which stipulated for a benevolent
neutrality in case one of the two should be attacked
by another Power. The negotiations had not been
altogether easy. "It was not with much enthusiasm that Austria entered into engagements with a
neighbour who was her most dreaded rival; and
Russia, on her side, manifested some distrust towards
these friends who had made their own alliance
against herself." [1]   After concluding the Triple
Alliance against Russia, Bismarck had accomplished
the stroke of genius which consisted in getting Russia
to guarantee it. Under pretext of defending the
"monarchic principle," Germany strengthened her
hold on Europe. The isolation of France was
absolute. An additional ring encircled those which
had already been passed round her in 1879 and 1882.

It will be understood without difficulty that
Bismarck was anxious to preserve this masterpiece;
and, indeed, whatever could be done to make it
secure, he did. In 1885, he welcomed Mr. de Giers,
his Russian colleague, to Friedrichsruhe. In 1886,
he met him at Franzenbad, and, with a view to
conferring more importance on the meeting, five
Russian diplomatists — Mr. de Staal, Ambassador
at London; the Baron de Mohrenheim, Ambassador
at Paris; Prince Cantacuzene, Chargé d'Affaires at

[1] See Paul Matter's *Bismarck and his Times*, Volume III.

Vienna; Mr. de Toll, Minister at Copenhagen; and
Mr. de Struwe, Minister at Washington — were all
present at it. In November, 1887, the Czar,
Alexander III, arrived at Berlin. At this moment
(March 21, 1887) the Counter-Assurance of the
Three Emperors had been for three months without
force, it having expired, and Russia not having been
willing to renew it on account of her fears over the
Eastern question. On the 18th of November, while
the Czar was staying at Berlin, Bismarck extorted
a fresh treaty from him, similar to the previous one,
except that, instead of binding three Powers, the
engagement was between Germany and Russia
only. It was a repetition of Skiernevice, with two
signataries. The Counter-Assurance was resus-
citated with an equal value for Germany. Sure of
the future, Bismarck was convinced that for long
to come he had averted the danger of a Franco-
Russian coalition.

At the same time, he contrived, by his supple
diplomacy, to keep England in his game. To tell
the truth, it was not so hard as "recapturing"
Russia. England had quitted the Congress of
Berlin in a satisfied frame of mind. Egypt had
caused her to fall out with France. She was content
to remain in her "splendid isolation," and was
without prejudices against Germany. Not that
she had been pleased to see her acquire the Marshall
Isles in 1878, Luderitzland, New Guinea, Togo, and
the Cameroons in 1884, and install herself in Eastern
Africa in 1886. But she did not yet believe in the

German peril which, ten years later, was to cause
her such anxiety. At certain times, there was
some tension between London and Berlin, for instance, when Germany and France prevented Great
Britain from ratifying the Treaty with Portugal
which would in advance have made her supreme in
the Congo (1884). Now and again, also, the *North
German Gazette* had disputes with the *Times* (1884).
But not much attention was paid to this. In
1885, Bismarck declared he was confident of the
future. "With England," he said, "we are on good
terms. That England, with her persuasion she
rules the seas, should feel some surprise on suddenly
seeing her cousin land-rats, as she calls us, begin
to navigate, is not astonishing. . . . But we have
old relations of friendship with England; and the
two countries are anxious to preserve them."
(January 10.)

In the month of February following, Lord Granville protested against the idea of any coolness
having arisen between Downing Street and Wilhelmstrasse. In his turn, Bismarck disclaimed "having
ever blamed the English policy in Egypt." (March
3.) On the 4th, Count Herbert von Bismarck, who
was privy to his father's intentions, paid a visit
of courtesy to London. And, on the 22d, the Prince
of Wales, in person, went to Berlin to testify to the
cordiality of the two countries' relations. In 1886,
three Anglo-German colonial agreements were signed
successively, the first relative to the Pacific (April
6), the second, to the possessions in the Gulf of

Guinea (August 2), the third, to Zanzibar and
East Africa (November 1). Moreover, through
Italy, Bismarck did not despair of sooner or later
entering into closer relations with London. He
was aware of his Ally's exchanges of views with
Great Britain. He knew that if the Italians had
gone to Massowah, it was with the consent of the
English Cabinet. And, in fine, he was not ignorant
that Austria also, in a large measure, could rely on
British support. He was quite confident, therefore,
and, as he followed on a map of the world the
progress of our expansion outside Europe, he promised himself the joy of witnessing, — *suave mari
magno,* — "the shock of the English and French
locomotives"; a fresh opportunity for his acting the
part of a kind and "honest" broker.

On the French side, he found entire security in
the prodigious ardour which made us, in all parts
of the world, rush after colonies, whatever they
might be. Jules Ferry had said in 1882: "France
must have colonial power. Every portion of her
colonial domain, even its least fragments, must be
held sacred by us. . . . It is not the future of
to-morrow that is concerned, but that of fifty and
a hundred years hence, that of the mother-country
herself." This eloquent appeal had been heard,
and even listened to with too great readiness, so
that the action of France had been scattered, and
carried to spots in which we had no interests. The
Tunisian protectorate in 1882, the annexation of
the towns of Mzab, six hundred kilometres from

Algiers (1882); the Senegal and Niger expeditions
against Ahmadou and Samory (1883); the conquest
of Dahomey (1883–1892); the settlement in the
Congo (1884); the Madagascar war (1882–1885);
the settlement at Djibouti (1882–1885); the conquest of Tonkin and Annam (1885–1888); all these
proved our vitality, and rendered us inoffensive in
Europe. To this French expansion Bismarck was
favourable. "We have every reason to rejoice at
it," he said after Tunis. And, in his generosity,
he wished us to have Morocco, respecting which,
in 1880, he had instructed his delegates at the Conference of Madrid "to regulate their attitude by
that of their French colleague." In September,
1884, he placed himself in agreement with our
Ambassador at Berlin, the Baron de Courcel, on the
question of opposing England. And in agreement
with him also, he summoned the Congo Conference.
On the 24th of December, 1885, he signed a delimitation treaty respecting the French and German
colonies in West Africa. In October, 1886, Mr.
Herbette's appointment, in the place of Mr. de Courcel, furnished the Chancellor's newspapers with an
occasion to say that Mr. de Freycinet was coming
round to Jules Ferry's policy. In reality, Bismarck
had no anxiety that was caused by France; and, for
this reason, he proclaimed in the Reichstag "that
the two Governments had full confidence in the
sincerity and loyalty of their mutual relations."

This did not, however, hinder him from sometimes brandishing his big sabre with a view to

depriving the French neighbour of any inclination to budge, and more especially for the purpose of inculcating in the German tax-payers and their Parliamentary representatives a taste for military expenses. He had not waited for that till Boulangism arose, and had never ceased mingling threats with his advances. In 1883, the *North German Gazette,* speaking of the risks of war, wrote with reference to France: "One may paint the devil so often on the wall that at last one sees him appear." On the 4th of September in the same year, the same semi-official paper declared: "Germany will maintain the Treaty of Frankfort as long as she is left with a man." And gracefully the paper added: "And now let there be no more said about it." Ten days after at Skiernevice, Bismarck warned the Three Emperors of the revolutionary peril, that is to say, of the French peril. On the 28th of November, 1885, he condescended to address to the French Government an assurance of his confidence; but, at the same time, complained bitterly of the French press and people. On the 26th of March, 1886, he seized the occasion of the Decazeville strikes to express the opinion that, after all, the French Army, which was then occupied in restraining the workmen on strike, might well one day become again, as in 1792, the army of social subversion. On the outbreak of Boulangism, his tone naturally rose. On the 31st of January, 1887, there was an article in the *Post,* entitled "Under the Knife," which violently denounced French provocations. In April,

there was the Schnaebele incident; in September,
the Brignon affair.[1] The *North German Gazette*, between times, lauded "German patience" in terms
that hinted this patience was at an end. And, on
the 19th of May, a circular, courteously conceived,
it is true, made public the fact that Germany would
not take part in the Universal Exhibition of 1889.

Why all this fuss and bluster? No doubt, to
secure the voting of the War Credits. The Seven
Years' Period, adopted in 1880, expired on the 31st
of March, 1888. At the opening of the session of
1886–1887, the Royal Speech had announced the necessity of increasing the country's military strength.
"In the Army," it said, "is the only sure guarantee for the lasting protection of the blessings of
peace; and, although the Empire's policy continues to be pacific, Germany is not able, in presence
of the development of military institutions in States
bordering on our own, to abstain longer from increasing her military force and, in particular, its
present peace footing." The new Seven Years'
Period, in fact, comprised an augmentation of 61,000
men and increased credits of 47 million marks.
On the 11th of January, 1887, Bismarck made a
strong personal appeal.[2]

The question," he said, "of our future relations with France
is one that I am not so sure about . . . Between ourselves and
France the work of maintaining peace is difficult, since the two
countries have long been divided by a dispute that is historical,
to wit, the fixing of the frontier line, which has been doubtful

[1] Incidents on the French-German border.
[2] See Paul Matter's book already cited.

and contested from the time when France acquired her complete unity and Royal Power.   This dispute is not ended; and we must expect to see it continued on the French side.   At present it is we who are in possession of the coveted portion, if I may so speak of Alsace.   We consequently have no motive ourselves for fighting about it.   But no one can pretend that France does not dream of reconquering it, no one of those who have any real knowledge of what is published in the French press.   They who desire a war with us seek only in the meantime for the possibility of entering upon it with the greatest forces possible.   Their task is to keep alive the sacred fire of revenge. . . .   I have confidence in the pacific intentions of the French Government, and of the French people; but I cannot on this account lull myself with such assurance as to be able to say: We have no fear of France attacking us!   I am convinced that an attack by France is to be feared.   Whether it may happen in ten days or in ten years is something I cannot venture to settle. . . .   His Majesty cannot disavow the work to which he has devoted the last thirty years of his life — the creation of the German Army, the creation of the German Empire. . . .   If to the Confederate Government's solicitude for the defensive strength of Germany you do not give satisfaction by a prompt and complete adoption of our project, we shall then prefer to continue the discussion with more chance of success by resuming it in another Reichstag than the one I see before me.

Being beaten, Bismarck read the decree dissolving the national Parliament; and at once let loose the official press, the *Post* in particular.   The elections of the 21st of February, 1887, gave him his majority.   But the military effort was not yet achieved, whence the occurrence of fresh frontier incidents, which continued until the eve of the January discussions in 1888.   In December, there was a new project for increasing the numbers of the *Landwehr* and *Landsturm*, which, following on the inauguration of the fresh Seven Years' Period,

caused considerable anxiety in the Russian press.
Deeming his situation impregnable, since he had
just concluded his second Treaty of Counter-Assurance with Russia (November, 1887) and France
was in the midst of her civil discord, Bismarck now
resolved to strike a decisive blow. On the 3d of
February, 1888, he gave order for the text of the
Austro-German Treaty to be published. Any one
who reads it through again will be able to judge
what an effect was produced by its becoming known
at Saint Petersburg. On the 8th of the same month,
he made a speech in the Reichstag, using language
of unprecedented harshness, aimed not only against
France, but still more against Russia: —

The fears that have arisen in the course of the present year
have been caused by Russia more even than by France, chiefly
through an exchange of provocations, threats, insults, and reciprocal instigations which have occurred during the past summer
in the Russian and French press.

He added, however, that the pacific assurances
which he had received from the Czar in 1887, had
more weight with him than newspaper articles.
As to the movements of Russian troops on the
frontier since 1879, they had tended to create the
impression of an approaching aggression, *at some
unexpected moment*, against one of the neighbouring
countries. He declared, nevertheless, that he did
not believe in the existence of such an intention:—

I am convinced that even if some French explosion or other
were to involve us in a war with France, it would not immediately bring us into immediate hostilities with Russia, at any
rate not necessarily. But, on the other hand, should we be

engaged in a war with Russia, war with France would be certain. No French Government would be strong enough to hinder it.

Bismarck went on to speak of the military expenses France had made, of "her hatred against all her neighbours," and said: —

Our geographic situation imposes greater efforts upon us. We have to protect ourselves on three sides. . . . More than any other nation, we are exposed to the dangers of a coalition. God has given us on our flank the French, who are the most warlike and turbulent nation that exists, and he has permitted the development in Russia of warlike propensities which, until lately, did not manifest themselves to the same extent.

He then retraced the history of Russo-German relations, insisting more peculiarly on his own rôle at the Congress of Berlin, where, with fine cynicism, he claimed to have behaved as if he had been "a fourth Russian plenipotentiary." He declared that throughout the Congress, no Russian wish had been expressed, to his knowledge, without his immediately satisfying it. At the same time, he overwhelmed Gortchakoff with his retrospective irony: "If I had not then been long in possession of the highest Russian Order, I should have well earned it." In fine, he accused Russia of having excited him against Austria. Thence had been born the Triple Alliance. And he concluded: —

The threats of the press are nothing else than sheer folly. Can any one believe that, by dint of ink and words, it is possible to intimidate a Power of Germany's pride and power? By means of courtesy and kind methods we may be easily — too easily perhaps — influenced, but by means of threats, never. We Germans fear God and nothing else in the world. It is fear of God which has caused us to love and cultivate peace. If any

L

one should break it, he will soon be convinced that the combative patriotism which, in 1813, called to arms the entire people of Prussia,—who were then weak and vanquished,—is to-day the common property of the whole German nation; and he will find them animated by one soul, with the strong belief existing in each soldier's heart that God is with us!

This *Quos Ego*, which was, as it were, Bismarck's political will and testament, ripened the Franco-Russian Alliance ten years sooner than might have otherwise been the case. Never had the *pax Germanica* uttered a prouder language. Never had the Chancellor made Europe feel, in a harsher way, that she had a master and would have to keep him. Would she have kept him, if, two years later, William II, in his feverish haste to reign alone, had not dismissed this master and freed Europe at the same time that he freed himself? We leave the question to be answered by amateurs of conjecture. As for Bismarck, such an hypothesis never entered into his head. A few months later, he made the statement that "he was sure he would remain Chancellor till he died." The ordering of the future was one of his favourite cards. Yet it was this card that deceived him. After struggling in secret for eighteen months with the new Sovereign, Bismarck retired on the 8th of March, 1890. Would his successors be able to play his game and prolong his success?

III

The conclusion of the Franco-Russian Alliance occurred a few months after the accession of William

II and Bismarck's retirement. As early as 1888,
the victim of 1888 had come into unmistakably
closer relations with the victim of 1871. True, on
the 30th of June, 1888, the *Gazette of the Cross* persisted in announcing that Bismarck had definitely
turned Russia from the French Alliance, and that,
in order to confirm the Russo-German understanding, William II, as soon as he was crowned, would
commence his visits to the various foreign courts by
going to see the Czar. The interview took place;
but its effect was not to bring Germany any nearer
to Alexander III. On the 10th of May, 1890, after
his dismissal of the month of March, Bismarck began his polemical revelations against his Sovereign
and his successor; and, in a published interview,
declared that "the existence of France was necessary
to Russia." On the 14th of the same month, when
defending a military project in the Reichstag, Moltke
contrived to couple Paris and Saint Petersburg in
his speech. He said: "The pacific assurances given
to us by our neighbours in the East and in the West
— assurances which do not prevent them from continuing their armaments — are certainly precious
to us. But it is for us to find our security in ourselves." A few months later, himself intervening
in the debates, William II exclaimed: "The times
in which we live are serious; and, perhaps in coming
years, we shall have trouble." When it is recollected
that, only ten weeks afterwards, the welcome accorded by the Russian people to Admiral Gervais'
squadron at Cronstadt, manifested to the world at

large, as the Czar put it, "the deep bonds of sympathy uniting France and Russia," these words of the German Emperor assume their full significance. From that moment, the Franco-Russian Alliance was made, if not signed; and the coalition which Bismarck, until his death, boasted of having dreaded and hindered as long as he was in power, — the coalition which, in several speeches, Caprivi was subsequently to declare inevitable and, indeed, inoffensive, — was thenceforth assured.

At first, this political event appeared to German policy as a discomfiture. When bringing in two new military bills on the 23d of November, 1893, Caprivi, in spite of his habitual optimism, did not dissimulate the change in the situation. "France," he said in substance, "has numerous and well-organized army corps, fortresses, and intrenched camps. And we should no longer find in Russia the same forbearance as in the commencement of the War of 1870. . . . The Emperor of Russia is a powerful partisan of peace. But the sentiments of the Russian people are against us. The Russian mobilization, moreover, proves that Saint Petersburg believes the next war will be in the West. . . . There can be no doubt that a *rapprochement* has come about between France and Russia. Its origins date far back. But, to-day, everything, Cronstadt included, leads us to suppose that an alliance is meditated. We do not mean to attack. But we do mean to be able to hold our own on both sides." This, it may be said, was an oratorical artifice, calculated to ob-

tain the voting of the military credits; an artifice
perhaps, but yet testifying to sincere anxiety and
real disappointment. Thanks to the Russian Alliance, France escaped from the forced inaction in
which she had remained for twenty years. Count
Schouvaloff's expression: "You are suffering from
a Coalition nightmare," took on an appearance
of prophecy in the light of events. The "Western
neighbour" passed from the state of passive peace
to one of voluntary peace. Germany, forsooth, did
not lack means to defend the territorial *statu quo;*
but the political *statu quo* was modified; and the
European balance of power, reëstablished to the
profit of Bismarck's two victims, took from the German Empire the dictatorship which it had held so
long. In 1879, Bismarck wrote to the King of Ba-
varia: "The danger of war complications (with
Russia) is, in my opinion, not imminent. It would
only become serious if France were ready to march
in agreement with Russia. Up to the present, such
is not the case." After 1891, "such was the case";
and it is easy to understand that the change represented a material and moral diminution for Germany.

A policy of sentiment and impressionism would
not have accepted this *fait nouveau* without anger.
German policy, being positive and realistic, sought
to get out of it what was possible. Without much
trouble, she recognized that the conclusion of the
Dual Alliance did not constitute an immediate
threat. Granted, the inheritors of Boulangism and

their naïve supporters attributed to the Franco
Russian Alliance a revenge of counter-value and
approaching reparation. And they relied on it for
the reconquest of Alsace and Lorraine. But, in the
Chancelleries, and even among the well-informed
public, it was understood that this Alliance was
purely defensive and that, if, in case of aggression,
it afforded France a guarantee, it did not in any degree or under any form encourage her to undertake
an offensive policy. What did the Cronstadt toasts
say? That the new Alliance was an element of
peace. What did the Russian papers say? That
Europe's tranquillity gained additional security by
the union of the two peoples. But peace meant the
statu quo; and the *statu quo* was the Treaty of
Frankfort. Germany, therefore, could put up with
the Dual Alliance, on condition it did not escape from
her control and turn against her. Within a few
months, her decision was made. She would resign
herself to the Franco-Russian Alliance, first because
no useful end would have been served by her not
resigning herself, and secondly because the Alliance
might become, in her hands, a fresh means of action.
Consequently, there was an end to bitter speeches,
an end to hints of possible or likely war which had
so recently been heard. Instead, were exhibited
constant amiability towards France, a visible desire
to act in concert with her, in concert with Russia;
to draw, when occasion offered, the two Allies into
coöperation with Berlin outside Europe, a coöperation having the double advantage of diverting France

more and more from Continental matters, and of involving her more deeply in the Colonial policy which, in 1881, had caused her to fall out with Italy, and had always, especially since the Egyptian question, brought her into conflict with England.

To this policy of relaxation and advances, William II contributed in person. When he ascended the throne, just after the Boulangist agitation and the Schnaebele incident, he brought with him, rightly or wrongly, a reputation for rashness, and for being ready to embark on any wild enterprise. Already, before the death of his grandfather, William I, he had protested that this reputation was undeserved. At the commencement of 1888, he declared: "I am quite aware that, among people in general and especially abroad, I am accused of frivolous desires of warlike fame. God preserve me from such cruel folly. I indignantly spurn these unworthy imputations." None the less, the reputation has remained, and has served as a foil to all his pacific affirmations. First, there was the Workmen's Conference at Berlin in 1890, and the fascination he exercised upon Jules Simon — things which marked the dawn of a fresh point of view in the French press with regard to the German Emperor. Jules Simon, who wrote a great deal, could not say enough in eulogy of the Imperial host, who entertained him royally. He repeated the favourable opinion held by William II respecting our Army, its progress, its fitness. And our *amour-propre* was flattered by this. Then, there was a series of courtesies which, coming

one after another, fell, like so many germs of peace,
upon the ground that had been so well prepared.
If there was some anniversary of 1870 to be com-
memorated, the Emperor did not fail to render
homage to "the chivalrous enemy" (December 14,
1891); to "the brave French soldiers fighting with
the courage of despair for their laurels, their
past, their Emperor" (December 2, 1895). When
Marshal MacMahon died, he instructed Count Münster, on the same day, to convey to the Duchess
of Magenta the respectful expression of his sympathy" (October 18, 1893). When President Carnot was assassinated at Lyons, he once more contrived to say just the right thing; and, first among
foreign monarchs, expressed his sympathy with the
widow of the President who, "worthy of his great
name, had died on the field of honour." On this
occasion, and in spite of some resistance manifested
by German opinion, he gave orders for the liberation
of two French naval officers who had been arrested
for espionage. Afterwards, there were similar pro-
ceedings on the death of General Canrobert (January 29, 1895); of Jules Simon (June 8, 1896); on
the morrow of the fire at the *Bazar de la Charité*
(May 4, 1897); and of the loss of the *Bourgogne*
(July, 1898); and again, still more recently, at the
funeral of Felix Faure, where, by his choice, he was
represented by one of the German princes nearest to
France by his family relations, Prince Anthony
Radzivill (February, 1899). On the 6th of July of
the same year, being in Norwegian waters, he visited

the French training-ship, *Iphigenia*, and telegraphed
to Mr. Loubet to express his gratification, "both as
a sailor and as a comrade" at the amiable reception
accorded him. In 1900, he personally superintended the organization of the German section of
the Exhibition, with a view to increasing its brill-
iance and success. In 1901, General Bonnal having been invited by him to the German military
manœuvres, he received this officer at Berlin and
loaded him with attentions. And, not so long ago,
the catastrophe of Martinique Island furnished him
with another opportunity to send us one of those
sympathetic telegrams in which he excels, and to
foster a friendly atmosphere which, while somewhat
artificial, perhaps, is none the less useful by reason
of the greater facility of relations that results from
it. The extreme shrewdness of Prince Münster, the
amenity of Prince Radolin, the smiling skill of the
Marquis de Noailles, for whom the Emperor felt an
especial friendship, aided in the improvement. On
our part, we did not cease to contribute what lay in
our power, with the reserve imposed on our dignity
by souvenirs ever present, but with correctness and
perfect grace. And, on each occasion that called for
it, notably at the time of the Kiel fêtes and of the
inundations in Silesia, the Government of the Republic were not backward in replying with courtesy
to the courteous advances made to them by the
German Emperor.

Politically, these advances bore their fruit; and
Germany derived profit from them. Being sure, or

at least believing he was sure, of the friendship of England, with whom he had signed successive Colonial agreements, William II managed to find or create opportunities of exhibiting his relations with the Dual Alliance. Already, in 1891, Mr. de Giers, Russia's Minister of Foreign Affairs, after a journey to Paris, had ostentatiously visited the three Capitals of the *Triplice*, Rome, Vienna, and Berlin. Four years later, the war between China and Japan brought about the threefold action of Russia, France, and Germany, which snatched from Japan the fruit of her victory (1895). In the same year, the inauguration of the Kiel Canal, which was honoured by the simultaneous presence of a French and a Russian squadron, was the outward and visible sign of a *rapprochement* that Saint Petersburg would seem to have counselled in Paris. On the 31st of May and the 10th of June, Mr. Hanotaux, being challenged in Parliament, defended his policy and secured its approval. To Mr. Millerand, who said to him: "France will never be false to the fidelity she has vowed to the provinces that have been taken from her," the Minister replied : —

We have done no more than other Powers in manifesting a behaviour of international politeness corresponding to an act of international policy that was addressed to all the Powers. . . .

In open peace, the relations of the various nations must be regulated by a sentiment, at once worthy and simple, of international politeness."

And further : —

Our sailors will go to Kiel, representing, not a resigned and discouraged France, but a France free and strong, sure enough of herself to remain calm, proud enough and rich enough in glory to fear no comparison, to disown no souvenir.

In what will this France be diminished in her prestige, her authority, her interests, because of her vessels' presence at an international ceremony where they will meet, among a hundred others, the vessels of a nation that is her friend, and that has replied in the same conditions as ourselves to the same invitation?

Now, by a curious coincidence, the sitting of Parliament in which the French Minister held this extremely polite language with regard to Germany, was just the one in which, in accord with the Prime Minister, he proclaimed officially, for the first time, the existence of the Franco-Russian Alliance. The feeling of the *rapprochement* was thereby rendered more sensible. In 1896, there was another symptom: Germany announced her intention to participate in our Universal Exhibition of 1900; and, a few weeks later, William II made a speech in honour of the European solidarity. In 1897, Count Mouraview, then Russian Minister of Foreign Affairs, came to Paris; but, with a certain manifestation of intention, he stopped at Berlin on his way back to Russia. On the 23d of July in the same year, a Franco-German agreement was signed relative to the Togo delimitation. And, at that moment, overtures were made to us from Berlin with a view to an understanding between the two countries, — overtures the particulars of which were unknown, but the reality of which was undeniable. More and more it would seem that circumstances were leading us towards a *rapprochement* with Germany on the

basis of the Continental *status quo* and of Colonial
action in harmony. The Fashoda alarm, and the
threatening prospect of a naval war for which we
were not ready, disturbed public opinion greatly,
which again turned to the advantage of Berlin,
since French Nationalists both past and future,
Mr. Jules Lemaître among them, advocated an
understanding with our neighbours on the East
against Great Britain. True, when once the English peril was averted, the Dreyfus Affair awoke the
old historic resentment. But the correct attitude
of the German Imperial Government removed all
risks of clashing and conflict. On several occasions,
the German Ministers were able to congratulate
themselves that this "*Affaire* which raised so much
dust, had not troubled the correctness of France and
Germany's relations with each other." And when
the crisis was over, it was once more the Colonial
understanding with France, which appeared to be
Germany's object, when Count von Buelow, speaking in the Reichstag in December, 1899, and defining the world-policy of Greater Germany, added:
"With France we have always, so far, easily and
willingly come to an arrangement in matters concerning Colonial interests." The events that occurred in China in 1900, the appointment of General
von Waldersee, as Commander-in-Chief of the International troops, the confraternity of arms instituted
between the adversaries of Sedan, confraternity
which William II celebrated in the ensuing year by
receiving General Bonnal at Berlin — everything

seemed to favour German plans. Again (March 15,
1901) the Chancellor insisted on the fact that, between France and Germany, there was no longer any
real conflict of interests, whether in the Far East or
in the many parts of the world. More and more,
Germany availed herself of a diplomatic combination which increased the security of her State-pos-
session, and allowed her, both in Europe and out of
Europe, to use either her own Allies, or ours, or ourselves.

The Triple Alliance, moreover, continued in force,
as in the past. Austria remained constantly faithful to it, and, absorbed by her domestic struggles,
in no way modified her foreign policy. Italy was no
less docile. She had fêted Chancellor von Caprivi
in November, 1890, William II in 1892 and in
1897. King Humbert had gone to Potsdam in 1892
and 1897; and the Prince of Naples, to the Lorraine
manœuvres in 1893. Her defeats in Ethiopia and
her economic difficulties, besides, dissuaded Italy
from the fits of Gallophobia that she had indulged in
during the early period of the Triple Alliance. In
June, 1991, this Treaty had been renewed for twelve
years, with the option of denouncing it in 1898. But
none of the three Allies had made use of the option.
Consequently, the Bismarckian system subsisted,
without any appearance of umbrage or prejudice
being caused by the Franco-Russian Alliance. Turkey and Roumania had been drawn further and
further into the German wake. The Empire's prosperity was brilliant. Its military strength was un-

diminished. The *Triplice* was no longer alone; but
it was not eclipsed. Never had the international
situation appeared to be more favourable to her
than it then was. William II exercised a personal
ascendency over Nicholas II which was maintained
by frequent interviews and regular correspondence.
Russia's Asiatic policy inclined her to accept in
Europe the German lead, which she had already
obeyed in China, by doing at Port Arthur what Germany had done at Kiao-Tcheou. The Austro-Russian agreement of 1897, relative to Turkish affairs
and intended to preserve the *statu quo*, prevented
risks arising from Eastern complications; and, if the
Bismarckian Counter-Assurance of 1884 and 1887
no longer existed, this had happened through the
operation of facts, not of engagements. Strengthened by her naval programme of 1900, Germany
saw opened to her, by the firman granting her the
Bagdad Railway, which had been obtained from the
Sultan in January, 1902, the fairest economic and
political prospects in Nearer Asia. Her purchase of
the Spanish colonies in the Pacific had also served
her world-policy (1899). She had made her appearance at Pekin, in 1900, under the auspices of
Marshal Waldersee, as Europe's dictator. Nothing
hindered her from wielding a discreet and profitable
influence over the Latin nations at the time when
they manifested a tendency to come nearer together.
The abolition of the dictature paragraph applying to
Lorraine had produced a good impression in Paris.
Negotiations had been opened respecting the Bagdad

Railway, which, with a little more moderation, Germany might have brought to a successful conclusion. It depended on Berlin, by coupling such negotiations with African affairs, to preside at the elaboration of the various Mediterranean understandings, instead of leaving the honour and benefit of them to others.

It seemed even that, to the political domination established by Bismarck, the Germany of William II had added an economic supremacy. Allusion has already been made to the prodigious progress of her commerce and industry. As ideas always run in the same mould, the Germany of trade had the like conception of success as the Germany of government. Under colour of serving the people's needs and German prestige, the German speculators attempted to impose their combinations on the world without respecting or even recognizing the rights and preferences of others. These economic conquerors on land and sea contrived to bring the nation's force and influence into the service of their unbounded appetites. Germany had become an "Industrial State." After supplying herself with the most scientific machinery and requisites that had ever been introduced into the economic struggle — canals, railways, harbours, technical schools, manufactories, and banks, — she abandoned Bismarck's system of protection. In 1895, she broke down the barriers which, not so long before, were a hindrance to her expansion, and started out to conquer fresh markets. She began with the countries of the Continent. But soon Europe no longer sufficed to her progress. Asia

Minor, India, Siam, Japan, China, Africa, the United
States, South America, were invaded by her products;
her commercial travellers, with imperial, dominating
manners, never failing to utilize the strength of the
Empire on behalf of their merchandise. Thus understood, the *Weltpolitik* was the mercantile continuation of the Bismarckian policy.

In spite of the perils attaching to such a system,
circumstances at the commencement of the twentieth century enabled Germany to consolidate it. She
had it in her power to draw along her borders, for
her own advantage, the "Continental line" which
seemed at certain moments to be the Emperor William's supreme aim. For three years, England had
been paralyzed by the Transvaal war. The rest of
Europe was in a hesitating frame of mind, easy to be
gained over and to be guided. There was a fine game
to be played, a game not difficult to be won by Mr.
von Buelow, who, since 1897, had been the guiding
hand of the Empire's diplomacy. "There is but one
favourable moment in affairs," said Bismarck, in
1878; "the thing is to know when to seize it. Mr.
Von Buelow did not seize it. Led away, now by the
"grand Continental designs" of the Emperor, now by
the attraction of immediate profits at the expense of
one and another, he was unable to choose; and,
through his contradictions, inspired distrust in all.
A few months later, peace was signed in the Transvaal (June, 1902); and this, following on the Anglo-
Japanese Alliance (January, 1902), restored to
England a liberty of action which new men, the King

and Lord Lansdowne, were ready to make good use
of. The opportunity which Germany had allowed
to escape vanished; and fresh combinations arose in
the midst of astonished Europe.

IV

As a matter of fact, at this time, acting on the
idea — a true one, indeed — that the Russian Alliance, which neither could have nor should have been
for us an instrument of revenge, yet, at least, could
and should leave us free in our movements, for the
settlement of our own affairs and the pursuit of our
interests, French policy, first in the direction of Italy,
next in the direction of England, and, last of all, in
the direction of Spain, began a triple campaign of
rapprochement. After playing, in Crispi's time, the
offensive rôle of the Triple Alliance against us, Italy
effected her reconciliation with us, first commercially and then politically (1898–1902). Not many
months after, an explanation of the same kind led
us to liquidate with Great Britain a whole past of
colonial rivalry and ancestral resentment. And this
liquidation, more striking and more important than
that of the quarrel between France and Italy, was
recorded, on the 8th of April, 1904, in a public treaty.
Finally, six months later, Spain, in her turn, gave
adhesion to this agreement. The local consequence
of these negotiations was to give us a free hand in
Morocco. That, however, was a small thing compared with the general scope of the liquidation,

M

which extended the field opened to our activity by
the Franco-Russian Alliance, guaranteed us our material and moral autonomy in Western Europe, and
made us a centre of attraction.

This was something new and disquieting to Germany, who, while it was still time, had not known
how to assume the direction of the movement. The
fresh Continental grouping, added to the Dual Alliance, was, in fact, calculated to substitute for the
German hegemony an equilibrium independent of
her influence. Being deeply imbued with Bismarck's principles, William II had no illusions on
the subject. The very system was in danger, which
it was his mission to safeguard. If any one will read
over the seven hundred and some odd speeches pronounced, since his accession, by the voluble orator
who presides over the destinies of the German Empire, a fixed idea will be found in them, by the side
of accidental opinions and ephemeral theories. This
idea is that Germany must retain the position she
acquired through her victorious war against France
— position accruing at once from the territorial conquests realized at our expense and from the passivity
to which our diplomacy was reduced. At the very
commencement of his reign, William II said plainly
what he conceived his task to be, and that he would
allow no breach to be made in the Imperial work:
"There are people," he exclaimed, "who do not fear
to assert that my father would have been willing to
give up what he, with my grandfather, had won by
the sword. We knew the Emperor Frederick too

well to permit, even for an instant, such an outrage
on his memory. Like ourself, he was convinced
that nothing must be abandoned of the conquests of
the heroic epoch. We would sooner sacrifice our
eighteen Army Corps and our forty-two millions of
inhabitants than let one stone fall of the edifice
raised by William I." The tenor of this speech,
which was made on the 16th of August, 1888, found
its echo in a series of similar manifestations during a
period of seventeen years. And it was always the
same thought that recurred: "To preserve the glorious conquests with which God has rewarded Germany's struggles for independence and unity is the
most sacred of duties." For this work of preservation two conditions were required, — those indeed
which Bismarck had always known how to realize.
First, it was necessary that the German Empire —
in security with regard to one of its two vanquished
rivals, to wit, Austro-Hungary — should be in a
position to repel an aggression of the other, to wit,
France, if, perchance, the aggression occurred. Next,
it was necessary that any risk of it should be averted
by the incapacity of France to practise and even to
conceive a policy of action. Thus and thus only
would the hegemony of Germany be maintained.
Thus and thus only would the "coalition nightmare" be removed from her. In 1903 and 1904,
William II was again seized by this nightmare.
Europe was escaping from his control, and he felt it.
Seeing her organize herself without him, and perhaps against him, he was troubled and alarmed.

Moreover, at this moment, Germany was but ill-prepared to look coolly at a disagreeable situation, finding, as she did, within herself and near her, things that might well make her nervous. The very progress which was her pride and which aroused anger and was prejudicial to interests abroad, was, by its rapidity and far-reaching character, a source of difficulties at home. In 1901, an economic crisis commenced to rage, which took more than two years to exhaust itself. "Between 1890 and 1895, seven hundred and eleven Joint-stock Companies were founded, with a nominal capital of 755 million francs. And between 1895 and 1900, fifteen hundred and fifty-one were founded, with a capital of 2 billions 800 millions. If to these figures be added the 600 millions represented by the various augmentations of capital belonging to older Companies and the two billions of bonds issued by them, it may be said that since 1895 the sums invested in German industry have attained the enormous figure of six billions." [1] Now the German Empire does not possess anything like the capital of England or France. Money fell short. The banks, becoming more and more daring, continued to go right on. And the returns were not sufficient to cover the overdraft. Failures, bankruptcies, and scandals occurred; notably there was the disaster of the *Leipziger Bank*,[1] which in 1904 was hardly liquidated. Agriculture was as much in debt as Industry. People began to ask themselves

---

[1] See Francis Delaisy's book, *German Force*.
[2] See Victor Bérard's *William II and France*.

whether it was not possible that the economic giant's feet were made of clay. Certain persons even thought that war was still the most profitable national career. Even the more moderate lacked the calmness needed in order properly to appreciate the European events by which the Continent was escaping from German preponderance.

Did it not seem, indeed, that the Triple Alliance itself was languishing? True, it subsisted still; and nothing was falser than to believe that its real existence had ever been threatened. Yet, certain disquieting symptoms were noticeable. Italy showed a somewhat indiscreet joy over the balance of power that she had managed to reëstablish to her advantage among the nations of Central Europe. She congratulated herself on having added to the prestige which for the last twenty years had accrued to her from the *Triplice*, the political influence which, to use Mr. von Buelow's expression, results from the "play of counterweight." However anxious she was to preserve her alliances, she was no longer, as at the beginning, condemned to them by her isolation. Slight modifications of attitude rendered the change perceptible. Germany no longer exercised over Rome the invincible prestige of yore. Visits were still paid, in which speeches were still pronounced in honour of reciprocal engagements. But the Italian speeches were colder than the German. And the reception accorded by Italy to William II, when he went there in 1904, seemed less hearty than the one given simultaneously to Mr. Loubet. On the other hand, it was impossible not to recognize that clouds were arising between Vienna and Rome. The *irredentist* incidents of Innsbruck, Trent, and Trieste, together with armaments that were symmetric and manifestations that were hostile, had on various occasions, in spite of the two Governments, brought out popular antipathies. Last of all, Italy's Balkan ambitions, the well-known theory of "the Adriatic equilibrium," which practically amounted to claiming for the Italians alone the supremacy of these seas, could not fail to give the Austrian Government serious food for thought. With the laudable desire of coming to an understanding, Rome and Vienna had elaborated agreements in view of the *statu quo — promesse di non fare*, as Signor Ugo Ojetti one day said. But such expedients were precarious. And the awakening of the Balkan problem might, whether Germany willed it or not, put her Italian Allies and her Austrian Allies at loggerheads.

The Emperor William's uneasiness was not long in showing itself. On the 8th of April, 1904, the Franco-English arrangement was signed. On the 28th of the same month, he spoke at Carlsruhe, and this is what he said: "Let us think of the great epoch when the German unity was created, of the battles of Woerth, Weissembourg, and Sedan. Present events invite us to forget our domestic discords. Let us be united in preparation for the occasion when we may be compelled to intervene in the policy of the world." On the 1st of May, when inaugu-

rating a bridge at Mainz, he spoke again and still
more clearly: "This work, which is intended to develop the pacific relations of our country, may have
to be used for purposes that are more serious." Finally, on the 14th of May, the same tone might be
remarked at Saarbrück. And, after congratulating
himself on the fact that the town in which he was
speaking had ceased, thanks to the German victories, being a frontier town, he unnecessarily boasted,
in the course of his peregrinations, of having visited
Metz, "the bulwark of Germany," which "sought no
quarrel with any one, but was ready to defend itself
against all the world." It is true that, for another
ten months, no act followed these words. The Chancellor of the Empire, who had made the Franco-
Italian *tour de valse* a subject for his jesting, who,
in 1902, had declared that the "Franco-Italian agreements respecting certain Mediterranean questions
were not directed against the Triple Alliance, and
did not, in fine, encroach on its scope, who, three
months later, had added: "We have no gable front
on the Mediterranean; we are pleased to see that
France and Italy, who each have great, important
interests there, have come to an understanding on
the question," — the Chancellor himself appeared
also to be as little disturbed by the Franco-English
agreement as he had been by that between France
and Italy. On the 12th of April, 1904, he said, when
commenting on the Treaty of the 8th of April: "We
have nothing to object to in it from the point of view
of German interests." On the 14th, he advocated a

"policy of calm reflection, and even of reserve," asserting his determination "not to embark the country on any adventurous scheme" — the reference being to Morocco. From that moment, however, the Emperor and Mr. von Buelow — the Emperor's *alter ego* — were conscious that the hour was approaching for them to enter, at least on the diplomatic if not on the military course which should decide about the future. They felt that an era of equilibrium was succeeding in Europe to the period of Germany's hegemony. About Morocco they cared but little. It was merely a pretext. Their preoccupation was "Germany's situation in the world," and by this they meant German preponderance based on the isolation of France. The preponderance, as they thought, was in peril. If they waited, it was because they hoped thereby to obtain circumstances more favourable. Since the month of February, 1904, Russia had been monopolized by the war in Manchuria. How would this war turn out? Before acting, they must know.

In the month of September, General Kouropatkin suffered a first disaster at Liao-Yang. In the month of February, 1905, that of Mukden was worse. The moment had arrived; the moment to defend, against European claims, "the edifice raised by the Emperor's grandfather," the moment to destroy coalitions that were forming, the moment to put in check the vanquished of the past or the aggressors of the future. On the 31st of March, 1905, William II, by disembarking at Tangier, proclaimed his hostility towards France. In reality, it was one system of Alliances which opposed itself to another. It was the Triple Alliance which was trying its strength against the Dual, the latter backed up by the *Entente Cordiale*. The diplomatic shock, which had been preparing since 1875, was about to take place. History would pursue its way with relentless logic.

CHAPTER V

CONFLICT OF THE ALLIANCES

I

It is impossible to justify, and difficult even to understand, Germany's Moroccan policy during the crisis of 1905–1906, if its manifestations only are considered. If, on the contrary, it is regarded as a functional part of her European policy, everything becomes clear; and it is seen to be an attempt to prove the value of the several international combinations made between 1902 and 1904, an effort to demolish these combinations by menace, if not by

violence, a Bismarckian operation carried out by
men who had neither enough of Bismarck's prestige
nor enough of his genius to succeed.

On the 11th of February, 1905, while Mr. Saint-
René Taillandier, our Minister in Morocco, was
engaged in explaining to the Sultan the plan of re-
forms that he had drawn up, Mr. von Kuhlmann,
Germany's Chargé d'Affaires at Tangier, said to
Comte de Chérisey, his French colleague: —

After the Franco-English agreement, we supposed the
French Government would wait, to put us into possession of
the facts concerning this new situation, until the Franco-Spanish understanding was effected, which was foreshadowed in the
arrangement of the 8th of April. But, to day, everything being definitely concluded, and the requisite Parliamentary ratifi-
cations having been obtained, we find that we have been
systematically kept ignorant of what was going on.

We have therefore regulated our attitude in accordance.

Do not imagine that I have laid down my line of conduct
on my own initiative. In presence of the contradictory interpretations of our newspapers, I thought it my duty to ask my
Government for formal instructions. Count von Buelow thereupon informed me that the Imperial Government had no
knowledge of the different agreements that had been made with
reference to Morocco, and did not recognize that he was in any
way bound as regards the question.[1]

These statements were calculated to surprise us.
As a matter of fact, it was false that Germany had
been kept in "systematic ignorance." On the 23d
of March, 1904, before the Franco-English agreement was signed, Mr. Delcassé informed Prince
von Radolin of its tenor. The Ambassador replied that he found the arrangement "very natural

[1] See Yellow Book, 1901–1905.

and perfectly justified." On the 25th of March, following on these verbal explanations, the *North German Gazette* wrote : —

As far as can be at present judged, German interests cannot be affected by the various exchanges of views concerning Morocco.

By reason of the reiterated assurance officially given on the French side that France has no conquest, no occupation in view, but is pursuing rather the opening of the Sultan's dominions in North West Africa to European civilization, there is ground for believing that Germany's commercial interests in Morocco have nothing to be afraid of.

With regard to this problem, therefore, there is no need, as far as the Germans are concerned, to take umbrage at the Franco-English understanding which is at present in force.[1]

A fortnight later, the text of the Agreement was published in London. On the 12th of April, Count von Buelow, Chancellor of the Empire, said in the Reichstag : —

We know of nothing that should lead us to think that this agreement is directed against any Power whatsoever. What it seems to indicate is an attempt to settle a series of disputes between France and England by means of an amicable understanding.

From the point of view of German interests, we have no objection to make against it. As a matter of fact, we cannot be desirous of a tension between France and England which would be a danger for the peace of the world, whereas we are sincerely anxious that peace should be maintained.

To speak more especially of Morocco, which constitutes the essential part of this agreement, we are interested in this country, as indeed in the rest of the Mediterranean, chiefly from an economic point of view.

Our interests there are, first and foremost, commercial. So

---

[1] See Yellow Book, 1901–1905.

we have important reasons for wishing tranquillity and order to reign in Morocco.

We owe it to ourselves to protect our commercial interests in Morocco, and we shall protect them. Nor is there anything to make us fear that they can be overlooked or injured by one Power or another.[1]

On the 14th of April, returning to the subject, the Chancellor expressed himself as follows:—

Count Reventlow pretends that the Anglo-French agreement, and especially the fundamental part of it referring to Morocco, called forth in Germany sentiments of dismay and discouragement.

He deems that we ought not to have suffered other Powers to acquire in Morocco a greater influence than ourselves.

That can only signify this: namely, that we ourselves ought to claim a part of Morocco. I should like to ask Count Reventlow one question, which is very simple.

Count Reventlow will certainly agree with me that, if a great Empire, like that of Germany, formulates such a claim, she must pursue the realization of the claim, cost what it may.

What now would Count Reventlow advise me to do, if a claim of this kind were to be resisted?

I do not say it is certain that such a claim would meet with resistance; I do not say this is likely; I say only that, in questions of such gravity, no eventuality should be lost sight of.

Would Count Reventlow advise me to unsheath the sword? Count Reventlow does not reply, and I understand his silence. (Laughter.)

I think, Gentlemen, it would be inconsiderate on my part,— and I am pleased to note that the leaders of all parties, except Count Reventlow, have expressed a similar opinion,— to decide unnecessarily on embarking the country in such an adventurous enterprise.

I think, too, Gentlemen, that, were I so to act, Count Reventlow, in whom the critical faculty seems to me to be strongly developed, would reproach me with my exaggerated ardour for action as keenly as he has blamed my so-called fear of action.

[1] See Yellow Book, 1901–1905.

On the 20th of April, Mr. Bihourd, French Ambassador at Berlin, saw Baron von Richthofen, then Minister of Foreign Affairs, and said to him: —

"I much appreciated the Chancellor's language, when he acknowledged in the Reichstag that the Franco-English understanding was not directed against any Power and in no wise threatened German commercial interests."

In reply, Mr. von Richthofen expressed no objection, made no reservation.

On the 7th of October, after the signature of the Franco-Spanish agreement, Mr. Bihourd informed Baron von Richthofen of the fact.

"Are you able," the Baron said to him, "to forecast the scope of the agreement with regard to Germany's commercial interests, which are what I have especially to think of?"

"The Franco-English declaration of the 8th of April last," replied Mr. Bihourd, "offers every guarantee on this point, nor can Spain's adhesion modify anything in the promises then made."

Finally, on the 13th of October, the French Ambassador communicated to Mr. von Richthofen the text of the Franco-Spanish declaration. Once more the Minister spoke to him of the exclusively economic interest that Germany took in Moroccan affairs. The Ambassador immediately answered, — renewing his assurances in Mr. Delcassé's name, — that "the Franco-English declaration of the 8th of April expressly guaranteed commercial liberty and that the Franco-Spanish declaration could not, in

his opinion, affect the securities already offered to
international commerce."

Consequently, Mr. von Kuhlmann's assertion was
entirely unwarranted. It constituted a *"bait"* —
founded on a pretext — in view of diplomatic action
dictated by reasons of a general and not a local nature. The reasons were likewise general, not local,
which guided the development of this action. On
the 15th of February, Mr. von Muhlberg, Under-
Secretary for State Affairs, when questioned by Mr.
Bihourd about Mr. von Kuhlmann's statements, replied that he had no cognizance of them. A fortnight later, the Russian Army suffered its decisive
defeat at Mukden, a defeat which was destined to
render the Saint Petersburg Cabinet powerless for
some time to come. Straightway, Germany's real
policy revealed itself. On the 21st of February, the
German Consul at Fez reported to headquarters that
Mr. Saint-René Taillandier, in order to back up his
plan of reforms, had claimed that he held a "man-
date from Europe." This assertion was false. On
the 7th of March, the same official denounced the
"aggressive Colonial tendencies of France." On the
12th of March, it was announced that William II
would call at Tangier in the course of his cruise in
the Mediterranean. On the 16th of March, Mr. von
Buelow, speaking ambiguously in the Reichstag,
said: —

Herr von Reventlow touches on the question whether
fresh agreements between third parties can affect our relations
with Morocco.

Herr von Reventlow seems to find that our policy is too inactive on this point, and that we are allowing ourselves to be guilty of negligence.

I quite understand the attention paid here to the events now taking place in Morocco and to their significance.

I consider it to be the duty of the German Government to see that, in the future, our economic interests in this country are not injured.

The moment is inopportune to make more particular statements.

I defer these till later.

On the 29th of March, the Chancellor said: —

The Emperor some time ago told the King of Spain that Germany seeks in Morocco no territorial advantage.

After a declaration so categoric, it is absurd to try to explain the Emperor's visit to Tangier by intentions directed against the integrity or independence of Morocco.

From this visit of the Emperor to Tangier, nothing can be deduced, as to its motive, that is of a nature to render any one uneasy who himself has no aggressive intentions there.

Herr Bebel has hinted that our policy with regard to Morocco has changed in the last year.

I must remind him that the language and attitude of diplomatists and politicians are regulated by circumstances.

The moment that I judge to be favourable for setting forth German interests, I choose according to my own estimation.

With this understood, nothing has changed in the tendencies of German policy on the point in question.

Whoever seeks anything new will not find it in German policy.

But if any attempt should be made to modify the international situation of Morocco or to establish any check on the open door in the country's economic development, we must see more than ever that our economic interests are not endangered.

We should first put ourselves into relations with the Sultan on the subject.

The threat, therefore, was rendered more precise. On the 31st of March, it was repeated with circum-

stance. Disembarking at Tangier, William II
spoke to the representative of Abd el Aziz as follows: —

> To-day, I pay my visit to the Sultan *in his character of in-
> dependent sovereign*.
>
> I hope that, under the Sultan's sovereignty, a free Morocco
> will remain open to the pacific competition of all nations, *without
> monopoly and without annexation*, on a footing of absolute equal-
> ity.
>
> My visit to Tangier is intended to make known the fact
> that I am resolved to do all that is in my power properly to safe-
> guard the interests of Germany, since I consider the Sultan *as
> being an absolutely free sovereign*.
>
> It is with him that I mean to come to an understanding
> respecting the best way of safeguarding such interests.
>
> As regards the reforms which the Sultan is intending to
> make, it seems to me that any action in this direction should be
> taken with great precaution, respect being had for the religious
> sentiments of the population in order that there may be no
> disturbance of public tranquillity.

By a circular addressed to the various German
Ambassadors on the 12th of April, the Chancellor
appealed to Europe. The die was cast. The substance of his communication was a reiteration of the
imaginary grievances already invoked by Mr. von
Kuhlmann, together with proposals for remedying
what was amiss. Relying on her rights and the
agreements she had made, France had endeavoured
to act alone. Mr. von Buelow demanded that an
International Conference should be summoned, composed of the signataries of the 1880 Convention of
Madrid.[1] This Convention, it was manifest, had

[1] See White Book for 1906.

N

nothing to do with the subject now raised, — and German jurisconsults themselves acknowledged this, — since it had merely settled the altogether special question of the protection to be granted to Moroccans by the several Foreign Legations. But, by forcing France to accept it, Europe was to be shown that, in spite of the agreements recently concluded, there was nothing changed in the world, and that Germany had only to oppose a certain policy for it to be altered in accordance with her wishes. On the 27th of May, the Moroccan "Notables," being assembled to hear what Mr. Saint-René Taillandier had to say, took up on their own account the German idea of a Conference. On the 30th, the Sultan made the proposal his own, and Abd el Aziz thus became the instrument of the European scheme which recent Western agreements had tempted Germany to try to carry out, which the Russian defeats had allowed her to initiate.

Considered by itself, the game was a magnificent one for the French Government to play. Thirty-four years had passed since the signing of the Treaty of Frankfort. After being vanquished, dismembered, threatened afresh in 1875, isolated until 1891, our country had, through the Russian Alliance, been restored to the possibility of diplomatic action. In spite of errors, she had pursued her way towards the attainment of an increasingly stable equilibrium, towards an autonomy more safely guarded on the outside. She had successively drawn nearer to Italy England, and Spain; and had utilized these *rap-*

prochements for the service of her most essential interests — her Mediterranean interests. The weight had grown lighter with which triumphant Germany pressed upon her; and it was in the plenitude of her good right that she had acquired such guarantees. After his installation at the Foreign Office in 1898, Mr. Delcassé had done more than any other Minister preceding him towards obtaining this result. Fortified by his patriotism, by Mr. Waldeck-Rousseau's confidence (1899-1902), by Mr. Combes' indifference respecting questions of foreign policy (1902-1905), he had methodically applied the plan that he had laid down for himself, probably without underestimating the risks attending it.

Unfortunately, when these risks revealed themselves, Mr. Delcassé had as yet done nothing to ward them off. Absorbed by his contemplation of the goal, with his eyes raised aloft, he no longer saw the snares that lay in his path. After the signing of the Franco-English agreement, he allowed ten months to go by without taking any action in Morocco, just as if he had been in sovereign disposal of a serene future. He had waited to act until the rout of the Russians at Liao-Yang, with those at Mukden and Tsusima, which were worse, deprived us of our best trump card, of our sole Alliance, of our only support on the Continent. Nor had he taken any measures to provide for the consequences of such conduct. Being split up into two parties by the Dreyfus Affair, and subsequently by the religious quarrel, France had lost her inclination for action abroad. Disheartened by the system of delation that prevailed, our Army and Navy had no leaders, no organization, no ammunition, no provisions adequate to the rôle they should have been ready at any minute to play. For some idea to be gained of their weakness at this time, it suffices to mention that the extraordinary credits, hastily spent in order to remedy the worst deficiencies, amounted, in 1905, to 225 millions; and this, "to execute in a few months what should have been spread over years, this, to fill up enormous shortage in the stock of ammunition, to place our four great fortresses in a proper state of defence, to complete the weapons and equipment of our armies, to construct the railways that were absolutely indispensable for operating the concentration set down in our plans of mobilization."[1] For months past and years past, the nation's "expenditure" had been cheese-pared to the profit of "Social" laws. For months past and years past, the Government had been living in a deceitful security, hiding from the country the consequences accruing from the policy — in itself excellent enough — which they were being compelled to carry out. And when the Minister of Foreign Affairs was anxiously asked for information respecting our military preparedness, he replied: —

"You are asking me too much. I do my own duty and presume that my colleagues do theirs."

It is not with "suppositions" that nations are led to victory. When Bismarck founded Germany, he

[1] See Pierre Baudin's book, *The Alarm.*

first consulted Moltke. Mr. Delcassé had questioned neither General André, nor yet Mr. Camille Pelletan, whose bad administration, however, he had no right to ignore. Being the dupe of a strange illusion, he believed that a diplomatic operation was self-sufficing. He forgot that the basis of a diplomatic operation is formed out of the military cash-in-hand of a nation, that, when one Power intends to uphold her rights and her designs, she prevails only by the consideration in which her strength is held, that, in order to be able to resist pressure in a state of peace, what is needed is the capacity for repelling an aggression through war. Being aware that German opposition would be made, sooner or later, not to his Moroccan but to his general policy, he, however, did not perceive that a France half-disarmed both materially and morally was fatally condemned to yield. He willed the end without willing the means. It was a ruinous aberration of mind in a good Frenchman who, by dint of regarding that which was desirable, had lost all notion of the real, and the sentiment of what was possible.

It was not long before the consequence of this mistake overwhelmed us. On the 31st of March and the 7th of April, Mr. Delcassé made two useless speeches, one in the Senate and one in the Chamber, in which he feigned not to understand the meaning of the discussion. On the 13th of April, he had a personal interview with Prince von Radolin, and on the 18th he caused a communication to be made to Mr. von Muhlberg, for the purpose of "removing the misunderstanding." But neither in Paris nor in Berlin did he receive a reply. On the 19th of April, a painful, alarming, humiliating discussion occurred in the Chamber of Deputies. The Minister of Foreign Affairs was not in his usual form. Mr. Rouvier, the Prime Minister, raised a corner of the veil when he exclaimed: —

What is it that we are reproached with?

With not informing Germany of the Franco-English agreement on the morrow of its being signed.

Rather should it be said *"with not informing other nations"*; since no notification was made of the agreement which the Chamber had approved.

Had not the Chancellor's speech the value of an acquiescence?

Did not the Chancellor declare himself satisfied on condition Germany's commercial interests were not threatened?

What has taken place since then?

Certain military happenings have weakened our Ally.

Perhaps, then, the neighbours with whom we wish to live in harmony thought that, by raising a debate, they might open a question which we were justified in deeming closed by reason even of the language held on the other side of the Vosges, and might thus obtain some commercial advantages.

This was the truth; but it was rather late in the day to utter it. After resigning for a first time, and then withdrawing his resignation on the 20th of April, Mr. Delcassé resumed the direction of his Department, but with diminished authority. It was just at this moment that Germany and Morocco demanded the assembling of a Conference. Mr. Delcassé attempted to reply by a refusal; as, however, he had neither previously arranged for the conditions of his refusal nor yet prepared them, his thesis was untenable. One needs trump cards in order to be able to resist a "bluff." And we had none. Every day, German pressure became increasingly insolent. Prince Henckel of Donnersmarck, whose colossal fortune assured him at the Court of Berlin a situation which he had not merited by his career, came to Paris as a bearer of comminatory language. After going over certain petty grievances, he came straight to the point, and said: —

We have, moreover, to complain of more serious grievances and grave lack of customary courtesy. You have endeavoured to detach from us the Power that was our ally and this on the advice of another Power with whom you have established a cordial understanding. You certainly have the right to choose your friends and your allies as you like; but we owe it to ourselves to protect ourselves against the consequences that may be involved for Germany by the agreements that you contract.

If your arrangements with England aimed only at the maintenance of peace in Europe, we should have sincerely applauded them. Unfortunately, the appreciations of newspapers that are supposed to reflect Government opinion, certain conversations having all the importance of official declarations, the speech made by King Edward VII in Paris, have convinced us that the chief object of the *Entente Cordiale* was to secure the isolation of Germany, preceding and preparing an aggression in the near future. Last of all, by disposing, without warning us or consulting us, of the Empire of Morocco, you have wounded the German Emperor and the German people to the quick.

Is this policy that of France, or must we consider it as being merely personal to Monsieur Delcassé?

If you are of opinion that your Minister of Foreign Affairs has engaged your country in too adventurous a course, acknowledge it by dispensing with his services, and especially by giving a new direction to your foreign policy.

We are not concerned with Monsieur Delcassé's person; but his policy is a threat to Germany; and you may rest assured that we shall not wait for it to be realized. The Emperor does not desire war. His chief care is to favour the development and expansion of German commerce. The German navy, which he means shall be large and powerful, is only a means for carrying out his exclusively pacific designs.

On this ground, the Emperor naturally finds himself in rivalry with England, who, by tradition, is bent on destroying the fleets of her neighbours, or rather on preventing their creation. It is for you to decide whether you prefer to serve England's interests, after taking into account the perils to which you expose yourselves by a verbal understanding which you are thinking of transforming into a written alliance.

The Emperor respects your Army, the high value of which he is far from underestimating. He is, however, warned, and it is better you yourselves should be so too, of the causes that may weaken it and of the germs of dissolution that have been sown throughout it.

In a war against Germany, you may possibly be victorious, since in her most tragic crises France has always found extraordinary resources in herself; but, if you are vanquished, — and my first hypothesis deprives my second of all offensive character,—if you are vanquished, as you probably will be, it is in Paris that peace will have to be signed.

Are you hoping that, faithful throughout to the friendship uniting you, England will make common cause with you, and attempt — on the German coast — a diversion from which you might derive advantage? That is possible. Let us assume the most favourable case for you. She bombards our ports, she destroys our fleets, she ruins our Colonies. With your billions, we shall repair the damage of all kinds that she may have caused us. She may deem herself impregnable at home; but, if we occupy your territory, she will be powerless to drive us away.

And now let us examine what I will call the other picture.

France does not threaten Germany. According to the desire of my friend Gambetta, she still thinks of Alsace and Lorraine; but she never talks about them. Other questions of more immediate importance solicit her attention; since the world is wide enough for a great nation like yours to be able to find the wherewith to satisfy her present ambitions, while adjourning hopes that are for the moment irrealizable.

Your country would assuredly have the finest and most glori-

ous rôle that a civilized nation can desire. Placed as an umpire
between friendly England and Germany, then, not hostile, she
might, by arbitrating in their eventual quarrel, spare the world
the horror of a general conflagration.

Believe the word of a German who has always had great
sympathies with you. Give up the Minister whose only aspira-
tion is to trouble the peace of Europe; and adopt with regard
to Germany a loyal and open policy, the only one which is worthy
of a great nation like yours, if you wish to preserve the peace of
the world.[1]

A few days later, the inevitable occurred. Conscious of our military weakness and Russia's powerlessness, Mr. Rouvier decided to yield. In opposition to Mr. Delcassé, who declined negotiations in
view of a Conference, he advocated the acceptance
of preliminary *pourparlers*. Being supported by the
majority of the Cabinet, he did not refuse the resignation of the Minister of Foreign Affairs when it
was handed in to him the second time. And by a
regrettable error, the disgrace of this retreat under
the enemy's fire was not even masked by a collective
resignation of the Ministry, which might have been
reconstituted on the morrow. Germany demolished
the Minister who had vaunted of holding his own
against her—without, indeed, his doing anything to
render himself capable of such action. She gained
the first bout. France was obliged, notwithstanding her alliances and friendships, to gainsay and
humble herself. And to enforce this success William
II bestowed on Count von Buelow the title of Prince.

[1] Conversation published by the *Gaulois* (June, 1905).

II

After this grave set-back, Mr. Rouvier found himself in a disadvantageous situation to negotiate. As a matter of fact, the two agreements which he concluded with Germany, on the 10th of July and the 10th of September, conceded Germany's claims.

If the Prime Minister hoped that, in the course of fresh *pourparlers*, the German Chancellor's exigencies would be lessened by Mr. Delcassé's retirement, he was soon obliged to undeceive himself. Since the immediate occasion of their dispute was not the fundamental cause of these exigencies, — no more in the second phase than it had been in the first, — any one would have been foolish to imagine that Mr. Rouvier's arguments on the subject of Morocco, however reasonable they might be, would have a determining influence at Wilhelmstrasse. In vain the Prime Minister remarked that projects were attributed to us which had not entered into our thoughts; that we had solicited the Sultan for no concession that could diminish his authority or hamper the freedom of trade within the boundaries of his Empire; that we had neither done nor dreamt of doing the same in Morocco as we had done in Tunis. In vain he added that a Conference would be "rather a complication than a solution"; that, if it assembled without a previous understanding being arrived at, it would turn out to be prejudicial; that, if it assembled after an understanding had been reached, it would be entirely useless. Prince von

Radolin, acting on the Chancellor's orders, continued obstinately to demand that the Conference should be summoned, adding (on the 10th of June, 1905): "We insist on the Conference. If it is not held, then the *statu quo* will remain in force. And you must know that we will back up Morocco with our entire strength." [1]

If the matter, thus put, had referred to Africa, and Africa only; if Germany had merely desired to obtain especial advantages in the Moorish Empire or elsewhere, such an attitude would have been inexplicable. On the other hand, it is understandable, if the Assembling of the Conference is regarded as a proof that the German Government was attempting to impose her hegemony on the world; if there is a consensus of opinion to the effect that the Moroccan dispute was the "occasion" only and that the object to be attained was something higher — and elsewhere. In this month of June, 1905, the Germans knew that Mr. Rouvier was willing to do more than pay the price of their good-will in Morocco. The financial help of France for their railways in Asia Minor might have been had by simply asking. They might even have obtained more, — perhaps the quoting of their public and private securities on the Paris Bourse. These advantages, although great, did not suffice to alter their attitude, since they were anticipating larger profit from the satisfaction being ac-

---

[1] See Yellow Book (1901–1905). The Yellow Book does not say "with our entire strength." But I am informed by Mr. Rouvier that this was the Ambassador's expression.

corded them that would publicly demonstrate the
continued existence of their preponderance.

Indeed, one has only to glance at the two agreements in virtue of which, during July and September, Mr. Rouvier prepared with Germany the meeting of the Conference. From the Moroccan point of
view, these agreements were not disadvantageous to
France, and procured her stronger guarantees than
those we had first hoped for. By the terms of the
former one, Germany declared that "she pursued no
object at the Conference that might compromise the
legitimate interests of France in Morocco or that was
contrary to the rights of France accruing from her
treaties or arrangements." She placed herself in
accordance with us respecting the principles themselves which had never ceased to inspire our policy,
— "the sovereignty and independence of the Sultan;
the integrity of his Empire; economic liberty without any inequality; the utility of police and financial
reforms, the introduction of which would be regulated for a short period through an international
agreement." Last of all, she acknowledged "the
situation enjoyed by France in Morocco by reason
of Algeria's contiguity to the Moorish Empire along
a vast extent of frontier, and of the particular relations that arise between two bordering countries,
there being also special reasons why France should
desire the reign of order throughout the Sultan's
dominions." The second agreement, which was the
consequence of the first, laid equal stress on our privileges. It provided for "the organization of a police

system by way of international arrangement"; but
"outside of the frontier region," there being an understanding to the effect that, in this region, police
questions should continue to be settled directly
and exclusively between France and the Sultan, and
should remain outside of the Conference programme."
There was a similar understanding with regard to
the repression of the smuggling of arms over the
area of the same region. The upshot of all this was
that Germany did not dispute our "peculiar interests." She admitted that we had in Morocco an
exceptional situation. She placed in our hands certain means of action, the value of which was incontestable, since, owing to them, we were able to obtain
at Algeciras the recognition of our rights and the
guarantee of our Moroccan interests.

But, if these various points were gained, if Germany
made us concessions which, though accorded reluctantly, were none the less precious, it was because,
by obtaining our adhesion to the Conference principle, she had secured that which she most desired.   In
the German press her conduct was characterized even
as a policy of *amour-propre* and show-off. We will
be more equitable towards the Chancellor. If he insisted so strongly on the Conference being held, it
was because alone the assembling of it would peremptorily establish that French understandings were
not self-sufficing when Germany was pleased to interfere; it was because this meeting, before which
would be heard the appeal of the policy that Germany had prevented us from carrying out at Fez,

would be a monument raised to German puissance, a warning for the future, a threat against whoever should bethink himself to aspire to political independence. On the 11th of April, the Chancellor wrote to Count Wolff Metternich, the German Ambassador in London: —

We are acting with a view to our interests, which apparently there seems to be an intention to dispose of without our assent. The importance of these interests is a secondary thing here. . . . If we, however, abandon them by our silence, we shall thus encourage the world, seeing us act so, to commit similar breaches of courtesy, to our prejudice in other questions perhaps more considerable.[1]

On the 4th of October, Prince von Buelow, receiving the author of this book at Baden-Baden, said to him: —

In the incidents which have arisen during the past six months or so, there are two distinct things to consider.

Morocco is the first; general policy is the second.

In Morocco we have important commercial interests: we intended and we still intend to safeguard them.

In a more general way, we were obliged to reply to a policy which threatened to isolate us and which, in consequence of this avowed aim, assumed a distinctly hostile character with regard to us.

The Moroccan affair was the most recent and most clearly manifested example of such policy. It furnished us with an opportunity to make a necessary retort.[2]

What should be thought of this pretended "isolation," the Chancellor had previously stated on the 14th of April 1904, when he said:—

[1] See White Book (1906).
[2] See *Le Temps* of the 5th of October, 1905.

The member, Mr. Bebel, has also spoken of an isolation of Germany. He seems to fear that we are drifting into complete solitude.

I answer him that we find ourselves at present *in solid bonds of alliance with two great Powers, in amicable relations with the five others*, that our relations with France are calm and pacific, and, as far as depends on us, will remain so.

I believe, moreover, that we shall not have much isolation to fear, as long as we continue to keep our swords well-whetted.

Germany is too powerful not to be capable of alliances.

There are many combinations possible for us; and, even if we had to remain alone, this would not be very terrible either.

Consequently, there is no need for anxiety.

Nothing had happened since this date, with regard to the distribution of alliances, that could justify the altogether different language which the Chancellor used to me in October. Germany had still her "two solid Alliances"; and was the only Power in Europe enjoying this situation. The isolation spoken of by Prince von Buelow was therefore imaginary. The truth was that the effect of the change he dreaded, the effect of the change which had induced him to employ the Moroccan question in order to make a "necessary return-thrust," the effect of the change which had caused him to pass from the policy of reserve to a policy of action and which he characterized as "isolation" by a conversational euphemism, this effect had been, not to reduce Germany to solitude, but to restore the balance of power in Europe. It had achieved, not the encircling of Germany, but the affranchisement of France. Throughout the dispute, the stake at issue for Germany was not the preserving of alli-

ances, which there was no likelihood of her losing,
but the safeguard of the diplomatic hegemony
secured by Bismarck as the outcome of the Congress
of Berlin. The stake was an important one, and,
far more than Morocco, warranted the efforts made
to win it.

At the end of 1905, Germany had grounds for
believing that she was nearing the desired goal. In
the conflict of Alliances that had just been fought
out, her triumph had been complete. She had
merely had to intervene at Fez for the policy to
crumble that had been established by the Franco-
English agreement of 1904. She had merely had
to threaten for France to sacrifice a Minister of
Foreign Affairs whom the Parliament had during
seven years supported by its confidence. Nothing
had been able to stand against her interference.
The paralysis of the Franco-Russian Alliance was
not astonishing, considering the difficulties both
exterior and interior in which our Allies were involved. But at its outset the *Entente Cordiale*
had shown itself no better, since it had not spared
France either discomfiture or humiliation. Indeed,
the military aid that England could have offered
would have done but little to make up for our own
weakness. The Franco-Italian and Franco-Spanish
agreements had not even been invoked against the
German pretensions. The Chancellor deemed himself sure of the morrow and spoke somewhat ironically
of English policy in its relations with ours.

In the conversation with me mentioned above,

the text of which was corrected by him before its
publication, he said: —

Your country has a useful rôle to play in tranquillizing minds
instead of exciting them.

In such a case as the present, the *suave mari magno* is not
applicable. International solidarity is too deep for any one to
be able to flatter himself on being the *tertius gaudens* — if I
may again use a Latin expression — in a quarrel, whatever its
nature may be.

If, between Germans and Englishmen, there are prejudices
which will vanish sooner or later, France can help in removing
them.

Allow me to add that she has set an example which proves
that it is always possible to become reconciled with England.

The Prince then went on to express his conviction
that the Conference would draw us nearer rather
than separate us. And he added in conclusion: —

One condition, however, is essential for the *rapprochement*,
namely, that the French public should quite understand that the
policy tending to isolate Germany is a thing of the past, and that
the course of conduct lately pursued is to-day definitely abandoned.

In spite of the courteous language that was subsequently employed in speaking of the Franco-English
and Franco-Italian *rapprochements*, Germany, not
without some curtness, expressed the wish that
nothing more should be said about the policy which
these *rapprochements* had emphasized. The meeting of the Conference appeared to sanction the
deference of France to this request. The debates
of this same Conference were about to prove to the
Chancellor that the *"evil"* was deeper seated than
he had imagined, and that Europe, after once shak-

o

ing off Germany's diplomatic yoke, did not intend
to submit to it again.

III

The Conference of 1906 was a disappointment to
Germany. The fact was that, owing to the ease
with which she had triumphed in the preceding
year, she had neglected to take into consideration
the durable realities underlying ephemeral appear-
ances.

When, on the 15th of January, 1906, the delegates
of the Powers met at Algeciras, the situation in
Europe was no longer what it had been six months
earlier. First of all, in France, a material and moral
change had occurred. A reflecting uneasiness had
succeeded the scare. Military measures had been
taken, and this was known. Ninety-four million
francs had been spent on ammunition, thirty millions on equipment, twenty-six millions on railways.
The press, which in the beginning had been divided
and hesitating, had now recovered itself, and had
rallied the minds of the public to the idea of resistance
being necessary, after so many concessions. On
the other hand, in August, 1905, Russia had signed
peace with Japan. And, in spite of the disorganization inevitably caused by an unsuccessful war, she
had resumed her place in Europe. England, who,
if France had been willing, would have made war
in 1905, had seen in Germany's success a fresh
motive for acting in conjunction with us for the

purpose of establishing the European balance of power. On the 1st of September, 1905, in view of the Conference, Spain had strengthened the ties that bound our two countries together. Last of all, and above all, the circumstances of an International Conference were less favourable than a *tête-à-tête* to the game of menace and "bluff" practised by Germany in the previous year. If a rupture were aimed at, it would be less easy to realize amidst the cumbersome machinery of an international gathering; and, by reason of the time lost, would appear less specious. If intimidation and moral pressure were the object, Europe's presence at the debates would allow us to find support and to create majorities. It was not so difficult for us to remain cool. Our risks were not so great.

This was not suspected at Berlin. There they relied on the docile aid of the two Powers of the *Triplice*. William II reserved to himself the task of personally influencing the Czar so as to get him to adopt a neutral attitude. From England and Spain an adhesion was reckoned on, which France alone would have paid for. What was simpler than to say to them: "You have treated with France about Morocco. You, English, have withdrawn in her favour; you, Spaniards, have pledged yourselves to her. Now, recover your liberty. You, English, have secured in Egypt the advantages promised you by the Franco-English agreement. You, Spaniards, have been obliged to give up, in favour of France, a considerable portion of the

profits you were hoping for in Morocco. Come, let
us talk, and talk about Morocco. Let us draw up a
scheme by which you will each get your share, and
we, ours. As to the solution, you will find us accom-
modating, since we have no fixed intention, or rather
we have only one, namely, to oust France, and to
publish her discomfiture to the world." This,
you may say, is hypothesis. No! not if the history
itself of the Conference demonstrates that such
was the policy of Germany; if it makes plain that,
while ready to accept all sorts of combinations which
France refused, she pursued one design only: to
wit, that of breaking down the diplomatic system
which Prince von Buelow, three months previously,
had said was a thing of the past, a thing that must
be abandoned forever.

The initial stage of the negotiations [1] lasted from
the 15th of January to the 19th of February and was
taken up with private conversations. On the 25th
of January, Mr. von Radowitz, the premier German
plenipotentiary, entered into *pourparlers* with his
French colleague, Mr. Révoil, yet without formulat-
ing any precise proposals concerning essential questions, such, for instance, as the police organization,
which France asked might be placed under her
control. At the same time, in order to entice Spain
away from us, Germany offered her the police of all
the ports, renewing the offer at Algeciras after
making it at Madrid. Through a semi-official
agency, the *South German Imperial Correspondence,*

---

[1] See our book on the *Algeciras Conference,* 2d edition (1907).

Italy received a similar offer. Finally, on the 3d of February, Count von Tattenbach, who was the second German plenipotentiary, suggested to England's representative the idea of separating from France. In the same week, four solutions, each differing from the others and from those that had been previously put forward, were proposed by Germany's representatives in interviews with the governmental delegates or communications to the Governments themselves of Spain, the United States, Russia, and Italy. There was thus a clear manifestation of attempts to dissociate these Powers from France, the sole, visible, and avowed aim being to isolate her, no respect being paid to the question at issue. On the 9th of February, one of the Wolff agency's telegrams announced that Germany had rejected the French proposals. This rejection, which was irregular in its form, occurred after the representatives of Russia, Italy, and the United States had informed Mr. von Radowitz that these proposals had their approbation. On the 19th of February, the Germans again rejected what was proposed both concerning the police and the question of finances; and, simultaneously, strong pressure was brought to bear on the Duke of Almodovar, Spain's plenipotentiary, with a view to securing his detachment from our side. Meanwhile, in Saint Petersburg, the German Ambassador, Mr. von Schoen, was trying to shake Count Lamsdorff in his fidelity to our cause. And in Rome, Count von Monts was advising Italy to "resume her liberty of action." At Madrid, Mr. von Stumm declared that, in case Spain behaved badly, the Emperor William would not be able to return the visit which he had received from the latter in 1905. In Algeciras every one believed that there would be a rupture. Every one found the French proposals reasonable. Every one was astonished at Germany's resistance. The astonishment was natural enough, if only the Moroccan question was regarded. But, on the other hand, no one had any need to wonder, who placed himself so as to see that the Chancellor's sole aim was to affirm Germany's supremacy in Europe through this thwarting of the French projects.

During the second period (February 20–March 14), the Conference held sittings for the discussion, first of the Bank question, next that of the Police. At the conclusion of the debates on the former subjects, German intransigence still continued to show itself, notwithstanding French concessions. In the meantime (February 21), Prince von Buelow, availing himself of Baron de Courcel's presence in Berlin, proposed a compromise to the eminent Ambassador which, since it went counter to the principles we had invoked from the beginning, would have certainly caused us to fall out with England and with Spain. On the 1st of March, William II replied to a communication of the Russian Prime Minister, Count Witte, by recommending the same compromise to him. To two telegrams of Mr. Roosevelt advocating the creation of a Franco-Spanish police checked by reports of the Italian Legation at Tangier, the Emperor replied by a double refusal. The "isolating" action therefore was being continued. The French Government was of opinion that they could not, without danger, allow it to develop further. On the 3d of March, seeing that no decisions were being reached with reference to the Bank, Mr. Révoil asked that the Police question should be brought up for discussion. Mr. von Radowitz opposing this, a vote was taken, with the result that ten delegates supported the French side, and three, the German. Although the point to be settled was merely one of procedure, it was seen that Europe had cast the die and won. Tired of Germany's injunctions, she had expressed her sentiments. The "Guardian" of European interests, as the Berlin papers called her, was deserted by all her wards except one; and, when the Conference had to decide as to the best way of entering upon reforms, she was backed up only by Austria and by the compromising help of Morocco, the latter being desirous of thwarting, by every means possible, the Conference's labours tending to reform.

This warning was understood at Berlin, since now, for the first time, either in Paris through the medium of the Prince of Monaco, or at Algeciras through the voice of Count von Tattenbach, the Chancellor's Government showed themselves disposed to be more conciliatory. It is in fact easy to see that, by demonstrating through its debates and votes the isolation of Germany, the Conference was upsetting the whole design which the Emperor had so striven to realize in his policy. Unfortunately, just at this moment, the French Chamber placed the Rouvier Cabinet in a minority, an act of folly which once more raised Germany's hopes. On the 10th and 11th of March, Mr. von Radowitz refused to keep the promises of concessions, that he had made during the morning of the 10th. On the 12th, the various German Ambassadors received a circular telegram from their Government, asserting that the majority of the delegates at Algeciras were hostile to France; that with a last effort she would be compelled to capitulate. On the same day, Prince von Buelow, through the medium of a German financier who was at Saint Petersburg, telegraphed to Count Witte: "Thanks to our concessions everything was going on favourably at the Conference when, suddenly, Mr. Révoil created fresh difficulties, to the surprise of all the other plenipotentiaries, who deem his pretensions unwarranted, and who, with even the English, incline in our favour. We hope that Mr. Witte will make his influential voice heard, if he desires to avoid a final rupture." Last of all, on the 13th, 15th, and 17th of March, in three personal telegrams, addressed to Mr. Roosevelt through the German Ambassador at Washington, William II appropriated the affirmation and declared that all the Powers, except the United States, had abandoned France, so that he urged the President to prevail upon us to consent.

Never had Germany's hold on the world been

asserted with such audacity. If France had yielded, and if her Allies and friends had not supported her, Germany would have won the game, not merely the Moroccan game, which forsooth was a small part of the Chancellor's great design, but that of the wider world, the Bismarckian game in favour of her hegemony against European equilibrium. Happily, France did not give up; and no one abandoned her. On the 14th of March, Mr. Léon Bourgeois, who succeeded Mr. Rouvier at the Foreign office, declared to the Ambassadors that he had maintained the instructions to Mr. Révoil in their entirety. Between the 13th and 14th, the British Government notified the Powers by a circular telegram that they supported France on all points and without either restriction or reserve. On the 18th, Mr. Roosevelt characterized the German proposals as being inacceptable. On the 19th, by a circular similar to the English one, the Russian Government informed the different Chancelleries that they unhesitatingly supported the French requests. In less than a week, we had recovered the advantage. Since our isolation had been asserted, we replied by a demonstration of the help on which we could count. The German manœuvre had failed. Europe had not yielded. In such conditions, the Algeciras debates had no further interest for Germany. She had now but one desire, to finish them off as quickly as possible, whatever the solution might be. On the 20th of March, Mr. von Tschirschky, Secretary of State, said to Mr. Bihourd: —

"I see no further difficulties, since we accept what you desire."

On the 28th, an agreement was established on all the principal points. Brutality of procedure, bad mental analysis, inaccurate estimation of the forces in presence — Germany's discomfiture exhibited all these. Obsessed with the idea of triumphing alone and gloriously, of leaving the Conference in her character of sovereign of the world, Germany had rejected with disdainful superciliousness the four offers of arbitration which had been made to her during the Conference, to wit, the Italian, Russian, American, and Austrian. To these four Powers, who, with but small difference of detail, were equally desirous of arriving at an honourable compromise, she rendered their task so difficult that, after being at first well-disposed intermediaries, they had become, with their varying means, the auxiliaries of our policy. The attempt made to entice England away had produced the contrary effect and joined London and Paris in closer bonds. Russia, who at the beginning had flattered herself she would be able to bring about an understanding, had subsequently been obliged, in presence of German exigence, to content herself with fulfilling her duty as our ally, and had fulfilled it loyally. Spain had remained faithful to us, seeing what little sincerity there was in advances that were continually accompanied by threats. Italy would have been only too glad to be spared the necessity of taking sides openly. Germany, however, forced her to do so; and, as she had given us positive pledges, whilst, on the other hand, through Germany's will, the Triple Alliance had always ignored the Mediterranean, she was bound to grant us her vote. The United States had supported us for the simple reason that our proposals appeared to them to be moderate. As for Austria, although devoted to Germany, she could not go against plain evidence, and had exercised a conciliatory action, which now and again inclined distinctly in favour of France. In short, throughout the three months, none of our supports had weakened; and some had even become more solid. It may also be said that fresh ones had been created through "reprobation of Germany," as Count Lamsdorff, on one occasion, put the matter.

The results of the Conference were important, gauged by the interest Germany had had in summoning it. The aim of German policy, manifesting, as it undoubtedly did, indifference with regard to Morocco, was to use the African conflict as an occasion for reprisals in Europe; to prove to France that the Anglo-French *Entente* was inefficacious; at the same time, to fortify the Triple Alliance by detaching Italy and Spain from the Western powers; in a word, to restore the situation which Bismarck had bequeathed to William II. And the undertaking was an utter failure. Not only had the two countries, reconciled by the agreement of the 8th of April, 1904, remained refractory to every effort made to disunite them, but, in the trial, their *En-*

tente had changed its character; and, after being
originally signed for the purpose of liquidating the
past, it had become a principle of action. This
action had influenced Madrid and Rome. The
visible solidarity of French and English policy had
likewise made its impression on the Italian and
Spanish nations. It had attracted them to the
extent of transforming the primitive *tour de valse*
into a durable connection. The Franco-English
binomial had acquired weight. It had changed
from the static to the dynamic condition. Even
the Franco-Russian Alliance was strengthened by
the crisis through which it had passed. On the
morrow of the Russian defeats, German threats
had shown to adversaries, as well as to friends,
of the Dual Alliance, the need there was for its existence. Last of all, for the first time at Algeciras
the representatives of Russia and England, brought
into contact by their coöperation in a work of general behoof, had exchanged amicable and reasonable views respecting the situation of both countries. The combinations in which France had her
place marked had lost nothing by this "experiment
of resistance." In accepting Europe's intervention
between the Sultan of Morocco and herself, our
country had done nothing more than record the
inevitable consequence of her set-back in 1905.
For the rest, her essential interests in the Moorish
Empire were safeguarded by the privilege of execution she shared with Spain, in putting into force
the police and finance reforms she had proposed.

In Europe, she maintained her rank; and her diplomatic resources were increased rather than diminished.

Germany's discomfiture was proved by the fact that what she had tried to demolish remained still in existence. The odds, therefore, turned against her. After winning the first two games, she lost the final one that should have given her complete victory. She was not any more isolated after Algeciras than she had been before, since she kept her two allies. But, if the term "isolation" is taken in the sense given to it by Prince von Buelow in 1905, to wit, a grouping of Powers outside of Germany's dictation, such isolation continued. Her own allies had made her understand that, while correctly fulfilling their obligations towards her, they were not willing to merely follow in her wake. Italy did not give up her Mediterranean agreements. To the theory of an autocratic Triple Alliance, she had opposed the doctrine of a constitutional *Triplice* in which each of the contracting parties proportioned their contributions to their profits. Austria, who was fulsomely congratulated by William II, had acted less as a "second" than as a mediatrix; she had contrived to show that she had her own policy, a thing many had doubted; and that she did not mean to accept peremptory orders from Berlin. So far, therefore, from having widened her field of action, Germany had, on the contrary, narrowed it. Instead of augmenting her authority, she had diminished it. Nothing of what was ma-

terial had been lost; but she had not obtained the
moral success on which she had relied.

This judgment was that which, in general, was
expressed by the German press. "Neither van-
quisher nor vanquished," said the *Cologne Gazette.*
The pronouncement would have been true, if, at
Algeciras, Germany had not been seeking victory.
"Neither Bismarck's genius nor Talleyrand's subt-
lety could have obtained more," was the opinion
of the *Berliner Tageblatt,* which, however, added:
"But Bismarck would never have gone to Algeciras." The *Tægliche Rundschau* spoke of Germany's
isolation; and the *Tageszeitung* summed up by saying: "After commencing with a flourish of trum-
pets, our Moroccan policy finishes by a surrender;"
while the *Hamburger Nachrichten* exclaimed: "In
reality, France has obtained everything at the Conference; her concessions are purely those of form.
On essential points, we have done nothing but
yield." A few months later, the *Hannoversche
Courrier* added, "Our diplomacy has been blind."
And at the end of 1906, the *Frankfort Gazette* summed
up the general impression by saying in substance:
"The Moroccan adventure has warded off none of
the risks against which it was pretended measures
were to be taken. . . . Germany's position has
been aggravated instead of being improved. German diplomacy has made itself disagreeable to everybody. . . . The telegram to President Kruger;
the propaganda against the Yellow Race or against
America; Pan-Islamic intrigues in Africa, — mistakes

and nothing but mistakes. . . . And what has it all resulted in? We have left the Boers to stew in their own juice. The Japanese have beaten the Russians. The Sultan of Morocco has to submit to Franco-Spanish police. Was it worth while raising such a hubbub?"

The official manifestations themselves were quite as little disposed to exult as the newspapers. On the 14th of November, 1906, Mr. Bassermann, one of the National Liberals in the Reichstag, said:—

We have entered upon an era of travels, speeches, telegrams, and amiable advances lavished on all sides.

To-day, the *Triplice* has no practical utility.

The Italian press and people incline more and more towards France.

Austria has been too much eulogized for playing the rôle of a "brilliant second," which she herself disclaimed.

The Franco-Russian Alliance remains intact; and the attitude of France towards us is not so good as it was.

The interview at Cronberg between the English and German sovereigns does not prevent England from pursuing her ancient policy, which tends to isolate us.

We are living in a period of alliances between other nations.

The Anglo-Russian understanding is fraught with grave consequences for us, and Bismarck already had the coalition nightmare.

Our policy lacks calmness and consistency; and one sees clumsy hands upset plans that had been well laid.

Abroad, all this is noticed with attention and distrust. We do not see that there is any imminent danger of war; but there is the danger that comes from a sudden relaxation of strain.

The Chancellor himself had altered his tone. Speaking during the same sitting, after Mr. Bassermann, he used language characterized by its extreme moderation, indifference, and resignation:—

I may remark here more especially that we have no thoughts of slipping in between France and Russia, or between France and England.

Nor have we any idea of producing a rupture of the friendship between any of the Western Powers. Such is not the object of our efforts whether secret or avowed.

The Franco-Russian Alliance, since its conclusion, has not been a danger to peace; on the contrary, it has acted as a weight contributing to the regular movement of the world's clock.

We hope that the same thing may be said of the Anglo-French *Entente Cordiale*.

The good relations between Germany and Russia have in no wise tended to break the Franco-Russian Alliance.

Nor can the good relations between Germany and England be in contradiction with the *Entente Cordiale* either, if its object is pacific.

He thus appeared to recognize the fresh conditions of equilibrium which, both before and during the Conference, the German semi-official press had not ceased denouncing as an attack on Germany's rights. The dream he had conceived, that of restoring, through Morocco, the threatened Bismarckian edifice, had not stood against the reality of things. In the ardour of the struggle, there was a good deal of indignation aroused, on this side the Vosges, by the manner in which Germany behaved. Without approving all that was said, one may recall, at this distance from the past, Bismarck's saying that "indignation is not a political state of mind." And as one understands better, one is less inclined to grow angry. The prodigious display of effort, activity, and intrigue which distinguished German policy during those three months could not be explained — and would be blamable and ridiculous —

if Morocco had been the only stake that was being played for, if the only questions had been those of deciding about a few gendarmes and meagre Customs duties. Let it rather be supposed that this effort and activity and intrigue were meant to build up, on the threshold of the twentieth century, the most extraordinary structure of political power that had ever been raised since the time of Napoleon I; to save Bismarck's work from the assaults of age; to secure Germany in the domination of Europe that had belonged to her from 1871 to 1891, — and even to 1902; to oppose these new combinations by an alliance that had gloriously won its laurels in a series of trials, and with it to overcome them. Then one may admit that the sometimes exaggerated ardour of German policy was not unjustifiable.

Its only crime, in the eyes of history, will be that of having been useless.

P

CHAPTER VI

THE NEW ASIATIC AND EUROPEAN UNDERSTANDINGS

I

DURING the last ten years, Asiatic policy has exercised on European policy an influence at once constant and considerable. Every Power that has
occupied the political stage in Europe possesses
territory in Asia. All the various diplomatic groupings, formed by reason of Asiatic interests, have
produced their counter-effect in Europe. Such
being the case, alliances and understandings referring to Asia can only be rightly comprehended
when viewed in connection with general policy.

The real *fait nouveau* of this period is Japan's entrance into the circle of the great Powers. Already, for a long time, the world had followed with sympathetic and astonished curiosity the efforts made by the Empire of the Rising Sun to superimpose, on its ancient and admirable civilization, the acquisitions of the West, which seemed to its patriotism the assurance of strength and an instrument of future greatness. For the first time, in 1894, Japan, being conscious of her power, put it to the test. Between herself and China, the Corean question had always been the subject of disputes, which, at length, grew embittered. On the 1st of August, 1894, the Mikado's Government transported the quarrel to the field of battle; and, on the 17th of April, 1895, the Treaty of Shimonasaki recorded their easy victory.[1] China, once for all, recognized Corea's entire, complete independence, renouncing all tribute from her and all ceremony indicative of vassalage. She gave Japan the perpetual right of possession over the peninsula of Leao-Tong, with Port Arthur, the island of Formosa, and the Pescadoras. Besides, she pledged herself to pay a war indemnity of 200 millions of taëls in eight instalments, the delay fixed being seven years at the outside, with a 5% interest on all payments in arrears; to appoint plenipotentiaries for the purpose of concluding with Japanese plenipotentiaries treaties of commerce and navigation, and arrangements relative to land communications and trade. She granted

[1] See Edouard Driault's book, *The Question of the Far East.*

Japan, in advance, the treatment of the most fa-
voured nation. She opened to Japanese trade the
ports of Chachi, Chung-King, Souchow, and Hang-
Chow. She accorded liberty of navigation on the
Yang-tse-kiang, beyond I-chang as far as Chung-
King, and on the river Wusung as far as Hang-Chow.
Moreover, Wei-hai-Wei was to be occupied by a
Japanese garrison until the first two instalments of
the indemnity had been paid.

Japan's joy of triumph did not last long. On the
20th of April, 1895, three days after the Treaty of
Shimonasaki had been signed, a group of Powers,
which seemed at this moment agreed to act together
in Europe and out of Europe, to wit, Germany,
Russia, and France, laid their embargo on Japan's
victories, and, out of the peace of the 17th, made a
second treaty of San Stefano. In friendly yet im-
perative language, the three Powers declared that
"a Japanese possession of the peninsula of Leao-
Tong would be a menace against the Capital of China
and would render Corea's independence merely
nominal." On the 5th of May, Japan yielded. She
announced that she accepted the advice of the Powers, not wishing to raise other difficulties. She
therefore contented herself with keeping the Pescadoras and Formosa, and renounced her right to Leao-
Tong and Port Arthur. In return, she obtained an
indemnity of 30 millions of taëls. The Treaty of
Pekin, of the 21st of July, 1895, set seal to this sacrifice, which was a painful one for Japanese pride to
make. Indeed, the sacrifice was not definitive, des-

tined, as it was, to be redeemed by another treaty
which the Mikado's plenipotentiaries were to sign ten
years later at Portsmouth in the United States.

The European intervention, which had just been
manifested so bluntly, would have been justifiable,
if it had been inspired by the principles that it appealed to.[1] The Powers were quite warranted in
insisting on the respect of Chinese independence,
which — then as to-day — appeared to be the best
pledge of peace in Asia. But throughout this interference, there was much less principle operating
than covetousness, which, in Saint Petersburg and
still more in Berlin, awaited only a more favourable
opportunity to satisfy itself. Since the time of Bismarck, Germany has always sought to tempt Russia
Asiawards, with a view to "getting rid of her influence" in Europe. The Chancellor used to say:
"Russia has nothing to do in the West. All that
she can get there is nihilism and other maladies.
Her mission is in Asia. There she represents civilization." In 1880, at the time of the Kouldja incident, this policy had been applied. Just then, a
diplomatist drew attention to "the incomprehen-
sible intimacy" of Russia's Minister, Mr. Koyander,
and Mr. von Brandt, who was Germany's, and to
their joint efforts to egg things on, the former acting from national ambition, and with an imprudent
and heedless desire of procuring his country fresh
conquests, the latter, on the contrary, reasonably
calculating that it was advantageous for Germany

[1] See René Pinon's book, *The Struggle for the Pacific.*

that Russia should be involved in adventures which he knew were perilous and which, if entered upon, would absorb her vital forces for long to come, and thus remove from Europe and the Vistula, men and generals whose proximity might hamper Germany at a moment when she wanted her hands free.[1] Fifteen years had gone by since then. And in their adoption of the *Weltpolitik*, the German Government had acquired also a taste for a Colonial Empire. To make in China a conquest of this kind and to drag in Russia behind them was killing two birds with one stone, a *coup* of the kind relished by Imperial diplomacy. From 1895, Germany had been working with this end in view.

Although having obtained excellent results during the whole of the nineteenth century by a policy of pacific penetration, Russia was not able to resist the lure of immediate profits that was held out to her. Being in the honeymoon period of the Alliance, France was hardly in a position to restrain her other half by a show of authority. So Germany had the game all to herself. On the 1st of November, 1897, the murder of two German missionaries at Chang-Tong furnished William II with the desired opportunity for making China feel his "iron-sheathed fist." After an expedition theatrically organized at Kiel under the command of Prince Henry of Prussia, China was obliged, on the 6th of March, 1898, to lease to Germany for ninety-nine years

[1] See André Chéradame's book, *The World and the Russo-Japanese War*.

the Bay of Kiao-Chow and a zone of fifty kilometres round it — an admirable footing on Chinese soil adapted to go with various other German vantage points in the Pacific, which latter were increased in the same year by the purchase of Spain's colonies in these seas. Three weeks later, on the 27th of March, without any pretext, and simply "with a view to protecting the Russian fleet and giving it a strong base on the western coast of China," Russia contrived to obtain, under the same conditions, the cession of Port Arthur, Talienwan, and a contiguous zone, as the terminus of the Trans-Manchurian Railway, for which, in August, 1896, Count Cassini had obtained the Tsong-li-Yamen's permission to be cut through Chinese territory. On the 11th of April, 1898, France exacted, in her turn, a lease of the bay of Kwang-Chow-Wan. Great Britain installed herself at Wei-hai-Wei. Even Italy, in 1899, tried, but in vain, to claim the Bay of San-Mun. It was the break-up of China of which Lord Charles Beresford had spoken some months earlier.

This quarry was the starting-point of the events which have since marked the history of Asia; and the situation thus created determined the trend of Far Eastern policy during the ensuing eight years. Though stripped of her conquests, Japan would, perhaps, have resigned herself to see them remain Chinese. What decided her to seek revenge was the substitution of the Russian for the Japanese flag at Port Arthur. With her integrity safeguarded

in 1895, China might have gone on in her lethargic
existence. She was roused and awakened by the
foreign invasion of her land. The Reform movement of Kang-yu-Wei, which failed in 1900, was
followed by that of the xenophobe Boxers. In the
month of June, 1900, the European Legations in
Pekin were attacked by the mob, with the intermittent complicity of the regular soldiers and of
the Chinese Government. Baron von Ketteler,
Germany's Minister, was assassinated whilst proceeding on horseback to the Tsong-li-Yamen. On
the 13th of August, an international army, which
was constituted at Tien-tsin, delivered the Legations,
the command of it being handed over, a few days
later, to Field-Marshal Count von Waldersee. Germany thus continued to play the premier rôle, or
at least the most ostentatious one, in Far Eastern
affairs. Assuming a high tone after the murder of
his Minister, William II peremptorily insisted on a
severe chastisement. He proposed his "military
protection" to the Emperor of China and refused to
evacuate Pekin. By an arrangement with England
(October 16, 1900), he seemed to reserve for his
own field of action the entire north of China, his
navigation companies, in the meantime, bidding
fair to destroy all competition in the South. At the
same moment, a Russian Army was systematically
occupying Manchuria. The European monopolization policy therefore still persisted, amidst a medley
of contradictions due to divergences among the
Powers; and it was becoming more and more alarm-

ing to China, who had to suffer by it, and to England and Japan, who, on different grounds, were forced to remain spectators of it only.

For many years, the progress of Russian influence in China had caused serious anxiety to the British Government, both commercially and politically. In 1900, their Consuls wrote: "The frontier routes take every year to Russian markets tea, either in blocks or in leaves, the total value of which must figure out in tens and hundreds of millions; and important cargoes also arrive at Odessa by sea. Although statistics are not forthcoming, there are a thousand indications which show from day to day the extent to which Russia has got hold of Northern China's trade. Even in the valley of Yang-tse-kiang, a rich colony of Russian merchants and commission agents has replaced the English agents who formerly made all Russia's purchases at Han-Kow, the great tea-market." [1] On the 16th of April, 1899, the London Cabinet, being already preoccupied by the prospect of war in South Africa, signed a treaty with Russia from which good results were hoped, for the protection of British interests. Russia pledged herself to ask for no railway concessions in the basin of the Yang-tse-kiang, whether for herself or for any of her subjects. England made a similar promise with regard to the Chinese provinces north of the Great Wall. The two signataries, moreover, expressed their intention to commit no act prejudicial to China's sovereign rights or to

[1] See Victor Bérard's book, *The Revolt of Asia*.

existing treaties. These stipulations, however, did not suffice to restrain the Russian infiltration. England then concluded (October 16, 1900) an agreement with Germany, — still with a view to "the preservation of her interests and her rights under the *régime* of existing treaties." But when an attempt was made by the London Cabinet to use this agreement for the purpose of protesting against the continued occupation of Manchuria, Berlin replied that, whilst the province in question belonged to the Chinese Empire, it did not, for all this, make part of the real "China," which latter country alone was the object of the treaty signed in October. Realizing how powerless she was to defend her interests in Asia as long as the Transvaal war occupied her military forces, Great Britain sought to get an Ally who might act in her place and stead. Japan offered, and she took Japan.

In silence and reflection, the statesmen of Tokio had been meditating many things during the past seven years; and, though they never spoke of their discomfiture of 1895, this was always in their mind. Throughout the crisis of 1900, forgetting their just grievances, they had loyally taken sides with Europe, had defended the cause of civilization, and had rendered eminent service to the international army, yet without losing the authority which they had acquired over the Chinese not only by their victories, but by the European spoliations that had followed them. At times, the presence of Russian armies in Manchuria caused them grave uneasiness. The occupation had lasted from 1900; and might any day be extended to Corea — the Corea so necessary to Japan economically, on account of the rice it produced, so necessary strategically by reason of the Continental base which it afforded her and which she as an island needed. On the other hand, Japan wanted money in order to go on with her transformation and complete her equipment; and none could be found except in Europe. She aspired, above all, in her legitimate pride, to be admitted as an equal into the company of the Nations, to see her efforts, magnificent in their intensity and discipline, openly acknowledged by the world. True, there were various ways of realizing such a design. And it does not seem that Marquis Ito, the Japanese Envoy, when he left for Europe in October, 1901, was altogether decided as to the particular solution he should adopt. He began his calls with Paris, staying a week in the French capital, when Mr. Delcassé would have been able, had he chosen, to conclude with him a piece of business advantageous to ourselves. He next went to Saint Petersburg, where they were no more clear-sighted than our statesmen had been here. Count Mouravieff, one of the most mediocre Ministers who have ever directed Russian policy, did not understand that despatch was necessary and that Japan would not wait. He allowed Marquis Ito to go away. In January, the latter arrived in London; and, on the 30th of the same month, the Alliance was signed and immediately published.

"Moved by the sole desire of preserving the *statu quo* and general peace in the Far East, being especially interested in guaranteeing the independence of China and Corea," the two Governments settled, for a period of five years, the following agreement: —

Article 2. — If Great Britain or Japan, for the defence of their respective interests before mentioned, should be engaged in a war with another Power, the second contracting party shall maintain strict neutrality and do her utmost to prevent other Powers from entering upon hostilities against her Ally.

Article 3. — If, in the case just mentioned, any other Power or Powers should enter upon hostilities against the said Ally, the other contracting party shall come to her aid and make war in common with her and conclude peace, with common accord.

This Treaty, the sudden conclusion of which astounded every one, had immediate consequences both in Europe and Asia. In Asia, Japan secured for her policy, not a military support, — since the *casus fœderis* was only to be brought into action in the contingency of a war with two Powers; and such a contingency was hardly probable — but a moral authority which was bound to encourage her in assuming an energetic attitude. On her side, England secured, for the aggregate of her possessions and the defence of her interests, the help of a Power installed in the very heart of the disputed country, and well equipped and armed. To the policy practised by Germany in 1897 and pursued also by Russia with increased vigour after 1900, the Anglo-Japanese Alliance gave a check, the efficacy of which was soon to make itself felt. In Europe, Russia received a set-back. And by the Franco-Russian declaration of the 19th of March, asserting the unity of views — a purely theoretic one — between Saint Petersburg and Paris as to questions in the Far East, France, without profit for Russia, took her part in this set-back.[1] From this moment, Russian policy, and the Franco-Russian Alliance in consequence, showed a growing tendency to drift farther East. Germany began to find fresh prospects of security and European preponderance, which the next three years were destined to develop to her advantage.

The Anglo-Japanese Alliance came into force on the 6th of February, 1902. On the 12th of April ensuing, Russia signed a treaty with China, fixing as successive dates for the evacuation of Manchuria the 8th of October, 1902, and the 8th of April and 8th of October, 1903. When the time came for the second zone to be restored to China, Russia contrived to maintain her troops in it, on the ground that the region was in a disturbed condition, this being, indeed, a fact. Three months later (August 13, 1903) the creation of a Russian Vice-Royalty in the Far East, and Admiral Alexeieff's appointment to it, seemed to indicate that a policy of expansion was being planned. The intrigues of Russian business men in Corea rendered Japan more and more uneasy. During this same summer of 1903, Mr. Kurino, the Japanese Minister at Saint Petersburg, informed Count Lamsdorff of his desire to enter

[1] See Chapter I.

into negotiations with reference to questions in the Far East. Russia complied, but appeared in no hurry to discuss. On the 3d of October, it became only too evident that the Russian and Japanese proposals were not in harmony. The crux of the dispute lay in Russia's refusal to come to any terms with Japan on the subject of the Chinese province of Manchuria. Three months passed by; and, on the 13th of January, 1904, this difficulty with regard to Manchuria still blocked the way. As a matter of fact, Japan required Russia to promise that she would "respect the integrity of China in Manchuria." Russia kept putting off her reply, and Japan lost patience. On the 5th of February, she broke off diplomatic relations; and on the 8th, her torpedo vessels attacked the Russian iron-clads, — *Cesarevitch, Retvisan,* and *Pallada,* — which were lying outside Port Arthur.

The war which thus commenced is too well known to require that an account of it in detail be given here. On the 1st of May, the Japanese crossed the Yalu. On the 30th, they invested Port Arthur. On the 15th of June, General Stackelberg, who had been sent to relieve it, was defeated at Vafangu. On the 8th of August, the outer positions of Port Arthur all fell into the hands of the Japanese. On the 2d and 3d of September, Kuropatkin was defeated at Leao-Yang. On the 1st of January, Port Arthur capitulated. Between the 23d of February and the 10th of March, the Russian Army was again beaten at Mukden. On the 27th of May, Rodjestvensky's fleet was annihilated at Tsusima. On the 8th of June, President Roosevelt induced the belligerents to negotiate. On the 5th of August, the Russian and Japanese plenipotentiaries met at Oyster Bay. And, on the 29th, peace was signed at Portsmouth. In a previous chapter was shown the immediate effect exercised by the Russian defeats not only on Europe at large, but more especially on France. Germany, being desirous of strengthening the hegemony that she feared to lose, profited by these defeats to act with greater freedom. A month after the fall of Port Arthur, Mr. von Kuhlmann gave us a hint of his approaching inimical behaviour. Three weeks after Mukden, William II manifested a clearer hostility at Tangier. A fortnight after Tsusima, Mr. Delcassé's resignation was imposed upon us by a campaign of intimidation. Only after the opening of the peace negotiations did Germany make the concessions which rendered the signing of the July and September agreements possible. Without exaggerating the rigour of this synchronism, it may be said that each defeat of Russia was followed by a set-back for France, and that the detestable policy entered upon in 1897, at Germany's instigation and from her example, had profited no one but this latter Power. In what position did the conclusion of peace leave us? What reasons did we find in it for uneasiness or for security?

If we had learned to our cost what an unsuccessful war waged in Asia by Russia meant, we were by no means sure, on the morrow of the Treaty of Ports-

mouth, not to see the peril reappear within a brief
delay. Both belligerents had been exhausted by
the war; and both—the vanquishers perhaps even
more than the vanquished — felt the urgent necessity of laying down their arms. But neither side
was content with the terms of peace; the Russians
first, which is easy to understand. On the 10th
of June, General Linevitch, who had become
the Commander-in-Chief; Generals Kuropatkin and
Kaulbars, Chiefs of Army Corps; Sakharoff, Chief of
the Staff; Rennenkampf, Zarubaieff, Bilderling, Lvof,
Samsonoff, Daniloff, and Korff had "energetically
and unanimously petitioned the Czar to continue
the war." In the heart of many Russians the regret
remained that this prayer had not been heard.
Corea was handed over to Japan; Port Arthur was
lost; the railway had been given up; half of
Saghalien had been ceded; a number of grants had
been made, notably in the way of fishing rights;
the Asiatic dream was deprived of its crown; and
all this was painful to Russian pride. The Japanese
were more irritated still. Intoxicated by their
victories, they were indignant at a peace which they
deemed to be shameful. When, on the 7th of September, the signing of the Treaty was known by
telegrams which the authorities had been keeping
back for two days, there was a formidable riot.
The Ministerial offices were attacked, and one of
them was set fire to. On the 9th, the Progressists
held a meeting at which all the members were
present; and a vote of censure on the Government

was passed. How long would a peace last which was received thus on either side?

In addition to the indirect peril threatening France from this situation, there was the more direct risk she ran of having compromised her relations with Japan through her friendly attitude towards Russia. During the war, on several occasions, the Japanese Government had reproached the French Government with failing to preserve neutrality out of courtesy towards Admiral Rodjestvensky. In the month of May, 1905, these reproaches assumed a character of sharp remonstrance. Basing herself on what had occurred at Cherbourg, Dakar, Algiers, Djibouti, Majunga, Nossi-Bé, and in the bays of Kam-ranh and Port-Dayot, Japan, through the voice of Mr. Motono, her Minister in Paris, stated: —

"1°. That, without incriminating the French Government's good faith, she was of opinion that the latter's orders had been insufficiently executed.

"2°. That, since her observations had been acted upon, after the things complained of had occurred, it was regrettable no better surveillance had been carried out before.

"3°. That, while not ignorant of the complexity of maritime neutrality questions and of the reasons France had for adhering to her own special regulations, she — Japan — considered that the aid given to the Russian fleet, through no proper surveillance being exercised, had greatly facilitated the accomplishment of its mission and had enabled it to reach the China seas."

Q

Mr. Motono concluded:

"What Japan defends against France is her very existence.

"What she invokes is the spirit of the duty of neutrality against the quibbles of the letter.

"What she affirms is that, on many distinct and successive occasions Rodjestvensky has utilized French waters, during his voyage on a war-expedition, either for staying to revictual his ships or else for the purpose of awaiting in safety the arrival of his reënforcements."

The French Government replied that in law they were completely covered by their neutrality regulations, drawn up, not on the occasion of the Russo-Japanese war, but at the beginning of that between Spain and the United States; that they had taken, in spite of the letter of these regulations, all the measures in their power to secure complete impartiality; that, except at Algiers, and there only in very small quantities, there had never been any direct purchase of coal in French ports; that purchases made even from French private persons, through the medium of trading vessels accompanying the squadron, had been insignificant; that all the stock of coal used by these vessels had been bought in England and Germany, without Japan's having made any protest on the matter; that it was impossible to exercise permanent surveillance along the whole of the Indo-Chinese coasts; that, moreover, the Japanese had done in the Dutch Indies and the Philippines the same things that they reproached the

Russians with doing in French waters. This discussion between the two Governments had no definite conclusion; but it left traces. A report, which was false, was published by some newspapers to the effect that the Japanese military Staff had elaborated a plan of invasion against Indo-China; and this produced a certain amount of sore feeling in France. Consequently, just after the end of the war, Franco-Japanese relations were less cordial than they had been before it.

Finally, if the Anglo-Japanese Alliance can be considered as one of the causes of the war of 1904, this cause subsisted more than ever on the morrow of the conclusion of peace. For the Alliance was renewed in London on the 12th of August, 1905, while negotiations were in progress and before they had finished. The common principles to which the two Governments subscribed were: —

1°. The consolidation and preservation of general peace in the regions of Eastern Asia and India.

2°. The upholding of the common interests of all the Powers in China, while assuring the independence and integrity of the Chinese Empire and the principle of equality for the commerce and industry of all nations, in China.

3°. The maintenance of the territorial rights of the high contracting parties in the regions of Eastern Asia and India.

Japan's political preponderance in Corea was recognized by England. On the other hand, Japan recognized that Great Britain, by virtue of "her es-

pecial interests along all the Indian frontier, had the
right to take, in the neighbourhood of this frontier,
such measures as she judged necessary for the protection of her possessions in India." The clause
respecting military coöperation remained the same
as in the first treaty, except that Article 7, relative
to "the means by which help should be rendered
available," allowed it to be understood that such
military coöperation might be given in Europe as
well as in Asia. The Alliance was concluded this
time for ten years, and was consequently extended
and strengthened. The article referring to the Indian frontiers and their "neighbourhood" lent itself
to all sorts of interpretations, even to that of a plan
of military action against Russia in Central Asia.
The Alliance was generalized in its object and made
more precise in its means.

For France, it brought out the disquieting possibility of a conflict no longer between Russia and
Japan, but between Russia and England. The
rivalry of the "elephant" and the "whale" was emphasized by the very precautions taken in London
to protect English possessions in Asia. In the course
of the war, the Dogger Bank incident had shown how
great the tension of minds was both in England and
Russia. The Saint Petersburg papers openly accused Great Britain not only of having excited Japan
and let loose the war, but of fostering Russian revolution with her gold. The English had not concealed
their sympathies for Japan, and had even given
them a distinctly aggressive form against the "heredi-

tary enemy," saying as the *Globe* did : "We shall not deviate from this line of conduct through fear of giving umbrage to Russia's friends on the Continent or through complaisance to the sentiments of Continental Powers." It was Lord Curzon's earlier policy which had most efficaciously contributed to prepare the way for the first Anglo-Japanese Alliance. The second one had the same character, in spite of the letter in which, on the 6th of September, Lord Lansdowne had announced it to Sir Charles Hardinge, the British Ambassador at Saint Petersburg. Notwithstanding the euphemisms in which the English guarantee was expressed when publicly spoken of, its consolidation of the Japanese victories caused the Russians an anxiety which was quite legitimate. The situation of France between Russia, her ally since 1891, and England, her friend since 1904, was about as difficult a one as could be conceived. The conciliation of our Alliance and our friendship might become impossible. And our entire policy risked being paralyzed in the attempt.

Whilst, through the conflict of alliances, which, in the month of September, 1905, was developing in Paris and Berlin, Germany derived an immediate advantage from her intervention, as proved by Mr. Delcassé's resignation and the forthcoming meeting of the Algeciras Conference, she was, therefore, benefited indirectly, but very appreciably also, by the events that had occurred in the Far East, although taking no part in them. The result for France was a false, precarious situation, perhaps even a dangerous one. Between an enfeebled Alliance and a triumphant friendship, our country must expect anything. In the past ten years, the intrusion of Asiatic affairs into European policy had always been prejudicial to us; and when the crisis closed, Asia weighed upon us more than ever, burdening our future with heavy uncertainty, all to Germany's profit.

II

It is to the honour of France that she succeeded in less than two years in warding off the three dangers threatening her — a conflict between Russia and Japan, a conflict between France and Japan, and a conflict between England and Russia — by means of three reconciliations, Russo-Japanese, Franco-Japanese, and Anglo-Russian.

The Russo-Japanese was the first one that needed securing; and, consequently, it was the first one essayed. Not to speak of the resentments already alluded to, the Treaty of Portsmouth had left material incertitudes subsisting. Arrangements it had provided for were still to be negotiated; and certain things remained to be defined more clearly, while there were also measures to be taken for the Treaty's execution. Between the month of December, 1905, and the end of 1906, the report was spread several times that these supplementary negotiations, which had commenced immediately after the signing of the Treaty, were making no progress. On the 1st of January, 1907, Mr. Motono, the Japanese Ambassador at Saint Petersburg, protested publicly against such rumours, in which the wish was father to the thought, being circulated both by Japanese and Russian newspapers. Thanks to the conciliatory spirit shown by the Ambassador, as also by Mr. Isvolsky, the year 1907 witnessed the conclusion of the necessary agreements. On the 13th of June, the Convention relative to the exploitation of the East China and South Manchurian railways was signed at Saint Petersburg; and also the protocol relative to the station in common at Kwang-Chung-tse.

On the 28th of July, 1907, an arrangement was made respecting the Fisheries question, which granted to Japanese subjects the right to fish, gather, and treat sea produce, seals and walruses excepted, in the seas of Japan, Okhotsk, and Behring, excluding only rivers and bays. Portions of land were to be offered on public lease to Japanese and Russian subjects, without distinction, for the preparation, etc., on shore of the fish that was caught. On the same day, a Treaty of Commerce and Navigation reciprocally recognized, on behalf of the subjects of both countries, rights and privileges which did not normally accrue from the most-favoured-nation clause. Finally, on the 30th of July, Mr. Isvolsky and Mr. Motono signed an agreement of more general scope. "Being desirous," it was said, "of fortifying the pacific, amicable, and neighbourly relations which have been happily reëstablished between Russia and Japan and to do away with the possibility of future misunderstanding between the

two Empires," the contracting parties made the
following stipulations: —

Article 1. — Each of the high contracting parties promises
to respect the present territorial integrity of the other, as also
all the rights accruing to either the one or the other of the high
contracting parties from the treaties in force, agreements or conventions in application at present between the high contracting
parties and China, the texts of which have been exchanged between the contracting Powers, this in the measure in which such
rights are not incompatible with the principle of equal treatment enunciated in the Treaty signed at Portsmouth, on the 5th
of September, 1905, and in the special conventions concluded
between Russia and Japan.

Article 2. — The two high contracting parties recognize the
independence and territorial integrity of the Empire of China,
as also the principle of equal treatment with regard to trade
and industry for all the nations of the said Empire. They likewise pledge themselves to uphold the *statu quo* and the respect
of this principle by all the pacific means at their disposal.

With praiseworthy clear-sightedness, Mr. Isvolsky
thus drew the inevitable consequences from a war
which had, indeed, cost Russia neither a kopeck of
indemnity nor an inch of her territory, and from
which, therefore, resulted no imperious duty of revenge. The Asiatic policy, as it had been practised
at Saint Petersburg since 1896, embraced more of a
chimera than a reality. It is not in the seas of China
that Russia has to seek for the free port promised
her by Peter the Great; not at four thousand kilometres from her Capital that a great Continental
Power must place the centre of her action. The
agreements of 1907, which recorded accomplished
facts and substituted friendship for distrust, were
consequently inspired by just views. Having played

a discreet and friendly rôle in the conclusion of these agreements, France saw the Russian Alliance replaced by them on its proper basis, that is to say, in Europe. The more immediate peril existing for her in the Far East was removed by the sincere reconciliation of those who so lately had been adversaries. And the field was thus opened for the pursuit of other guarantees.

If intellectual and moral ties have any value in the formation of international combinations, they should contribute something to the *rapprochement* of France and Japan. As was well said by the Japanese newspaper, the *Kokumin*, in the autumn of 1906, France, among the nations of Europe, was one of the most eager to encourage the Mikado and his people in the evolution which has made Japan a great Power. It was to France that the Japanese officers came who were sent to acquire instruction in military organization. And it was a Frenchman, Mr. Bertin, who created the Japanese fleet. The Japanese Code was modelled on that of Napoleon. Even during the course of the war, and in spite of the incidents mentioned above, a Japanese statesman of mark, Baron Suyematsu, son-in-law of the Marquis Ito, said to me: —

"No one in Japan is surprised at your sympathies for your allies. But we do not forget either — and we hope that France does not forget — the ancient, cordial relations uniting us to you, the services you have rendered us, the friendships you have formed among us. However ferocious a war may be, it is

only an incident in the history of the world. This
one has created between France and Japan a situation which is false and somewhat embarrassing. But
let us recollect two things — first, that France has
never been wronged by Japan, and secondly, that
Japan has never been wronged by France; and let
us in confidence wait for better days."

These days arrived. On the 5th of May, 1907, the
Havas Agency announced that a Franco-Japanese
understanding was about to be signed. The next
day, Mr. Pichon said: —

"The object of our negotiations with Japan, which
indeed are not yet terminated, is the signing of a convention which is calculated to add fresh guarantees
to those existing for the preservation of peace in the
Far East. They are the logical continuation of the
absolutely peaceful policy of France, a policy whose
only aim is to prevent all complications in whatsoever parts of the world, and more especially in those
where we have particular interests."

On the 7th of May, Baron Kurino, Japan's Ambassador, characterized the approaching agreement
as follows: —

"Our wish has been to achieve a work of good
sense and peace. The interests of France and Japan
are not at all contradictory. And the agreement will
set seal to their harmony. This arrangement com-
prises, on the one hand, a guarantee for the independence and integrity of China, and, on the other,
a security for the possessions of the two contracting
Powers. It gives sanction to the territorial status

accruing to Japan from the last war, and to France, from her situation in Indo-China. It constitutes a decisive proof of the moderation of our policy. The legend of the Yellow Peril and Japanese ambitions will, I hope, be definitely dissipated by the event now preparing. The old relations of friendship uniting Japan and France increase the value of this loyal arrangement, which the two countries have decided to conclude, by promising each other mutual support on the basis I have indicated to you."

The agreement was signed on the 10th of June following. It was conceived as hereafter: —

Declaration

The two Governments of Japan and France, while reserving to themselves the liberty to enter into *pourparlers* with a view to the conclusion of a commercial convention in regard to relations between Japan and French Indo-China, agree on the ensuing stipulations: —

The most-favoured-nation treatment shall be accorded to Japan's subjects and functionaries throughout French Indo-China in all that concerns their persons and the protection of their property; and this same treatment shall be applied to the subjects and protégés of French Indo-China throughout the Empire of Japan, and this, until the expiration of the Treaty of Commerce and Navigation signed between Japan and France on the 4th of August, 1896.

Arrangement

The Government of the French Republic and the Government of his Majesty, the Emperor of Japan, being animated by the desire to fortify the amicable relations existing between them and to remove for the future all cause of misunderstanding, have decided to conclude the following arrangement: —

The Governments of France and Japan, while agreeing to

respect the independence and integrity of China, as well as the principle of equal treatment in this country for the commerce and things touching the jurisdiction of all nations, and while having a special interest in securing order and a state of tranquillity, notably throughout the frontier regions of the Chinese Empire that are contiguous to territories over which they have rights of sovereignty, promise to support each other mutually in assuring peace and safety in these regions, with a view to preserving the respective situation and territorial rights of the two contracting parties on the Asiatic continent.

One has only to remember the anxiety experienced by France during the Russo-Japanese war, to appreciate rightly the diplomatic guarantee thus obtained from Japan for the integrity of her possessions. True, this guarantee depends only on the word of the Tokio Cabinet; and, whenever it might please Japan to attack Cochin-China, Annam, or Tonkin, it would be difficult for us, at so great a distance, to defend them. But to doubt of Japan's sincerity would be an insult. Her foreign policy has always been vigorous, and at times brutal. It has never been disloyal. It has kept the engagements to which it has given its seal. It has consistently announced in advance any decisions it intended to take. Moreover, everything dictates to Japan the advisability of maintaining amicable relations with France. The war having terminated without Russia's paying an indemnity, the financial situation of the Mikado's Empire has been rendered somewhat difficult. Japan's debt, which, in 1903, was 559 million *yens*, amounted, on the conclusion of peace at Portsmouth, to 1859 millions, this being an in-

crease of 1300 millions. France, therefore, being
an inexhaustible reservoir of capital, can be to Japan
the most useful of friends. Two loans of twenty-
three millions sterling have already been subscribed
by the French market. Provided the Japanese Government grants equitable advantages to our industry
in return, these operations are likely to be renewed.
The agreement, taken in itself, is, consequently, a
profitable one for both contracting parties. And it
becomes more valuable still, when taken in conjunction with the Anglo-Japanese Alliance, the Franco-
English friendship, and the Russo-Japanese conventions. It makes, in fact, an integral part of a
system of arrangements, the advantage of which for
France is twofold. In Asia, it eliminates all immediate risk of war, since three out of the four Powers
that have the greatest interests there have come to
an understanding for the maintenance of the *statu
quo*. In Europe, it removes risks of complications
arising from an Asiatic conflict. In order that such
a conflict, already rendered improbable, might become impossible, there remained one necessary condition to be fulfilled, and the one was sufficient: to
wit, the reconciliation of London and Saint Petersburg. Within less than three months after the
signing of the Franco-Japanese agreement, this last
condition was realized in its turn.

A few years ago, between August, 1900, and December, 1901, an English statesman published in the
Fortnightly Review, under the pseudonym Calchas, a
series of articles on British policy. In opposition to

current opinion, Calchas maintained that Great Britain might and should come to an understanding with Russia. "Why not a treaty with Russia?" he asked in October, 1900. And he drew the conclusion that, whether on the Bosphorus, or in the Balkans, or in Asia Minor, or in the Far East, there was room for the two countries, room also for an agreement between them. This press campaign, which attracted great attention at the time, may be considered as the origin of the oft-thwarted movement which, after seven years' waiting, resulted, in 1907, in the conclusion of the Anglo-Russian convention. In order to get so far, many prejudices had to be overcome. Since the mutiny of the Sepoys and its thorough repression, the Russian invasion had appeared to England to be the only peril with which India was threatened; and the history of Mediterranean Asia or Oriental Asia had, during half a century, been nothing but the record of Anglo-Russian disputes.[1] After the Crimean war, there was the struggle against Schamyl, the Caucasian Iman; that against Yacoub, the Sultan of Cashgar; then, there were Tchernaieff's, Romanowsky's, and Kaufmann's campaigns, the Turkestan campaign in 1870, that of Khiva in 1873, of Khokand in 1876, of Merv a few years later, and finally the Afghan war. Behind each of these native resistances, Russia thought she saw England. In 1885, just after the successes of General Komaroff, war appeared to be inevitable between the two Powers. However, it was avoided by the agree-

[1] See Rouire's book, *Anglo-Russian Rivalry in Asia.*

ments of 1885, 1887, 1895, and 1899. Russian expansion had slackened, and had to some extent turned aside. Still, it had not stopped. And soon, indeed, it was seen advancing over the plateaus of Mongolia and along the plains of Manchuria, filtering through into China and as far as Thibet, troubling once more the Hindu frontier, the defence of which dominates England's Asiatic policy, and adding the peril of the North to that of the Northwest. It was the time of the Transvaal war. On the 30th of January, 1902, the Anglo-Japanese Alliance was signed. The policy advocated in the *Fortnightly Review* seemed more than ever impossible. Anglo-Russian antagonism was at this moment aggravated by the rivalry raging between Russia and Japan; and a collision seemed to be imminent.

The very greatness of the peril acted as a brake. In spite of the occurrence of certain awkward incidents, — the Dogger Bank cannonade, for instance, — Great Britain and Russia remained at peace. For one thing, there was to be considered the importance of Anglo-Russian trade, which had grown continually since 1882. The English had increased their sales in the Empire of the Czars from eight to fourteen millions sterling, and their purchases from fifteen to twenty-five millions. Their consuls pointed out that Russia was an admirable field opened to their commercial progress, which everywhere else was hampered by Germany. Moreover, although Japan's Ally, England had no intention of handing the Far East over to her, Russia might be a useful counterweight against a friend that was too strong, while also offering an outlet for English industry. Last of all, the settlement of the Franco-English quarrel, on the 8th of April, 1904, gave a pertinent example to those partisans of a reconciliation who, though deeming it desirable, did not think it possible. In 1905, the Russian press, when examining into the causes of the Manchurian defeat, opined in favour of an agreement. The *Novoie Vremia*, in the September of this year, manifested a conciliatory attitude, which the *Times* at once took occasion to praise. In 1906, during the long weeks spent at Algeciras, the Russian Plenipotentiary, Count Cassini, had frequent chats with his English colleague, Sir Arthur Nicholson, and with Sir Donald Mackenzie Wallace, the king's personal friend, who subsequently paid a visit to Saint Petersburg. On being called to the Foreign Office in the May of the same year, Mr. Isvolsky, whose diplomatic skill was incontestable, showed his firm determination to place questions concerning the Far East in their proper relation to other Russian interests, without allowing them to encroach unduly, and his equally firm desire to establish a better understanding between Russia and England, on the basis of an equitable agreement. This desire was reciprocated by King Edward and his Government.

On the 23d of October, 1905, two months after the peace of Portsmouth, the *Times* correspondent at Saint Petersburg telegraphed to his paper: —

Saint Petersburg, October 23d. . . . I have reason to believe that the audience just granted by the Czar to Sir Charles Hardinge referred to the understanding which is being prepared between England and Russia. The arrangements to be made, in view of *pourparlers* concerning this question, require Sir Charles Hardinge's presence in London. I learn, on the other hand, that the Count Benckendorff, Russia's Ambassador in London, will proceed to Saint Petersburg for a similar purpose. The negotiations being intrusted to two Ambassadors who have already proved their ardent desire to see an improvement in the two countries' respective relations, the result of these negotiations can hardly be doubtful.

Faint denials greeted this information, which was perhaps premature. On the 22d of May, the *Temps* correspondent at Berlin telegraphed that every one in Germany was expecting the speedy conclusion of an Anglo-Russian agreement. Questioned on the 24th, in the House of Commons, Sir Edward Grey said : —

I cannot make any statements as to the alleged agreement which has been published in the press, since this agreement does not exist. But I may add that there is an increasing tendency on the part of England and Russia to give an amicable consideration to questions which concern them both, whenever such questions arise.

This tendency has lately led the two Governments to coöperate on more than one occasion.

It is a tendency which we shall be happy to encourage, it is a tendency which, if continued, will naturally bring about the progressive settlement of questions interesting each of the two countries, and the strengthening of the friendly relations existing between them.

In the month of July, the intended visit of an English squadron to Cronstadt was put off on account of the domestic difficulties with which Russia had

R

to cope at the time. However, in March, 1790, the
Russian sailors had a cordial reception in England.
And, on this occasion, a semi-official note, communi-
cated to the papers, said : —

The information published on the Continent, according to
which the negotiations relative to an understanding between
England and Russia have been broken off, is absolutely incor-
rect. On the contrary, these negotiations are being carried on
still between the Russian Minister of Foreign Affairs and the
British Ambassador at Saint Petersburg. It is expected that
the agreement will be signed in that Capital at no distant date,
unless something unexpected happens. However, as questions
relative to Afghanistan and Thibet are comprised in the negotiations, it is possible that some delay may occur before the agreement is concluded. In fact, certain of these questions have to
be submitted to the Emperor of China and the Ameer of Afghanistan.

As to the relations between the two countries, it may be
categorically announced that, even before the signing of any
agreement a real and definite understanding exists which has
permitted the two countries to act in complete harmony as
regards Persia; and, but for this understanding it is hardly
doubtful that recent events in Teheran would have led to grave
complications.

It is necessary to insist on this point that the Anglo-Russian
agreement is by no means a menace to any other Power. It
does not threaten the integrity of Persia, and interferes with no
interests invested in this country.

The existence of negotiations was therefore publicly recognized. On the 15th of June, 1907, the
English Government showed their determination
"not to admit any mixing up of Russia's domestic
concerns with discussions referring to the respective
frontiers of the two countries and aiming at the
prevention of difficulties that might otherwise

arise." On the 31st of August, the agreement was
signed at Saint Petersburg. This agreement dealt
with Persia, Afghanistan, Thibet, and, under the
form of some correspondence annexed, with the
Persian Gulf. In Persia, it fixed three zones of
influence, a Russian one to the north, an English
one to the southeast, and a third one, mixed in its
character, between the two others; the eventual
measures of financial control being left to future
settlement by common arrangement. In Afghanistan, under reserve of the maintenance of the political
statu quo and commercial liberty, Russia recognized
the preponderant influence of Great Britain, and
renounced the right to send diplomatic agents to
Cabool. In Thibet, the suzerainty of China was
recognized, as well as its territorial integrity. Russians and English pledged themselves to abstain
from all interference in the domestic administration
of the country, and to seek no concession there.
The letter relative to the Persian Gulf stated the
agreement of the two Powers to the maintenance of
the *statu quo*.

Of interest to England as being one of the routes
to India, Persia is of interest also to Russia, as being
one of the ways capable of conducting her to the
free sea. But on this ground, the nineteenth century
was far from being equally favourable to English
and to Russians. And, more especially in its last
quarter, Russian preponderance extended itself
over the greater part. In less than ten years,
between 1890 and 1900, Russian importations into

Persia doubled, increasing from ten millions of roubles to twenty-one millions. And exportations showed a similar progress. In 1904, the English Consuls at Bagdad, Kermanshah, and Teheran, as well as throughout the towns of the Iran, were unanimous in acknowledging the success of Russian commerce, to the detriment of British. It was not, however, so much by commerce as by banking that Russia conquered and held Persia during the last years of the nineteenth century. The Russian Loan Bank, which had existed for long years at Teheran, acquired much more importance at the accession of Mouzaffer ed Dine, father of the Shah now reigning. With the support of the Saint Petersburg State Bank, of which it was a branch, it granted a loan of twenty-two millions of roubles without special guarantee, and on the sole condition that all the other creditors of Persia should be reimbursed. Thus it became the unique creditor, with all the *de facto*, if not *de jure*, advantages attaching to this situation. Since the arrival of Lord Curzon in India, Great Britain had tried to react, not at Teheran itself, where the English bank, which was the "Persian Imperial Bank," had made so many mistakes that its influence was lost, but towards the South and East, by Koweit and the Seistan. In the Viceroy of India's eyes, it was a course necessary to that defence of the Empire which, about the same time, induced him to send Colonel Younghusband to Thibet. The understanding established between those who were considered, at this moment, as probable or possible adversaries marked a great change, therefore. The two Governments had been inspired by a spirit of prudence, moderation, and restraint. And it was the same spirit which had already guided their financial arrangement of October, 1906, by which they pledged themselves to lend Persia, on joint and equal account, the sum of £4,000,000 sterling. It may be further remarked that the convention provided for ulterior arrangements, particularly with regard to the eventual control to be established over the Persian revenues. The contracting Powers made a point of not only liquidating the past but preparing the future.

In Afghanistan, Great Britain's success was complete. England's relations with Afghanistan had been difficult for a long time past. But the Russians were not responsible for these difficulties, which they had profited by, even while they had not provoked them. Lord Roberts used to say, "The less the Afghans see of us, the less they will detest us." And, as a matter of fact, each forward movement of England, during a whole century, aroused Afghan resistance, generally followed by a Russo-Afghan *rapprochement*. The Burnes mission of 1838 led to the Alliance between Russia and the Ameer and the massacre of the British garrisons in 1841. In 1875, things turned out pretty much in the same way; attempts on the English side to resume negotiations resulting in the massacre of the Cavagnari mission. Afghanistan's policy, therefore, with regard to England seemed to be a

policy of reaction. Lord Curzon's somewhat restless activity had increased rather than dissipated
the distrust at Cabool. On the contrary, since
1905, a real alteration for the better had occurred.
In the course of his mission to Afghanistan, Mr.
Louis Dane obtained from the Ameer a confirmation
of previous pledges, and notably of the Treaty of
1893. Already, in 1904, the Ameer's son had paid a
visit to Calcutta, where he was received with the
most flattering attentions. During the winter of
1906–1907, the Ameer, Habib Hulla, in his turn, was
entertained by Lord Minto, who displayed in his
honour unprecedented magnificence. This visit reassured Great Britain on the Afghan side. The
Convention of the 31st of August reassured her on
the Russian side.

To tell the truth, Russia had not waited for this
agreement to declare that she had no ambitions
concerning Afghanistan. In the month of March,
1869, Prince Gortchakoff wrote to the Russian
Ambassador in London: "You may repeat in the
most positive terms to the Secretary of State
Affairs of her Britannic Majesty that his Imperial
Majesty considers Afghanistan as being completely
outside the sphere in which Russia can be called
upon to exercise her influence. Neither intervention nor interference of any kind detrimental to
the independence of this State enter into his calcu-
lations." In February, 1874, the Russian Chancellor renewed the same assurance to Lord Augustus
Loftus. In February, 1882, the Russian Ambassador

in London affirmed to Lord Granville that his Sovereign's intentions had not varied. In October, 1883, Mr. de Giers went further still; and, as the English Ambassador at Saint Petersburg asked him if it were true that a Russian envoy was to start for Cabool with a letter from the Czar to the Ameer, he replied: "It is impossible. All measures are taken in order to avoid there being any relations between Russia and Afghanistan, that country being considered as belonging to the English circle of influence." Certain apprehensions, however, still persisted. And traces of them may be found in the speech in which, on the 12th of January, 1905, Mr. Balfour identified "the problem of the British Army" with that of the defence of Afghanistan. Such fears were destined to be appeased by the Convention of the 31st of August, which determined a zone of English influence in Persia beyond the Afghan frontier and explicitly recognized Great Britain's "special situation" at Cabool. It even went so far as to admit the hypothesis of England's energetic action, in case the Ameer should not keep his engagements to her. It was a sort of *carte blanche* given her by Russia; and was valuable to England without costing the Czar's Government much.

On the other hand, in Thibet, Great Britain made a halt, at any rate, with respect to her policy of preceding years. For rather more than two centuries, the Dalaï-Lama, or pontiff, in whose person are supposed to be united the two halves of God,

Pope and Emperor, had been China's vassal. He is
assisted by a Chinese Resident Minister; and China
guarantees him the integrity of his States. In spite
of this Chinese guarantee, the British, in India,
have always exhibited an indiscreet tendency to
approach the Thibetan wall. They first subdued
half a dozen petty principalities. Then, in 1890,
they took the valley of the Tista in Thibet itself,
with the consent of China. This annexation, which
was insupportable to the proud patriotism of the
Thibetans, definitely alienated from the English
the sympathies they might eventually have secured
among the people of Lhassa. Russia, on her side,
all along the Siberian frontier, has, if not conveniences, at least possibilities of approach as far as
the "Roof of the World," — an approach long and
painful, but yet an approach all the same. Moreover, she has numerous Buddhist subjects, who
belong to the Buriat church, and whose chief receives
a twofold investiture: the one temporal, at Saint
Petersburg, the other spiritual, at Lhassa. On
several occasions there have been Thibetan embassies
despatched to Russia. In 1900, there were political
pourparlers, with a view to a sort of protectorate.
True, there is nothing to prove that these *pourparlers* aimed ultimately at an attack on British India,
which, indeed, is practically impossible of realization. But many English people, especially those
in India, believed this or affected to believe it.
Lord Curzon, in particular, proclaimed loudly the
necessity of raising British prestige, and, in order to

succeed in this, the advisability of penetrating into Thibet "by persuasion or by force." It was evident that such a proceeding risked provoking an Anglo-Russian conflict which in other parts of Asia had been prevented.

In November, 1903, overcoming the Conservative Government's prudent reluctance, Lord Curzon obtained permission to send Colonel Younghusband to Thibet, his purpose being, so it was asserted, to open up commercial negotiations. However, he was soon joined by General MacDonald's troops. Russia did not disguise her displeasure. But three months later, the war in Manchuria drew her attention away from Thibet. After encountering much opposition, and engaging in several combats, Colonel Younghusband reached Lhassa (September, 1904). He succeeded in getting — not from the Grand Lama, since the latter had fled, but from his Ministers — a Treaty opening the Thibetan markets to the British, making the promise of a large indemnity, and pledging the Thibetan Government to neither sell, lease, nor mortgage any portion of their territory to a foreign Power without the consent of Great Britain. The occupation of the Chumbi Valley was to serve as a guarantee. This was a success, which might, however, not be durable, and had been possible only owing to the Russo-Japanese war. Still, it marked on Great Britain's side a determination to play an increasingly active rôle in Thibet. In the light of what precedes, one is better able to understand the meaning of the Treaty of the 31st of

August. In the matter of Thibet, England and Russia were two adversaries, both formidably armed for a struggle, the prize of which appeared to be uncertain. In such a case, it was best to treat before measuring strength. This was what was done. Great Britain abandoned Lord Curzon's grandiose projects. But the *Standard* was able to write that even before the Treaty, all ulterior profit from the Younghusband Convention had been renounced. On the other hand, Russia declared that she would abstain from all interference in the domestic administration of the country. Yet she retained many discreet and powerful means of action through her Buriat subjects; and, in addition, England's identical promise of abstention was a precious security to her. It may, therefore, be concluded, without dwelling on useless comparisons, that the Treaty of the 31st of August, in the part relating to Thibet, was a work of Russo-English wisdom, and that it was happily inspired by the same conciliatory principles as those characterizing the whole agreement.

There was no mention made in the agreement of the Persian Gulf question. But, in a letter addressed on the 29th of August to Sir Arthur Nicholson, the English Ambassador in Russia, and made public at the same time as the Treaty, Sir Edward Grey wrote: "The arrangement concerning Persia is limited to the regions of this country that touch on the respective frontiers of Great Britain and Russia in Asia. The Persian Gulf is no portion of these regions, and is only partly in Persian territory. There seemed consequently no reason for introducing into the Convention a positive declaration concerning the special interests possessed by Great Britain in the Gulf,—interests which result from the British action which has been exercised in these waters during more than a hundred years." Sir Edward Grey added that the Russian Government had explicitly declared, in the course of the negotiations, that "they did not deny Great Britain's special interests in the Persian Gulf." If the agreement said nothing about them, the reason was that the Persian Gulf question is intimately connected with that of the Bagdad railway, and that, to discuss the latter, there were four Powers necessary, instead of two.

As a matter of fact, England had not waited till the year 1907 before she asserted her particular situation and her privileged influence in the Persian Gulf. For more than a century, her ships have cruised there. And she claims the honour of having, thanks to them, caused order and peace to prevail in its periphery. It is correct to say that, during the whole of the nineteenth century, the British flag was almost the only one that appeared in the Gulf, bound either on voyages of scientific exploration or on expeditions of police repression. The surrounding country naturally underwent the action of successive British officers and consuls. Indeed, it may easily be seen that the lower valley of the Tigris and Euphrates is attached to India by eco-

nomic ties that are indissoluble. In 1901, during
the Koweit incident, Lord Curzon upheld its rights,
or rather its claims, against suzerain Turkey and
Germany, Turkey's ally. And, in 1903, Lord
Lansdowne did not hesitate to declare that "the
creation of any naval base or warlike stronghold
on the Persian Gulf by any Power whatsoever would
be a direct menace to British interests, and that the
Government would offer every opposition possible
to such creation." This decided language could not
be gone back upon. And, in his letter of the 29th
of August, Sir Edward Grey did not fail to write,
"It is desirable to draw attention to previous
declarations relative to the British policy, to confirm
afresh, in a general way, what has already been said
concerning British interests in the Persian Gulf,
and to again assert the importance of maintaining
the said interests." It is allowable to suppose that
the Cabinet of Saint Petersburg — if one judges
by this letter of Sir Edward Grey and also by the
limits fixed by the zone of Russian influence in
Persia — had resigned itself to England's claims in
the Persian Gulf, and that the two Powers were
ready to discuss together the negotiations destined
to be opened, sooner or later, with regard to the
Bagdad railway. No doubt this hypothesis was
looked at in the course of the *pourparlers* between
Mr. Isvolsky and Sir Arthur Nicholson. The problem of the Gulf, which in the future is bound to
attract the attention of the Chancelleries, seemed
therefore implicitly settled between London and

Saint Petersburg. When the discussion comes on about Bagdad, it will be taken into account. It is true that such discussion is perhaps remote. For, if the Germans assert that they are in no hurry to enter upon it, France, Great Britain, and Russia are still less so.

At the close of these laborious negotiations, France was able to consider their product from a twofold point of view: that of the genesis, and that of the consequences. It is certain that the reconciliation of England and Russia was willed both on the side of Saint Petersburg and that of London; and it would certainly have come about even if no foreign influence had been brought to bear in these two Capitals. But, for several years past, our country had not ceased endeavouring to effect a *rapprochement;* and the signing of the Franco-English Treaty of the 8th of April, 1904, may be considered as marking the commencement of the evolution which was completed in 1907. This Treaty was at first, in general, badly received in Russia. However, two days after its conclusion, Mr. Nelidow, in an interview, expressed quite different views. "We are the allies and friends of France," he said. "As friends, we rejoice at whatever good fortune befalls you. As allies . . . we are glad of an understanding that delivers you from many cares and frees you from certain restrictions. . . . And, besides, is there not a proverb which says: 'The friends of our friends are our own friends.' Who knows if it will not be verified once again!"[1] More than one Russian newspaper reproached the Ambassador for having uttered this language. And yet, three years later, he was to be justified by events. In so far as the press can facilitate a movement of opinion parallel to diplomatic negotiations, our French press had seconded the efforts of our diplomacy. During three years, whether the question was Afghanistan, or Russia's domestic policy, or Persia, or the Far East, we had affirmed, in spite of passing clouds, the possibility and desirability of the Anglo-Russian understanding. On the other hand, at Algeciras, during the long, monotonous weeks of the Moroccan debate, our plenipotentiaries had not forborne to encourage the general conversation engaged in by Count Cassini, Sir Arthur Nicholson, and Sir Donald Mackenzie Wallace. Discreetly, but yet most usefully, we had avoided certain collisions: first, the military collision that the Dogger Bank cannonade might have caused, by suggesting the meeting of an International Commission of Inquiry in Paris; and next, diplomatic friction, either at the time of the renewal of the Anglo-Japanese Alliance, or during the negotiations themselves, which, a year before, had prepared the Convention of the 31st of August, 1907. Our amicable intervention had been vigilant and continuous. Our interests justified it.

As a matter of fact, the Anglo-Russian agreement completed the establishment of the Asiatic equilibrium upon a durable foundation. Henceforward,

[1] See our book, *Diplomatic Questions of the Year* 1904.

five series of agreements, the Anglo-Japanese Alliance, the Russo-Japanese, Franco-Japanese, and
Anglo-Russian agreements, and the Franco-Russian
Alliance, converged towards the same object; to wit,
the maintenance of the *statu quo*, which guaranteed
the independence and integrity of China. The
disturbed situation of the Chinese Empire, of which
France experienced the counter-effect on her Tonkin-
ese frontier in the spring of 1907, added fresh importance to the collective guarantee expressed by
these five agreements. The return to a policy of
preserving China's territorial integrity, the only
one calculated to avoid conflicts, received its most
solemn sanction. From what precedes it plainly
appears that such return constituted in itself a
profit for France, a profit which, indeed, was about
to be increased by the European development of
some of these agreements.

III

During half a century, the rivalry between England
and Russia had been Germany's favourite weapon
against France. It would be easy to follow, from
the Crimean War to that of 1870, Bismarckian policy
in the web of work of which we were the victims.
If Thiers' efforts to interest Europe in our cause
failed, it was because, under the auspices of Bismarck, Russians and English continued to pursue
designs that were opposed. It needed Germany's
formidable progress to unite in our favour the two

constant rivals during the crisis of 1875. This
coöperation was merely ephemeral. And, a few
years ago, in 1904, Mr. Theodore Schiemann, one
of the fiercest adversaries France has in Germany,
wrote joyfully that the Anglo-French understanding
was incompatible with the Franco-Russian Alliance,
since a *rapprochement* between Saint Petersburg
and London would never be possible. This *rapprochement* was thereafter accomplished. Supported by Russia, her Ally, and by Great Britain,
her friend, and the Ally and the friend being reconciled, France was possessed in Europe of peculiar
moral authority. And the new link that was riveted
in the chain of understandings procured her — in
the diplomatic order of things — the maximum of
securities it was permissible for her to wish for.

Neither by its text nor by its tendencies was the
Anglo-Russian agreement a menace to any one.
It was aimed at no one, and isolated no one. But it
added one more element to the combinations which,
since 1904, had contributed to free the balance of
power in Europe from the hold of Germany. Coming
after the Franco-Russian Alliance, after the Franco-
English, Franco-Italian, and Franco-Spanish understandings, it fortified European liberty and, like
them, dealt a blow to the Bismarckian system, to
the edifice of preponderance which William II had
striven in 1905 to restore, and which the Conference
of Algeciras had shown to be so fragile. To resume,
officially, in September, 1907, the attacks made two
years earlier against the "isolators" of Germany

would have been to discredit more clearly a
manœuvre already tried and found wanting. The
semi-official press of Berlin took care not to attempt this, and Prince von Buelow even thought it
advisable to say, in a speech he made during the
autumn, that neither the Empire's happiness nor
its greatness were built up from the divisions of
the other Powers. The Pan-German press was
less prudent. Those papers which had denounced
in the Franco-Japanese understanding a fresh essay
of "encirclement" did not fail to discover another
in the Anglo-Russian agreement. The *Deutsche
Tageszeitung* asserted that "Germany had no reason
to be satisfied on seeing certain difficulties removed
between the two nations, since, under given circumstances, the continued existence of such difficulties
might have been useful to her." The *Frankfort
Gazette* itself wrote: "The kingdom of English India
has not for a long time been so secure from Russia
as it is now. If England, therefore, without there
being any immediate need for it, is coming to this
understanding with her ancient adversary, the
motive of her doing so must be sought elsewhere.
Probably we are not making a mistake in seeking
for it in Europe."

German recriminations in 1905 had sufficed to
emphasize the character of the Franco-English
agreement of 1904. Those of 1907 likewise helped
to enlarge the scope of the Anglo-Russian one.
At the outset, the negotiators of this agreement
had not been thinking of Germany. They had

s

done their best to liquidate old Asiatic quarrels,
the possible revival of which was a source of anxiety
to them. Gradually, under the state of mind created
in Europe by the persistence of German ill-humour,
it occurred to the Cabinets of London and Saint
Petersburg that their colonial agreement might serve
as the guiding principle of their further coöperation
in Europe for the settlement of questions which
certain oppositions rendered difficult of solution.

In February, 1908, during a debate in the House
of Commons, Sir Edward Grey gave a hint of this
general value which he attributed to the Anglo-
Russian understanding. In the ensuing month
of June, Edward VII went to Revel on a visit to
Nicholas II; and, in the toasts that were proposed
when the Czar alluded to "the limited scope of the
1907 agreements," Edward VII added, "I believe
that the Convention recently made will contribute
to tighten the bonds uniting the people of our two
countries; and I am sure that it will lead to a
satisfactory, amicable settlement of some important
questions in the future." On the same day, a
semi-official note, telegraphed from Revel, emphasized the meaning of this declaration: "The *pourparlers*," it said, "which have been carried on, for
some time past, between the two Governments
concerning Macedonian affairs, may be considered
as about to result in a complete understanding.
Nothing now is wanting but a definite form to be
given to the agreement, which, it may be hoped,
will serve as a basis for a general understanding

between the Powers interested in the work of reforms in Macedonia." Though couched in the most correct terms with regard to the other Powers, this note, in reality, announced that the Anglo-Russian agreement of 1907 relative to the Far East had given birth to a new one, relative to the Near East, between the two countries.

On the 27th of January, 1908, Baron von Aehrenthal, Minister of Foreign Affairs in the Austro-Hungarian Government, announced to the Delegations that he hoped soon to obtain the Sultan's assent to the proposal he had made of prolonging the Austrian railways as far as Mitrovitza. This was an initiative allowed by the twenty-fifth article of the Treaty of Berlin, but one which was calculated greatly to consolidate Austria's situation in the Balkans. In its spirit, if not in the letter, this initiative was contrary to the Balkan agreement concluded in 1897, and renewed in 1903 between Austria and Russia, with a view to the maintenance of the *statu quo*. The almost exclusive place held by Asiatic questions in Russia's preoccupations between 1890 and 1905 had rendered the use of this agreement more profitable to Vienna than to Saint Petersburg. Under the nominal direction of the two "Powers sharing in the understanding," the reform policy had been pursued but slackly under the real control of Austria, to whom Russia accorded in every case a docile approbation. As a warrant for their intervention, the other Powers retained the rights bestowed on them by the Treaty of Berlin.

But their action, at first intermittent, remained
purely diplomatic. Russia and Austria alone,
through their "civil agents," acting in conjunction
with Hilmi Pacha, the Turkish Inspector-General
of Macedonia, played a political rôle on the spot.
It was only reluctantly that they had consented
to the creation of the "Financial Comptrollers"
who superintended the management of Macedonian
finances in the name of the other Powers. In reality, the Austro-Russian Syndicate's plan of reforms
pledged no one to anything. And Great Britain's
efforts to obtain more serious guarantees from the
Sultan were rewarded with but poor success. It
was quite clear that, benefiting by Russia's forced
adhesion, Austria, taking thought for her own
interests — at which no one need be astonished —
was practising in the Balkans a policy that was more
Austrian than European.

The project relative to the Mitrovitza railway
was merely a fresh manifestation of this policy.
But, at the moment when it was announced by the
Baron von Aehrenthal's speech, the situation was
no longer the same as it had been in preceding years.
After three years' peace, on the morrow of the signing of agreements with Japan and Great Britain
which liquidated the Asiatic dream, Russia made
"her reappearance in Europe" and Mr. Isvolsky
took no pains to hide the fact. "The Russians
intended to recover their prestige, which had been
diminished. They made it a point of honour with
themselves to preserve the highest rank on the his-

toric field of their military and diplomatic victories, on the territory they had sprinkled with their blood. They had renounced a direct domination over the Balkan peninsula. But they intended to remain for the people they had freed old friends and protectors for always." [1]

The Austrian scheme seemed to them a provocation. Being anxious to modify the policy of renunciation which had been imposed upon them by their understanding with Austria, they found in Austria's own action a reason or a pretext for such modification. They seized the opportunity to free themselves, and, by breaking the pact of 1897, to replace the Macedonian question on its historic footing, that is to say, before the six Powers.

Such was the object of Russian policy from the month of February, 1908. And the Anglo-Russian agreement acted as its lever. On the 3d of March, Sir Edward Grey had proposed to the Powers a programme of reforms much more radical than all previous ones. On the 26th of the same month, Russia addressed to all the Chancelleries, and no longer to Austria alone, a project which, though less "advanced" than the English one, yet showed a step forward, compared with previous proposals issuing from the Austro-Russian understanding. This project, in fact, indicated the Saint Petersburg Cabinet's abandonment of the understanding. On the 4th of April, Great Britain, who had probably

[1] See René Pinon's article, "Railways and Reforms," in the *Revue des Deux Mondes* for May 15, 1908.

boon advised beforehand, signified her adherence
to it; and, by standing aside for Russia, allowed
her the honour of resuming the moral direction of
Macedonian reforms in the presence of all the Powers.
Although every Government assented in principle
to the Russian scheme, there were slight differences
in the way in which the assent was given.

Great Britain, France, and Italy were favourable
to the Russian proposals without restriction. On
the contrary, Germany and Austria were, above all,
desirous of preserving and, indeed, of improving, the
intimate relations with Turkey by which they had till
then profited. Consequently, negotiations, in view
of a definitive understanding, were bound to be
long and difficult, when, in July, 1908, the revolution broke out. This event could not but help,
as the events of previous months, in turning Russian policy more towards London and Paris than
towards Vienna and Berlin. They, therefore, fitted
in with the general tendency manifested in Europe
since the Conference of Algeciras.

This tendency was still further brought out in
1907 by the dual agreement signed by Spain in the
month of May with France and England. The
Franco-Spanish and Franco-English *rapprochements*
had, by this time, entered into the general course of
things. Spain's treaties with France in 1904 and
1905, and the marriage of Alfonso XIII to Princess
Battenberg in 1906, permitted no doubt on the
point. The agreements of 1907, though not con-
stituting an alliance or involving military engage-

ments, marked progress in the political intimacy of the three nations. They were drawn up as follows (the text of the Anglo-Spanish agreement being identical in its terms with the Franco-Spanish one) : —

Animated by the desire to contribute by all possible means to the preservation of peace, and convinced that the maintenance of the territorial *statu quo* and of the rights of France and Spain in the Mediterranean and in the part of the Atlantic washing the coasts of Europe and Africa should serve efficaciously to attain this object, while being profitable to the two nations, who, moreover, are united by ties of ancient friendship and community of interests : —

The Government of the French Republic desire to inform the Government of his Catholic Majesty of the following declaration, with the firm hope that it will help not only to strengthen the good understanding so happily existing between the two Governments, but also to serve the cause of peace.

The general policy of the Government of the French Republic, in the regions above indicated, aims at the maintenance of the territorial *statu quo*, and, in conformity with this policy, the Government are firmly resolved to preserve intact the rights of the French Republic over their insular possessions as well as their maritime ones situated in the said regions.

In case fresh circumstances should arise, which, in the opinion of the Government of the French Republic, are calculated to modify or to contribute to modify the present territorial *statu quo*, the Government will enter into communication with the Government of his Catholic Majesty, in order to enable the two Governments to concert together, if judged desirable, as to the measures to be taken in common.

A Spanish note, expressed in similar language, replied to the French note. Thus fresh precision was added to existing arrangements. Spain, France, and Great Britain have, all three of them, possessions in the Western Mediterranean and in the East

Atlantic. Some are insular, others European, and others again African. The governments of Madrid, Paris, and London, being united by ties of friendship, have an evident interest in there being no modification, without their consent, of the *statu quo* in these regions. And still greater is the interest they have in maintaining constant communication with their respective possessions, if complications should arise. Their understanding helped them to procure this twofold security. The necessity of Franco-Spanish coöperation in Morocco, resulting not only from bilateral treaties, but from the general provisions of the Algeciras Conference, was an additional reason for making an arrangement which, neither in reality nor yet in its form, was a threat or an attack against any one.

The German Press, none the less, denounced the offensive intention of the dual declaration of the 16th of May — just as, in the months to come, she was to denounce the aggressive character of the Franco-Japanese agreement, the Anglo-Russian agreement in Asia, and the Anglo-Russian agreement in Macedonia. Thus was pursued, in the same terms, and with parallel consequences, the diplomatic debate which we have seen arise and develop; on the one hand, after twenty-five years' diplomatic servitude, Europe claiming the right to settle her own affairs and to guarantee her balance of power; on the other, Germany seeing in this activity a proof of hostile intention and an effort to isolate her. Bismarck had disappeared twenty years before; but still round him, and his work, his plans, his dreams, this world-game was played. The dead man continued "to speak." And doubtless for long to come Europe will hear the muffled echoes of this great voice from beyond the tomb.

CHAPTER VII

FRANCE AND THE UNITED STATES

I

BETWEEN the United States and France there exist no political ties in the form of an alliance, just as there exists none between the United States and any other country in Europe. Such ties are forbidden by the Monroe doctrine, which, at the same time that it proclaims the moral control of the Union over the whole of America, affirms, by way of counterbalance, the Union's indifference to European questions. A similar prohibition comes from General

266

Washington's political testament, which advised his fellow-countrymen never to contract alliances. However, a nation of eighty million souls, materially or morally master of a whole continent, mingling with increasing activity in the economic life of the world, at present possessed of a first-class navy and of strength which is destined to grow still more, a nation animated by ardent patriotism and a lofty national pride, cannot live "huddled up like a petty shopkeeper in a tiny shop." Whether they wish it or not, the United States have a policy of world importance. During the last ten years, they have been seen participating, sometimes in the first rank, not only in the solution of American problems, but in that also of Asiatic questions, and even of European ones. It is therefore impossible to avoid giving them a place, among our allies, our friends, and our rivals, in the aggregate tableau of our foreign action.

Until now, at the base of relations established between France and abroad, we have found there was interest. In the case of the United States the basis is in sentiment. Franco-American relations have developed in an atmosphere of reciprocal sympathy. And it is such sympathy which confers on them, still to-day, their best originality. To exaggerate the action of this "imponderable" would be to expose one's self to errors. To deny it would be to run into them. If certain events had not occurred, if some others had happened which the march of history has thwarted, perhaps these sentiments would have lost a part of their sincerity and ardour. But, favoured by circumstances, they have flourished without let or hindrance; and the twentieth century American not only feels no embarrassment in expressing them, but feels none either in inspiring himself with them. The American gratitude is a fact, and as, in the order of facts, nothing contradicts or hampers it, there is a readiness to translate it into deeds. As Elihu Root, Secretary of State, lately said, it is a reality with which one must count and on which we can rely.

One of the most distinguished historians of America wrote recently: —

On two occasions, the conduct of the French Government was decisive in affecting the future of the Union, so much so that one may wonder what would have been its destiny if France had acted otherwise. Without the help of France, the thirteen revolted colonies would not perhaps have succeeded in conquering their independence at the time they did, and, even if they had, would not perhaps have secured the boundaries which, in fact, were their guarantees. Without the purchase of Louisiana — and it must be remembered that France took the initiative of the transaction, — the movement of expansion towards the West, although inevitable in any case, would have brought about other results. If France had kept Louisiana long enough to settle there a considerable French population, there might, to-day, have been among the whites of the Southwest a struggle between two rival nationalities for the supremacy. Or else, if England had conquered it and added it to her possessions in Canada, what would have been the future of the United States? [1]

It may be said that the American people, in their aggregate, however much they are modified every year by immigration, have the feelings attributed to

[1] Archibald Cary Coolidge, *The United States as a World Power*.

them by their historians. The statues of Lafayette and Rochambeau standing opposite the White House, their portraits placed in the Congress Hall by the side of Washington's, are not the cold affirmation of an official courtesy, but the living expression of a national friendship. As Archbishop Ireland said to me: "The United States have forgotten nothing. An American learns to love France when learning the history of his country. The past has not ceased to act on the present. American sentiment cannot detach itself from France. The immigrants that arrive on our shores are numerous, it is true. But in the air we breathe there is something that assimilates them in less than a generation. And the newcomers are like those that have American ancestors. When learning the history of their new country, they also learn to love France, the great benefactress of our Republic. During the first fifty years of our history, the souvenirs of French help and friendship were almost contemporary. They have now become definitely incorporated in our traditions."

To patriotic gratitude Republican confraternity is added. In spite of profound and numerous differences of temperament and constitution, the Americans respect in France the apostle of liberty. Thomas Jefferson was the friend of Lafayette, Barnave, the Lameth brothers, and all the chiefs of the Feuillants Club. From the very first day, he was in favour of the French Revolution; and even the counter sentiments called forth in the United States by the excesses of our Convention were not able to uproot the original sympathy arising from an identity of principles if not of actions. In spite of temporary difficulties, — the conflict of 1799, the Mexican expedition, the Panama affair, — this sympathy has persisted. When the "citizens" of America look on the side of Europe, they feel themselves drawn naturally towards the "citizens" of France. By its duration, the Republic has borne witness in favour of our political stability, and her American elder, while blaming certain of her tendencies, particularly in religious matters, has accorded her an esteem which continues to grow as time goes on. No doubt, in the eyes of Americans, as of the rest of the world, we still carry the weight of our defeats. But the consistency of our action abroad, the amplitude of our colonial expansion, and the diplomatic combinations that we have succeeded in signing, have procured us suffrages and assured us friendships which, in any estimation of international forces, must be appreciated at their value.

Never, indeed, has Franco-American intimacy taken more trouble to manifest itself than in the course of the last few years. Following on the inauguration of the monument to Rochambeau, there was the Saint Louis Exhibition in 1904, which supplied the manifestation with the most magnificent of settings. In the month of February, 1905, Mr. Jusserand, the French Ambassador, officially handed over to the Congress of the United States Washington's bust by David d'Angers, of which the original had been burnt in

1851, and the rough clay model had been recently found at Angers. In the ensuing month of July, an American squadron came to Cherbourg to fetch Admiral Paul Jones's coffin, which had been discovered in Paris through the investigations of the United States Ambassador; and the sailors of the two nations associated themselves together in brotherly homage paid to one of the most glorious combatants in the American War of Independence. During the same year, the retirement of General Porter was made the occasion of a spontaneous demonstration of affection, which contrasted with the official ceremony usually accompanying the departure of a diplomatist. In 1890, an American squadron came to pay a visit to our French ports in the Mediterranean. In the month of April following, one of our naval divisions, being invited to take part in the fêtes given in honour of Paul Jones's memory, was triumphantly received in America. The second centenary of Franklin, both in Paris and in the States, was solemnly celebrated with ceremonies in which the two Governments were united. In 1907, Admiral Stockton's visit to Brest, and the Tricentenary fêtes of Jamestown again furnished an opportunity for publicly manifesting the reciprocal sympathy existing between France and America.

The speeches made on these various occasions deserve to be remembered, since they emphasize, often with happy stress, the special character of intimacy and confidence in the relations existing between the two Republics. In 1905, Mr. MacCormick, when handing his credentials to Mr. Loubet, said: "During the century and more that this Franco-American alliance has lasted, which, on account of the souvenirs left in our minds by the services rendered to the cause of liberty, has a much greater solidity than if it had been inscribed in treaties, no cloud has come to trouble the amicable understanding subsisting between the two nations." A few days later, in the farewell dinner offered to him, General Porter expressed the same sentiments: "As iron is welded in the fire of the forge, so friendships," he said, "are welded in the fire of battle. . . . America is still too young not to be grateful. . . . She will never fail to remember that, when Washington, Rochambeau, and Lafayette met before the enemy at Yorktown, the contact of these great minds lighted the electric spark which showed the way to victory and led the new world once for all towards justice and liberty based on legal order and the rights of man." On this same occasion, Mr. Delcassé spoke, "of the two countries whom nothing separates at present and whose legitimate aspirations, however far one may look into the future, are not perceived to run any risk of being ever opposed to each other." In April, 1906, at the fêtes given at Philadelphia in honour of Franklin's memory, Mr. Root added, as he handed to the French Ambassador for his Government a gold medal struck by order of Congress after a special vote: "What we are offering is nothing compared with the immense service rendered to us by great French hearts. Yet, at least, it is a token that, amid changing conditions and the afflux of citizens from all countries of the world, Americans have not forgotten their ancestors. You will thus know that, amongst Americans, there is a sentiment in favour of France that persists, and that such a sentiment, amongst such a people, is a real and great fact, which must be taken into account. As far as we are concerned, we remain true and loyal friends to France." Then there was Mr. Roosevelt, who telegraphed to Mr. Fallières to assure him of the special place occupied by France in the heart of the United States, to whom she "rendered invaluable services in what was certainly the most critical period of their history." Again, on the 23d of March, 1907, Mr. Henry White, the Union's new Ambassador, when entering on his functions, declared to Mr. Fallières that the American Government esteemed it an honour to "strengthen" the ties of friendship binding them to France. And, once more, he made use of the same language when assisting, on the 4th of July, at the celebration of the American National Fête.

These speeches define the altogether peculiar nature of the bonds created between France and the United States by a tradition of more than a century old. True, one may wish these ties to become still closer, through a reciprocal, more complete, and better informed comprehension of the respective virtues of the two nations. The wish may be expressed that Americans, instead of merely seeing in France a country of elegance, literature, and art, might have a juster notion of her resources, strength, and aspira-

T

tions. This is a progress to be desired and one that
is realizable. But, while working with a view to its
being brought about, there should be no under-esti-
mation of what has already been achieved. If the
French established in the United States are few in
number and exercise but small influence; if the Irish
immigrants, not long ago our warmest friends, have
been alienated from us by our religious policy, on
the other hand, our ideas and our culture are the
object of sympathetic curiosity all over the territory
of the Union. The efforts of the *Alliance Française,*
which have been crowned with success, the exchange of lectures and lecturers between the Sorbonne, for instance, and Harvard University, have
contributed largely to make us known and appreciated on the other side of the Atlantic. The cordial
welcome given to French travellers in America, and to
the American Colony in Paris, has added individual
friendships to collective sympathies. In Franco-
American relations, sentiment, which usually occupies so small a place in politics, plays an indispu-
tably important rôle. It is the most active leaven in
coöperations sometimes imposed by circumstances on
the two peoples. There was no need of the Arbitration
Treaty of 1908 to guarantee that questions arising
between Paris and Washington will always be settled
in a spirit of good faith, good grace, and good will.

However, commercial interests, quite as much as
ancient sympathies, justify the maintenance of cordial relations between France and the United States.
Bismarck used to assert that history and politics

have nothing to do with trade; that tariff wars
prevent neither alliances nor friendships, and that,
conversely, the consequence of the latter is not always an increase of trade.   The example of France
and Italy has allowed it to be seen that this assertion is not strictly accurate.   And the example of
France and the United States tends also to discredit
it, since there is no doubt that the two countries'
intimacy has favoured and encouraged the exchange
of merchandise between them.   If the trouble is
taken to glance at the sales made by France to the
United States, it will be seen that the upward movement has been almost constant, showing an increase
of about 75 per cent in less than forty years.   In
reality, these sales have passed through the following phases (*Special commerce*) : —

						In millions of francs
1860	.	.	.	.	.	219
1870	.	.	.	.	.	306
1880	.	.	.	.	.	332
1890	.	.	.	.	.	328
1900	.	.	.	.	.	355
1907	.	.	.	.	.	402

We sell to the Americans more than we buy from
them.   However, our purchases have gone up in the
same proportion as our sales.

						In millions of francs
1860	.	.	.	.	.	139
1870	.	.	.	.	.	217
1880	.	.	.	.	.	731
1890	.	.	.	.	.	317
1900	.	.	.	.	.	509
1907	.	.	.	.	.	632

In considering these figures, it must be borne in mind that the development of such exchanges had to contend against the double obstacle of American and French Protectionism. France was the first nation to be favoured by the United States with a reduction in the duties on imported articles. By the Treaty of the 30th of April, 1803, which settled the terms of the cession of Louisiana to the States, certain privileges were accorded to our ships and our products. In 1831, a second agreement, which restricted in various particulars the advantages of the previous ones, balanced the modification by lowering, during a period of ten years, the import duties on our red and white wines. After this, a long time passed without any further negotiations. When, in the year 1882, the United States began, by reason of their commercial development, to feel the need of having recourse to commercial reciprocity, the agreements they negotiated were applied first to the States of South America. The Dingley Tariff, which became law on the 24th of July, 1897, enlarged the possibility of fresh understandings. On the 28th of May, 1898, the Paris and Washington Governments, "with a view to improving their respective countries' commercial relations," concluded a first arrangement comprising various reductions of duties. On the 24th of July, 1899, a Treaty of Reciprocity was signed. But it called forth keen opposition more especially on the part of the New York and New Jersey jewellers and goldsmiths. Indeed, none of the treaties negotiated, in virtue of Section 4 of the

Dingley Tariff, were ratified by Congress. Consequently, the agreement of 1898 had to be fallen back upon. On the 20th of August, 1902, an additional protocol extended its provisions to Porto Rico and Algeria. Finally, in 1907, the United States having signed a commercial agreement with Germany which benefited, to the detriment of French champagnes, German sparkling wines arbitrarily called by the same name, France expressed the desire, at once acceded to by the Government of the Union, to enter into negotiations calculated to reëstablish an equality of treatment. The Treaty of the 28th of January, 1908, was the result. By the terms of this Treaty, which, as its preamble indicated, was intended to "complete previous ones," French champagne wines were to benefit by a reduction of twenty per cent in the import duty, France continuing to apply her minimum tariff to Colonial produce and articles of consumption coming from the United States and Porto Rico, exception made for tobacco, sugar, and things manufactured with them. Moreover, a technical commission of six members, three being Americans and three French, was intrusted with the task of studying certain modifications to be introduced into the Customs regulations of the two countries. This friendly coöperation is likely to facilitate and develop exchanges between them.

Indeed, if the nature of such exchanges is examined in detail, it will be seen that they are capable of being increased in the case of numerous articles. It is true that our tissues, which form the most important portion of our sales, are threatened by the creation of fresh manufactures.   But, as in the case of our skins, our Paris articles, our wines, our comestibles, it lies in our power, by an improved organization of our sales, to secure them a larger market.   In his excellent report on the Saint Louis Exhibition, Mr. André Lesourd writes: "The French trader has certain false ideas which are hard to eradicate.   He thinks that all rich Americans come every year to Paris and can consequently buy in Paris.   He thinks that, as his business house is well known in Paris, it is well known all over the world, and that those Americans who wish to give him orders can do so from America, simply from seeing his catalogues. Now, though the rich Americans who visit Europe every year are very numerous, still they do not constitute more than quite a small minority of the wealthy class."   In the same order of ideas, Mr. Lucien Bonzom, our Deputy Consul General at New York, proposed in his 1906 report to create, in Fifth Avenue, a sort of *maison d'art*, where our artistic industries might be all represented.   He estimated that, from the very first day, "the turn-over would be enormous."   The equally enormous amount of general expenses and the cost of installation have so far caused French tradespeople to hold back.   But there is nothing to prevent the hope that the idea will sooner or later be carried into effect.

The economic crisis which, between the autumn of 1907 and the spring of 1908, raged in America was prejudicial to Franco-American commerce.   As might be expected, it diminished purchases and what may be called touring expenses. Moreover, it created some erroneous notions which needed explanation for them to disappear. In the month of November, 1907, being in want of specie, the American market applied to the Bank of France. Acting in accordance with its statutes, the latter had already sent to the Bank of England eighty millions of American gold eagles, which had naturally been despatched to New York. The direct operation which it was now asked to effect had a precedent. At the time of the Baring crisis, the Bank of France had lent the Bank of England seventy-five millions in gold, against which the latter, as a guarantee of its indebtedness, had handed in a check, being a British Treasury Bond payable at three months' date. The Bank of France replied, therefore, that it was ready to intervene on the same terms, that is to say, with the guarantee of the American Treasury. This condition, as was most justly remarked, was all the more legitimate, since there exists no central Issue Bank in the United States similar to the Bank of England, and it is the Treasury which, in reality, acts as a State Bank with regard to the American market. There was, consequently, a double reason why its intervention should be stipulated. Having been informed of this reply, the American Government, for constitutional reasons, did not think fit to give the guarantee requested. The Bank of France, therefore, being no longer in presence of a State guarantee, but of a private operation, was bound to obey its statutes, which forbade such a transaction. Not being correctly informed, the American press was annoyed and took no trouble to disguise the fact. "This refusal," wrote the *New York Herald* on the 17th of November, "is a measure as shortsighted as it is useless." And yet we might say that it was somewhat unwarrantable to seek to impose a responsibility on the Bank of France which the American Treasury refused to join in assuming. Moreover, no one could be ignorant that our Bank of France has no right to give gold against credit paper. On the other hand, how could it be supposed that the Bank would take part in the issue of the three per cent American Treasury Bonds, when it is forbidden to buy securities on its own account and those that it can accept in guarantee of its advances are exclusively French? One ought here to add that, through the medium of the Bank of England, the Bank of France sent, during the crisis, more than a hundred million dollars in gold to America. This appreciable service is sufficient to prove that, in conforming itself to its regulations, our National Bank was in no wise animated by hostile sentiments towards the American market.

Indeed, it is a well-known fact that, for some years past, a more active share has been taken in American business by French capital than in times gone by. No doubt, the scare of 1907 will, to some extent, lessen this coöperation for a while, but it will not stop it. In spite of the competition resulting from the rapid progress of American industry, the production of the two countries remains commercially, in a large degree, complementary. The cotton, cereals, tobacco, cotton-seed and oils, fruits, meat, wood, mineral oils, both natural and refined, and the machines that France buys each year, come to fill up the lack of her soil or of her industry. In return, French industry is distinguished so sharply by the finish of its manufacture from that of the United States that it is certain always to find on the other side of the Atlantic a market which can still be extended in notable proportions. Therefore, business as well as sentiment justifies the intimacy of our relations with America. How are these relations to stand the test imposed on them by the necessities of contemporary politics?

II

On the 2d of December, 1823, President James Monroe wrote : —

Seeing the free and independent attitude assumed by the American continents, they ought not to be considered by any European Power as a territory lending itself to more ample colonization. We owe it to the frankness and friendly relations that exist between the United States and the various European Powers to declare that we should consider as being dangerous for our peace and security any attempt on their part to extend their system to whatsoever portion of this hemisphere.

We have never mixed ourselves up with the wars that these Powers have engaged in with each other on questions concerning themselves; and it is not in our policy to do so.

We have not intervened, and we shall not intervene, in the present colonies or dependencies of any European Power. But in the States which have declared their independence and have maintained it, and whose independence we have recognised, after mature reflection and in accordance with the laws of justice, we can only consider the intervention of any European Power whatsoever, for the purpose of oppressing them or controlling their destiny in any way, as being a manifestation of hostile sentiments towards the United States.

These rules, which, in their author's mind, applied only to the special situation created by the revolt of the Spanish colonies, have become the guiding principle of American policy. The practice of non-annexation and, before long, of non-intervention which was thus opposed to the European Powers in matters affecting the New World, has assumed the value of a dogma. And, by the attitude of the Powers with regard to it, Americans have judged what sentiments were held respecting themselves. With but few exceptions, France has never caused them any anxiety. The deplorable intervention of Napoleon III in Mexico was the only occasion of a dispute that risked bringing us into open conflict with them. No doubt, this conflict would have broken out, if the war of Secession, at the beginning of the Mexican adventure, had not monopolized the forces of the Union, and if the Emperor Maximilian's tragic end had not closed the incident later. However, it left a certain coldness between Paris and Washington, which made itself felt to our prejudice in 1870. Since that time no further difficulty has arisen. The making of the Panama Canal by France might have been the cause of some fresh unpleasantness, if we had carried it through. Being resolved on getting the control of the Canal into their own hands, the

United States would not have resigned themselves to see it managed by a foreign company.   The failure of the French enterprise, painful as it was to our national pride, spared us by its completeness any danger of future complications on this score.   In all other circumstances we have contrived, without detriment to ourselves, to conform our action to the doctrine of Monroe.   We keep our colonies of Saint-Pierre and Miquelon, with that of Guyana and what else belongs to us of the European possessions in the West Indies.   But the United States do not threaten them.   Each time that a dispute has arisen between us and a Latin Republic, the loyal and moderate character of our action has always been appreciated at Washington.   Our controversy with Brazil respecting the frontiers of Guyana was settled by amicable arrangement.   In dealing with Venezuela and its dictator Castro, we have shown a patience that has been carried to excess, and has often been spoken of as inclining to weakness by the Americans themselves.   At any rate, they were gratified by our not joining in the naval demonstration against Venezuela undertaken in 1902 by the three Powers, Germany, Italy, and Great Britain.   And satisfaction was expressed likewise when the Franco-English agreement relative to Newfoundland settled a question of difficulty in which American fishermen risked being sooner or later implicated.[1]

In a general way, France may be said to accept the Monroe Doctrine.   She accepts, at the outset

[1] See Coolidge's book, already quoted.

of this twentieth century, even the larger scope of
the doctrine, known under the nickname of the "big
stick." There is no need to explain this term; and
every one, to-day, is aware of the causes that have
brought about the gradual development of the original doctrine and made it what it is. The immediate object of the United States was to prevent all
European military action in the Latin Republics,
and, what is more, all European occupation of territory. They could not, however, claim to protect
these Republics against the consequences of the
disregard certain of them only too often manifested
for their international engagements. The United
States were, therefore, compelled to exercise a sort
of preventive control over them, to act as an intermediary between them and Europe, and to assume
the rôle, with regard to them, of a benevolent but
vigilant gendarme. It was in this character that
the Washington Government intervened in San Do-
mingo; and, similarly, they will probably be obliged
to intervene in Venezuela. Having no desire to
acquire fresh territory in any part of the New World,
France is, consequently, without any motive for
seeking to oppose a system which, while it has no
juridical value, is of vital necessity to the Government of the Union. She is, on the contrary, quite
disposed to acknowledge the "special interests"
which the United States claim in America, the more
so as she herself puts forward a like claim with regard to Northwest Africa. Moreover, the United
States Government has never called on her to make

sacrifices incompatible with her dignity. And, whenever she happens to be at loggerheads with any one of the lawless Republics of South America, she is accustomed, of her own accord, to acquaint Washington with her intentions; and to have recourse, in the largest degree possible, to the good offices of American diplomacy. This attitude is so much the more agreeable to the Government of the Union, as they have not always met with it, to the same extent, in the various other Powers. Bismarck used to characterize the Monroe Doctrine as an "international impertinence." And, a dozen years ago, Great Britain, who since then has adopted a more conciliatory tone, did not seem far from approving this sentiment. By repudiating any design in opposition to the principles that lie at the base of the doctrine, France has strengthened the favourable disposition of mind existing towards her in Washington.

Indeed, it is no longer on the American soil only that the various European Powers are to-day exposed to find themselves face to face with the United States. If the Monroe Doctrine has evolved in its reference to the New World, it has evolved also with regard to the Old. What Boutmy wrote is true: "A nation of eighty million souls that sells wheat, and coal, and iron, and cotton, to the whole world cannot remain in an isolated condition. Her very power lays obligations upon her. Her strength confers on her a right. The right changes into a claim. The claim resolves itself into the duty of

pronouncing on all the divers questions formerly
settled by the agreement of European Powers alone.
These Powers themselves, in critical moments, turn
towards the United States, being anxious to know
the latter's opinion. And the Government of the
Union would lessen their influence in the eyes of the
world, if they shut themselves up in negative abstention. Henceforward, the United States have a
policy of world-wide reference." Said Mr. Roosevelt to me one day : "What is most lacking in our de-
mocracy is the sense of their larger responsibility."
This sense has developed with singular rapidity in
the last ten years. In order to be on good terms
with Americans, it is no longer enough not to interfere with them in America. It is also necessary to
be in agreement with them in other parts of the
world.[1]

When they ceased limiting their policy to America, they first extended their preoccupations to Asia.
This was a foregone conclusion. The law of their
expansion, in fact, carries them from east to west.
When, under cover of their high tariffs, their industry needed outlets, they were obliged to seek them
towards the Pacific, in Asia. They began by peo-
pling California. Then they looked farther on.
They conceived the dream of a Pacific which should
be "an American Mediterranean." On this ocean
the Hawaiian Islands, Samoa, part of the Marianne
Islands, the Philippines, and, last of all, the zone of
the Panama Canal, all these have staked out for

[1] See our book, *Notes on the United States.*

them the routes of the future. "Our products," Mr. Shaw, Secretary of the Treasury, exclaimed one day, "will be transported over all the seas, and the United States will become in reality, as they are destined by nature to become, masters of the vastest of oceans." As a matter of fact, American policy in the Pacific and in Asia has been, above all, an economic one. Between 1896 and 1905, American importations into China increased from thirty-five millions of francs to two hundred and sixty-five millions. In Corea, they rose, between 1903 and 1905, from one million nine hundred and fifty thousand francs to no less than ten millions. Within ten years, they increased in Japan from forty to two hundred and sixty-five millions. In these different countries, it was commercial interests which held diplomacy in their leading strings.

At certain times these interests may have seemed to clash with French ones. Not that France had intentions of annexation or monopoly in any region of the Far East, but because her alliance with Russia necessarily associated her with the projects of the Saint Petersburg Cabinet. These projects, which aimed at a Russian annexation of Manchuria, and after that, of Corea, had for some years past, caused anxiety in the United States. The latter advocated the "Open Door"; and, since Japan advocated the same thing, Americans espoused the cause of the "dear little Japs." As one of them wrote: "Japan represents in this conflict the civilized element, the modern, liberal principle of national policy, the promise of pacific development." This *parti pris* was further aggravated by the rancour existing against Russia among the American, Polish, and Jewish immigrants. And to some extent the Government was influenced by it. In the early days of the war between Russia and Japan, Mr. John Hay, the Secretary for State Affairs, proposed to the Powers measures for insuring that "the neutrality of China and her administrative entity should be respected." Under an appearance of impartiality, this was a precaution taken against Russia. As all the Neutral Powers were interested in the neutrality and the territorial integrity of China, the American proposal was adopted. In Saint Petersburg it was considered as not being very amicable in its intention, even though it was correct in its form. And French opinion, which was favourable to Russia, found itself on this account in opposition with American opinion, which continued to be on the side of Japan.

Since then, the situation has changed. Most prudently, President Roosevelt and his Ministers had abstained from mixing themselves up in the manifestations of public opinion. Did they, even then, foresee that the success of Japan would make her the future rival of the United States in the Pacific? The war was hardly finished before popular sentiment in both countries underwent a change. The Japanese reproached the Americans with the rôle played by Mr. Roosevelt during the peace negotiations of 1905. And the Americans were, in return, astonished at the tone assumed towards them by the Japanese newspapers. A year later, the incident of the San Francisco schools called attention to the immigration question, which, after being the cause of animosity, twenty years previous, against the Chinese, now aroused similar feelings against the Japanese, who were rivals far more to be dreaded. Between the autumn of 1906 and the spring of 1908, the conflict went through its successive phases with alternating periods of agitation and tranquillity, fears of war and hopes of appeasement. The cruise of the American fleet and Mr. Taft's voyage to Japan were its last incidents. An agreement was subsequently established, the text of which was not published. In it was manifested the unanimous desire of the Americans for their country not to be over-run by Japanese coolies, and that also of the Japanese to keep their labour at home. The agreement was a purely opportunist one, since neither party abandoned the principles they upheld, — on the one side, the right to enter, on the other, the right to exclude.

With this conflict France had nothing to do. However, she had to suffer its counter-effect. As a matter of fact, the Franco-Japanese Treaty, which was justified by the reasons that have been stated in a previous chapter, was signed on the 16th of May, 1907; that is to say, just when the Nippo-American crisis was in its most acute phase. In spite of the restricted character of this agreement, a disagreeable impression was produced in the

U

United States. The financial help granted by
France to Japan, our engagement to respect and,
in accordance with her, to see that others respect
the territorial integrity of China, to join her in assuring the maintenance of order in certain provinces
of the Celestial Empire, not to speak of the guarantee we afforded to her own territorial situation in
Asia,—all this caused the Americans to feel uneasy.
"Some among us," writes Mr. Coolidge (who, indeed, refuses to share in these fears), "may see in the
Franco-Japanese Treaty a proof that, in the rivalry
of the United States and Japan on the Pacific,
France is taking the side of Japan. If they should
persuade themselves, besides, that, in the event of
the United States vanquishing Japan in war and
deciding to deprive her of Formosa, France would
be bound to intervene by the terms of this Treaty,
their irritation might be very great." Such irritation has not yet been shown; but still there is a
sort of hesitation, which France should have no
difficulty in removing. In reality, the Franco-
Japanese Treaty ought not to be considered alone,
as we have already seen above. It belongs to a
series of understandings constituted by the Anglo-
Japanese Alliance, the Franco-Russian Alliance,
the *Entente Cordiale* and the Russo-Japanese *rapprochement*. Even though Japan were to form
aggressive designs against the United States,—and
this is not proved to be likely, as indeed for the
moment it is impossible,—Great Britain, Russia,
and France, who are all three against such designs,

would have, by reason of the ties that connect them with the Tokio Cabinet, much greater authority to restrain and advise the Japanese Government, with a firmness that could scarcely fail to produce its effect and to bring about a peaceful solution.   Paris, London, and Saint Petersburg are equally concerned in the balance of power in the Pacific remaining what it is to-day, and equally concerned also in preserving the independence of China.   Far from compromising this equilibrium, their agreements with Tokio confer on it an additional guarantee.   Consequently, the relations of France with the United States cannot, under present circumstances, suffer anything from our policy in Asia. This policy favours the elements of stability, and American efforts should tend to multiply them.

The identity of views and interests existing between the world-wide policy of the United States and the general policy of France has manifested itself in Europe even more clearly than elsewhere. On the 15th of January, 1906, the representatives of the various Powers met at Algeciras, at the request of Germany, who wished this Assembly of the Conference to confirm our country's discomfiture. The United States occupied at the Conference a position that was altogether unique.   Of the eight Powers participating in it, she alone was free of all pledges given to either side.   Her Plenipotentiary, Mr. Henry White, had been instructed to share in the deliberations, first, because the United States Government had signed the Madrid Convention of 1880, secondly, because it was interested in the maintenance of freedom and commercial equality, and, lastly, because it might be able to contribute to the adopting of conciliatory solutions. Save for an intervention which he had promised to the Jewish Societies in behalf of the Moroccan Jews, Mr. Root had not bound Mr. White to any particular initiative. He left him free to appreciate the relative value of each different proposal and to sign the final protocol *ad referendum*. There is hardly any need to observe that, by the very force of things, this attitude of impartiality was destined to lead to the American Plenipotentiary's acting the rôle of a veritable arbitrator at Algeciras. A Power of the United States' rank and strength could not, in fact, take part in such a debate without its action making itself almost immediately felt. In spite of the Monroe Doctrine and the apparent abstention which was its logical consequence, the United States were about to play their part in the most important diplomatic encounter of the Chancelleries that had occurred since the Congress of Berlin.

It is no more than a just homage rendered to American diplomacy to recognize that, on this occasion, it exhibited quite as much clear-sightedness as loyalty. We are pleased to think that America's sympathies towards France were not without some influence on her attitude. But it would be wronging her to ignore the fact that her paramount desire was to decide equitably and to work in the cause

of peace.   When the United States are in presence of
Europe, they have only one preoccupation : to maintain the balance of power, while opposing any attempt at one-sided domination.   This was their
first and decisive reason for showing themselves
favourable to France, who, in this particular case,
represented the cause of European equilibrium
against German hegemony.   Moreover, they were
in a position better to understand than any other
Power the nature of the double interest we claimed
in Morocco, the negative one, that of removing all
other European influence than our own from the
Moorish Empire, the positive one, that of preparing
the reëstablishment of order.   This double interest,
in fact, was identical with that which had created
the doctrine of Monroe.   What we wished to do at
Fez and Tangier, the United States, for similar
reasons, had done in different parts of the world,
notably in Cuba.   If, therefore, faithful to our
engagements, we offered every commercial guarantee in proposing reforms that respected the integrity
of the Moroccan Empire, as also the Sultan's Sovereignty, we were favourably situated for being able
to rely on America's support.   From the first to the
last day, this support was granted us.

To tell the truth, it had not waited for the meeting of the Conference in order to show itself.   In
the month of June, 1905, on the morrow of Mr.
Delcassé's resignation, President Roosevelt had
personally asked William II to make the acceptance
of the Conference, which at the same time he urged

upon us, an occasion for assuming a conciliatory attitude. When the debates were entered upon, Mr. Henry White, with all the frankness of his character, expressed his opinion concerning the solutions proposed by Mr. Révoil (Franco-Spanish police). On the 5th of February, he declared himself favourable to them, during a conversation he had with Mr. von Radowitz. When these proposals had been put aside by a first German refusal, it was Mr. White, again, who, approving of the further concession made by France (Reports of the Italian Legation concerning the Franco-Spanish police), undertook to introduce this combination, which was a sort of compromise (February 15). After supporting the first solution, Mr. Roosevelt also supported the second, not because it emanated from France, but because it corresponded to the principles proclaimed at the opening of the Conference. When, on the 3d of March, at our request, a vote was taken as to the advisability of placing the police question on the order for the day, Mr. White gave us his vote, still in the objective interests of an understanding, against which obstacles were being raised, not on the side of Paris. On the 7th of March, at the moment when, after this vote, Germany seemed, at last, disposed to make concessions, Mr. Roosevelt, for the third time, recommended to William II the combination adopted on the 15th of February. After the fall of the Rouvier Cabinet, the American policy did not vary one jot or tittle, remaining faithful at once to its aim and to France.

When William II sent his three telegrams (13th, 15th, and 17th of March), urging the President to exercise pressure on us, Mr. Roosevelt opposed to him the most courteous, but, at the same time, the most resolute firmness, exhibiting, to the very end, his intention of executing, from the Moroccan point of view, a work of justice and good sense, and, from the European point of view, a work of equilibrium and peace.[1]

Is there any need to recall what comments were passed upon the intervention of American diplomacy? Attempts were made to explain it by anterior grievances against German policy. But it would seem that this interpretation cannot legitimately be maintained. It is quite true, that, during the last twenty years, Germany has often caused anxiety at Washington. Refractory to the Monroe Doctrine, she has allowed Americans to think, by her acts on several occasions, that she did not intend to be governed by it. Since the dispute that arose in connection with Samoa in 1888, which it required eleven years to appease, numerous incidents have occurred. In 1898, the enigmatic arrival of Admiral Dietrich's entire squadron at Manila, on the day after Dewey's victory, aroused lasting distrust in American political circles. Moreover, it is the fear of Germany which has recently given such an impetus to the construction of warships in the United States. The occupation of Kiao-Chow, the purchase of the remainder of the Spanish colonies in

[1] See our work, *The Conference of Algeciras*.

the Pacific, Marshal Waldersee's behaviour during
the Chinese crisis of 1900, the 1902 naval demonstration against Venezuela, the project attributed
to Germany of purchasing the Danish Islands in
the West Indies, have alarmed and irritated the
Americans.   The restless activity of the Germans
in South America, especially in Brazil, the hypothesis of territorial ambitions, of which immigration
would have been only the preface, have caused apprehensions still more precise.   Last of all, between
the two most modern "World Firms " — Germany
and the United States — commercial rivalry is intense and cannot be otherwise.   And yet, these
things notwithstanding, it seems certain that, in
1906, the remembrance of the difficulties they
caused was to some extent less vivid, if not entirely
wiped out.   Prince Henry of Prussia's voyage to
the United States; the frequent exchange of courteous messages between William II and Mr. Roosevelt, as, for instance, in 1906, at the time of the
lectures delivered by Professor Burgess in Berlin;
and, more recently, the signing of a commercial
agreement which settled a long controversy, had
all contributed to a better state of feeling between
the two countries.   And the Americans, who admire
Germany on account of her strength and her me-
thodic way of doing things, were quite willing to
live on good terms with her.   Consequently, the
approval of French action during the Moroccan
crisis was not to be explained merely by the existence of a long-standing grudge against Germany.

It had political value and a more general signification.

To the special reasons explained above, two other motives were to be added, which, since then, have continued to produce their effect. The first was that France, who herself possessed the sympathies of the United States, was thenceforward the ally or the friend of the two Powers with whom they have the most lively desire to maintain cordial relations. Russia, who, three years previously, had been an object of suspicion to the Americans, was now regarded by them as a necessary counterweight to the Japanese Power. The slow, but already, as it would seem, normal evolution of the Russian Empire towards a *régime* of legality facilitated this reconciliation, which was determined by common interest. To-day, except in Jewish circles, there is no longer any hatred against Russia. It appears even that, in Washington and Saint Petersburg, equal regret is felt for the neglect to profit by opportunities of getting to know each other better in the past. As regards England, she has consistently sought, during the last ten years, to gain the friendship of the United States. The Venezuelan dispute of 1896 was the last vestige of a century-old quarrel. And by then accepting the haughty interpretation of the Monroe Doctrine, opposed to him by Mr. Richard Olney, President Cleveland's Secretary of State, Lord Salisbury rendered the *rapprochement* definitive. The war with Spain enabled Great Britain to make it more cordial. The Hay-Pauncefote Treaty, which restored to the United States their liberty of action in Panama, and the subsequent settlement of the Alaskan frontier difficulty, were the outward and visible signs of this improved state of affairs. Nor has the Anglo-Japanese Alliance, which, indeed, was concluded before any difficulties arose between Japan and America, done anything to hinder the *rapprochement*. It is most favourably regarded in Washington; and the *Entente Cordiale* has extended to France its advantages. Was it not, moreover, Mr. MacCormick, the United States Ambassador in Paris, who, in an official speech, made in 1905, said: "I am happy to notice the development of ideas which, in recent times, have gradually brought about an amicable understanding between France and the mother country of Americans. *Rapprochements* of this kind render powerful service to commercial and pacific interests, which are those of the world of work. For my part, I shall endeavour to encourage them."

The second motive is more general than the first. Still more than by historic souvenirs, still more than by our intimacy with London and Saint Petersburg, our possession of the United States' good-will is favoured by the object which our policy constantly pursues. Our aim is peace; our means towards it is the balance of power. Both end and means correspond equally to American desires. Being in full economic progress, playing her part in the world-game, the United States would not be able to regard without apprehension the subjection of Europe to any single Power. They are aware that William II, when he is not preaching a crusade against the Yellow Race or against England, takes pleasure in denouncing the American peril to the "United States of Europe," which he would like to form beneath his rule. They are ready to respect Germany's legitimate interests whenever they meet with them. But, on the other hand, by reason and by instinct they are on the side of France, when, in defence of her diplomatic autonomy, the latter country undertakes, as a necessary condition, the defence of the balance of power in Europe. This is a moral guarantee for our policy as strong as any written engagements. Is it not for the said policy, at the same time, the best of justifications?

CHAPTER VIII

FRANCE AND PEACE

In less than forty years, our diplomatic situation has undergone a thorough change. In spite of rapidly succeeding Ministries, and notwithstanding the mistakes that have been made, France has accomplished the duty which history marked out for her to perform. By means of the Russian Alliance, she has broken out of the circle of solitude in which Bismarck had confined her. By means of her understandings with Great Britain, Italy, and Spain, she has restored the balance of power which the German hegemony had destroyed in 1871. By means of the Russo-Japanese, Franco-Japanese, and Anglo-Russian *rapprochements*, she has secured complementary guarantees to her reconquered liberty. But being now at the goal of this evolution, the policy, dictated to her by preoccupation concerning her future, places her more than ever in opposition to that suggested to Germany by this country's devotion to Germany's past.

It is useless to wonder at a conflict which everything rendered inevitable. Being vanquished, France could do no otherwise than strive to get back, if not her provinces by war, at least her autonomy and her safety in peace. And Germany, being victori-

ous, could do no otherwise than take alarm at this
effort. On the one side, the struggle was for equilibrium; on the other, for supremacy. Balance of
power was necessary to France; supremacy was
habitual to Germany. France was as fatally bound
to claim the one as Germany was to endeavour to
safeguard the other. The history of Europe has
been working during the last quarter of a century at
this problem of political psychology and seeking for
its solution. In the conflict itself there is nothing
of the contingent. It results from the very nature
of things; and has its origin in the Treaty of Frankfort, not in the caprices of Sovereigns or in the
passions of Peoples.

In order for the peril to be removed, either France
would have to sacrifice her interests or Germany
would have to reform her state of mind. The first
hypothesis is inadmissible. On the contrary, the
second contains nothing that is unacceptable. If,
instead of looking ever to the past, the Germans
would live more in the present, the irritation that
acts upon them would thereby be appeased. The
Germany of the twentieth century is no longer the
dominating power in Europe. However, she holds
among its various nations a rank that is still eminent. She has admirable economic resources. Her
vigorous natality assures the necessary elements
of her military organization, which, from above,
made up of method and, from below, of discipline,
is unsurpassable in solidity. She is allied with
Austria and also with Italy, both of which Powers

are anxious to preserve the Alliance. She is the pivot of the sole *Triplice* that exists in Europe. Germany is not isolated. Germany is not diminished. She has the right to be proud, in an equal degree, of her material strength and her moral authority.

She is none the less uneasy; and is continually showing signs of her nervousness. The Emperor, although he sometimes blames those that always look on the black side of things (*Schwarzseher*), seems sometimes also to share in their pessimism. Even from the Chancellery words of bitterness are heard, no doubt because during the last fifteen years a number of agreements — alliances, understandings, friendships — have been concluded in Europe without Germany's being called upon to participate in them. These different groupings, while formed outside of her, have not broken up the one of which she is head. She has, however, the impression that an attempt is being made to isolate her. This impression is erroneous, yet it is easily explicable by history. When the habit has been acquired of reigning without any one to dispute the right, there is a tendency to find in the divisions of others a guarantee of the power one exercises. What Germany dreads is not being reduced to solitude, but to see her neighbours issue from theirs. She feels herself isolated, because they are ceasing to be so. The warrant of *her* peace is in *their* remaining alone. "*Ubi solitudinem facit pacem appellat.*"[1]

[1] The German Moroccan policy in August and September 1908, with regard to Muley Hafid's recognition, confirms the fact of the existence in Berlin of a systematic opposition against France always and everywhere.

Who is there, however, that does not see the impossibility of her intervening in these recent agreements? In the diplomatic order of things, as also in the military, she had managed to get too far ahead. As early as 1882, she reared up in the midst of Europe the "block" of her alliances. Was it likely that the new groupings would themselves also choose Germany as a pivot; that is to say, as a dictator? Was it not rather a necessity, in virtue of a law of equilibrium imposed in turn on Charles V, Louis XIV, and Napoleon I, that these groupings should constitute themselves outside of Germany's control? Against her? No. But without her. If what was wished at Berlin had occurred, Europe would have no longer been Europe. And since Europe did exist, it was necessary that diplomatic action should load the other scale of the balance and reëstablish the equilibrium. Where Germans see a deliberate menace, there is nothing more than the action of a law of political physics guiding international elements towards a position of stability.

If Germany would accept this conception of European equilibrium, if she would admit that a river which overflows returns sooner or later to its bed and that what it loses in width it regains in regularity, she would contribute the most powerful guarantee of durability to the world's peace and her own puissance. As a matter of fact, this is far from being the case. Germany has not resigned herself to the loss of her supremacy. It is true that, for thirty-seven years, she has continued to be pacific.

But since, during twenty of them, she dominated Europe by means of peace, there was no real reason for her to declare war. More lately, she has allowed opportunities to go by of doing so which Bismarck would have seized. For this were responsible the Emperor William's honourable scruples, the fear of risking a glory that was already acquired, and the new way of thinking of people for whom war is no longer the only trade. But, during this same period, the German peace has been a nervous, enervating peace, reluctantly and ill-humouredly accorded, a precarious peace that no one is sure of, either in Germany or out of it. The doubts that agitate the minds of the Emperor and his Ministers, that incline them, one day, to accept the inevitable and, the next day, to try some decisive blow, have their counter-effect on Europe, which suffers from the morbid mentality of Berlin.

If this state of things persists, the risks of war will soon become greater than the chances of peace. The less Germany is disposed to resign herself to the restored situation of diplomatic equality, the more the other Powers will apply themselves to fortify such equality and to keep it free from her attack. And the more also, in order to mate them, war will appear to her as the only solution. Experience is here decisive. Each time that Germany essays to regain Bismarck's sceptre, a fresh grouping of Powers rears itself in her way. The Russo-Japanese War, which was the outcome of her policy in Asia, renders her supreme in Europe; the *Entente Cordiale* reëstablishes the equilibrium. Mr. Delcassé's fall is a German apotheosis; the Conference of Algeciras reduces to a triumph of *amour-propre* what seemed, but lately, likely to be a lasting success. And, all at once, there is a creation of agreements that, both in Asia and in Europe, break the levers by means of which, a quarter of a century before, Germany had moved and manipulated the world. By dint of such an exercise of pressure and counter-pressure, one ultimately drifts into war; Prince von Buelow has said as much, and he was right to say it. But what should be added is that the pressure, in the first instance, came from Germany, and that the solution of the difficulty should come from Berlin, since Berlin is responsible.

As a matter of fact, France has no offensive designs. Whether it be a matter for congratulation or regret, she has lost the vocation to attack. Her conscience forbids her to do anything which resembles an acceptance of the wound she bears in her side. But the sentiment of revenge has ceased to animate her. Having accustomed herself not to speak of it, she has at length given up thinking of it. Nations that wish to avenge themselves do not wait forty years. Between Shimonasaki and Mukden, ten years only intervened. France has shown less moral force, and has not known how to fix the goal of her national life in the prompt reconstitution of her territory. She is capable of making war; but she does not desire it. She would be a redoubtable adversary, and no one has the right to underestimate her chances of

x

success. But if her mobilization plans are formed in view of an offensive, her policy, on the other hand, is refractory to it.

Her right, therefore, to require that this policy, such as it is, should be admitted, is all the more unattackable. Instead of seeking for her revenge on the field of battle, she has taken it in the Chancelleries; and this is the very least of what she owed to herself. She will, therefore, yield nothing of what she has conquered on this ground. She was determined not to remain the eternal vanquished. She was determined that peace, in default of war, should restore honour and independence to her. German threats have proved to her the necessity of being strong. She has repaired transient errors; and, having limited her designs, she is bound to carry them out without weakness. Henceforward, any "bluff," like that of 1905, would produce no effect. She will not allow the edifice of her alliances or her friendships to be touched. If, at any time, an attack should be made on it, the people, who have pledged themselves most deeply to peace, would, as the Socialists themselves have declared, all of them rise ready for war.[1]

However, in the Europe of the present day, a Franco-German dispute is not the only thing that might cause war. In the world-game of nations, it is no longer France, but England, who, at present, first faces Germany. Commercial rivalry, naval rivalry, hostility of minds, an equally uncompro-

[1] Speech of Mr. Jaurès, June 19, 1908.

mising attitude, everything indicates that a conflict is to be feared. It is true that, in such a conflict, France ought to wish to remain neutral. She ought, since she is not England's ally. She ought, because her geographic situation, by exposing her to the enemy's blows, bids her be prudent. She ought, because her patience in waiting to avenge her own quarrel forbids her to engage, except for this, in that of others. If England should attack Germany, France is not pledged to attack with her. If Germany should attack England, France has not promised to back up the British fleet by creating a diversion in the Vosges. Her intervention would be a contradiction to her past, and an act of heedlessness with regard to the future. It would be her right and her duty to preserve her neutrality. But would she be able to exercise this right? Would she be able to fulfil this duty?

She had formerly to encounter the hostage theory. This barbarous theory has since developed; and now, somewhat apologetically, it is taken up in another form. The German Army, we are told, being reduced to impotence by a naval war, would not put up with the first defeat. It would insist on fighting,—on fighting for the mere sake of fighting, at any cost, against the first persons to hand, against the nearest neighbour, in short against France. Consequently, our pacific intentions would not be sufficient to guarantee us peace. We should be attacked, not even as hostages, but without reason, without pretext, simply in order to find the German

Army something to do. In vain we should have renounced waging a war of revenge, and sacrificed our sympathies for our friends to the higher claim of our interests. War would lay hold of us all the same.

This hypothesis dictates our duty to us. As Clausewitz remarks, all war must cease whenever the conclusion of peace is less onerous than the continuation of war. Turning this formula round, it may be said that the only way to avoid the outbreak of war is to render it more onerous to one's adversaries than the maintenance of peace. If, in presence of an Anglo-German struggle, France and Russia were to be enfeebled so as to offer an easy prey to the aggressor, the German Army's need of action would doubtless be manifested at their expense, and this without much trouble. But if, on the contrary, France and Russia are both strong, and are capable, each being sure of the other, of making any one pay dear for an attack on their neutrality, then Germany, however ardent for war, will prefer not to utilize her army, foreseeing that she would only fail in the attempt. She will shrink from a course of action the risk of which would be greater than the profit.

The Franco-Russian Alliance, therefore, on condition it holds itself ready for emergencies, is the sole guarantee, if not of the preservation of peace, at least of the circumscription of any war. It is the only foundation on which to establish the league of neutrals which will be, perhaps, the formula of the near future. In a period of crisis, the world's security will be gauged by the power of France and Russia.

Diplomacy has sufficed to restore the condition of equilibrium. It cannot pretend to be sufficient for the avoiding of war. Our right to act politically depends on our capacity to act militarily. We can only safeguard the freedom of our alliances and our friendships if we are in a position to defend them on a field of battle. Our army would have been the key of our future if we had wished to render peace impossible. It is the key likewise, if we wish to maintain it.

There would be a want of frankness in not looking these embarrassing contingencies plainly in the face, the more so as the uncertainty of mind that prevails in Berlin respecting the best course to be followed, and the increasing irritation caused by this uncertainty in London, may, at any time, in a few hours, transform such contingencies into facts. However, nothing yet proves that the bad is bound to change into the worse. Through a wholesome fear of the irreparable, an unstable situation may last for years. Who indeed can say whether Germany, being satisfied with what is definite in her gains, will not abandon all idea of compromising them by insisting on their increase, whether she will not rather make up her mind to consolidate by a durable equilibrium what was originally secured to her by an ephemeral hegemony? Should she sincerely adopt this system, Germany might count on our help in preserving a peace which would be equal for all. And the agreement, by setting its seal to our recovered status, would become, among the nations of Europe, the natural leaven of reasonable reconciliations.

INDEX OF NAMES

The United States as a World Power

By ARCHIBALD CARY COOLIDGE, Ph.D.

Harvard University

Cloth, 8vo, $2.00 net; by mail, $2.14

The work is of international importance and appears at once in English, French, and German editions.

The material of which the book is constructed was originally gathered for use in the lectures delivered by the author at the Sorbonne as Harvard lecturer on the Hyde foundation. Since then it has been entirely recast and retested, but still retains its broadly international and neutral attitude. It is therefore more likely to give an unbiased and rightly proportioned knowledge of the situation than if its view were specifically American.

" The extreme lucidity, broad generalizations, and rapid glances at long historical periods which the character of the audience demanded are among the chief merits and charms of the book.

" We know of no volume which sums up so well and in so brief a space the wide interests which have attracted public attention during the last decade, and which, incidentally, are certain, in view of our development, to loom still larger on the national horizon. Many Americans will doubtless welcome the opportunity of not only reducing to order and simplicity in their minds the vast mass of information relating to the movements and interests of the United States as a world power which they have acquired from desultory reading, but also of refreshing their memory as to the historical development of which these movements form, for the present at least, the climax." — *The Inter-Ocean*, Chicago.

No work covers this broad field, full of controverted points, so fully, clearly, and interestingly, as does this book.

PUBLISHED BY

THE MACMILLAN COMPANY

64-66 FIFTH AVENUE, NEW YORK

The Government of England

By A. LAWRENCE LOWELL

Professor of the Science of Government in Harvard University
Author of "Colonial Civil Service," etc.

*In two volumes. Bound in the style of Bryce's
"American Commonwealth." Cloth, 8vo, $4 net*

PUBLISHED BY

THE MACMILLAN COMPANY

64-66 FIFTH AVENUE, NEW YORK